# KAREN BROWN'S

# *French Country Inns & Chateaux*

## BOOKS IN KAREN BROWN'S COUNTRY INN SERIES

*Austrian Country Inns & Castles*

*California Country Inns & Itineraries*

*English, Welsh & Scottish Country Inns*

*European Country Cuisine - Romantic Inns & Recipes*

*European Country Inns - Best on a Budget*

*French Country Bed & Breakfasts*

*French Country Inns & Chateaux*

*German Country Inns & Castles*

*Irish Country Inns*

*Italian Country Inns & Villas*

*Portuguese Country Inns & Pousadas*

*Scandinavian Country Inns & Manors*

*Spanish Country Inns & Paradors*

*Swiss Country Inns & Chalets*

# KAREN BROWN'S

# *French Country Inns & Chateaux*

Written by

**KAREN BROWN**

Illustrated by Barbara Tapp

**Karen Brown's Country Inn Series**

**WARNER BOOKS**

TRAVEL PRESS editors: Clare Brown, CTC, Karen Brown, June Brown, CTC, Iris Sandilands

Illustrations: Sherry Scharschmidt, Barbara Tapp, Richard Kerr
Cover painting: Barbara Tapp
Country Maps: Keith Cassell, Itinerary Maps: Karen Herbert

This book is written in cooperation with:
Town and Country - Hillsdale Travel
16 East Third Avenue, San Mateo, California 94401

This Warner Books edition is published by arrangement with Travel Press, San Mateo, California 94401

Warner Books, Inc., 666 Fifth Avenue, New York, NY 10103
Ⓦ A Warner Communications Company

Printed in the United States of America
First Warner Books Trade Paperback Printing: February 1988
10 9 8 7 6 5 4 3 2 1

LIBRARY OF CONGRESS
Library of Congress Cataloging-in-Publication Data
Brown, Karen.
    French country inns & chateaux / Karen Brown.
        p.   cm.
    Includes index.
    ISBN 0-446-38814-9 (pbk.) (U.S.A.) / 0-446-38951-X(pbk.) (Canada)
    1. Hotels, taverns, etc. ·· France ·· Guide-books. 2. Castles ··
France ·· Guide--Books. 3. France ··Description and travel ·· 1975 -
·· Guide-books. I. Title. II. Title: French country inns and chateaux.
    TX910.F8B76 1988
    647 .944401 ·· dc19                          87-26574
                                                      CIP

To Rick with Love

# Contents

# COUNTRYSIDE HOTELS

# INDEXES

 # Introduction

Yes, you can fly to Paris, eat hamburgers, stay in an Americanized hotel and return home safely with stacks of snapshots. If you choose, though, you can travel to France and explore it. You can eat, sleep and drink France, venture off into the country, meet the French and return home with a load of memories and pleasures as well as snapshots to recall them.

To tempt you, hundreds of magnificent chateaux, cozy inns and elegant manors owned and managed by some of the warmest and most fascinating people, are tucked away in the French countryside. Many of them, designed and built centuries ago as private residences, are in superb locations, have beautiful surroundings and, fortunately for the traveller, have been turned into hotels. As travellers, we can take full advantage of this opportunity to live France every minute, twenty-four hours a day.

France has so much to offer the inventive and adventurous traveller. This book strives to supply enough information to stimulate the interest of just such people. The French provinces are as different as individual countries and deserve to be visited and explored.

## PURPOSE OF THIS GUIDE

This guide is written with two main objectives: to describe the most charming, small, beguiling hotels throughout France and to "tie" these hotels together with itineraries that include enough details so that travellers can plan their own holiday. We aim not simply to inform you of the fact that these places exist, but to encourage you to explore towns and villages not emphasized on tours and to stay at these inns and, perhaps most of all, to convince you that it is not difficult to do. This book contains all of the necessary ingredients to make you confident about planning your own trip. With easy-to-follow itineraries to serve as guidelines, and with a list, sketches and descriptions of over one hundred and ninety charming hotels throughout France to choose from, the task of planning your trip will become a pleasure.

Any guide which tries to be all things to all people fails. This guide does not try to give in-depth information on sightseeing - just highlights of some of the most interesting and appealing places. It will be necessary to supplement this guide with a detailed reference such as Michelin's Green Guides to the provinces of France, an excellent, reliable source for town maps, addresses and dates and times museums are open. This guide does not try to give a complete, but, rather, selective listing of hotels in France. An extensive research trip was just completed for this fifth edition. Any new discovery that sounded promising was visited and any hotel included in previous editions that sounded as if it no longer maintained the same standards of welcome and accommodation was revisited. "French Country Inns & Chateaux" has been reformatted and devotes an entire page to each of the one hundred and ninety hotels, sixty of which are new to this fifth edition. The list of hotels is stronger than ever and it reflects only the very best of what France has to offer.

This guide does not try to appeal to everyone. Tastes and preferences vary. This book is definitely prejudiced: the hotels included are ones I have seen and liked. It might be an elegant chateau dominating a bank of the Loire or a cozy converted mill tucked into the landscape of the Dordogne Valley. But there is a common denominator from country cottage to stately mansion - they all have charm. Our theory is that where you stay each night matters. Your hotels should add the touch of perfection that makes your holiday very special: the memories you bring home should be more than just of museums, theaters and tours through palaces. These are important, but this guide takes you through the enchanting back roads of France and introduces you to the pleasure of staying in romantic hideaways.

## CLOTHING

France is a country that stretches some twelve hundred kilometers from Calais in the north to Nice on the Riviera. Expect changes in the weather, regardless of the season and particularly if you are making a grand tour. For winter bring warm coats, sweaters, gloves, snug hats and boots. The rest of the year a layered effect will equip you for any kind of weather: skirts or trousers combined with blouses or shirts which can then be "built upon" with layers of sweaters depending upon the chill of the day. A raincoat is a must, along with a folding umbrella. Sturdy, comfortable walking shoes are recommended not only for roaming beckoning mountain trails, but also for negotiating cobbled streets. Daytime dress is casual, but in the evening it is appropriate to dress for dinner. Consider yourself a guest in a private home, as that is often the situation.

# CREDIT CARDS

Most major cards are accepted widely by stores, restaurants and hotels. However, there are a number of small inns that do not accept credit cards. Those hotels which do welcome "plastic payment" are indicated in the hotel description section using the following abbreviations: AX - American Express, VS - Visa, MC - Master Card, DC - Diner's Club, or simply - All major.

# CURRENT

If you are taking any electrical appliances made for use in the United States you will need a transformer plus a Continental two-pin adapter. A voltage of 220 AC current at 50 cycles per second is almost countrywide, though in remote areas you may encounter 120V. The voltage is often displayed on the socket.

# DRIVING

*BELTS:* It is mandatory and strictly enforced in France that every passenger wears a seatbelt. Children under ten years of age must not sit in the front seat.

*CAR RENTAL*: All major car rental companies are represented throughout France at airports and in major cities, but it is wise to consult your travel agent on details of car hire. Reservation and prepayment in the United States is not necessarily cheaper but will ensure a guaranteed fixed price. Car companies in collaboration with airlines often offer a variety of rental packages. Be sure to investigate the options available as it might prove financially beneficial to book a car at the same time you purchase your airline ticket. However, taxes and insurance must be paid locally and there are often surcharges for returning the vehicle to a place other than the originating rental location.

*DRIVER'S LICENSE*:   A valid driver's license is accepted in France if a stay does not exceed one year.   An International Driver's License, however, is a useful supplement to your travel documents.   The minimum driving age is eighteen.

*DRUNK DRIVING*:   It is a very serious offense to drive when you have been drinking.   Therefore, do not drink and drive: save your liquid refreshments for evening meals when your driving is finished for the day.

*GASOLINE*:   Prices are generally double those in the United States and remember that autoroute filling stations generally charge well above the average. There are two grades throughout France: "Essense" (lower octane ratings) and "Super".   "Faites le plein, s'il vous plait", translates as "Fill her up, please".   At some self-service stations one must pay in advance, before using the pumps.

*PARKING*:   It is illegal to park a car in the same place for more than twenty-four hours.   In larger towns it is often customary that on the first fifteen days of a month parking is permitted on the side of the road whose building addresses are odd numbers, and from the sixteenth to the end of the month on the even-numbered side of the road.   Parking is prohibited in front of hospitals, police stations and post offices.   Blue Zones restrict parking to just one hour and require that you place a disc in your car window on Monday to Saturday from 9:00AM to 12:30PM and again from 2:30PM to 7:00PM. Discs can be purchased at police stations and tobacco shops. Grey Zones are metered zones and a fee must be paid between the hours of 9:00AM and 7:00PM.

*ROADS*: The French highway network consists of autoroutes (similar to our freeways), Peages (autoroutes on which a toll is charged) and secondary roads (also excellent highways). In recent years the policy concerning drivers who exceed speed limits has changed drastically. Posted speed limits are now strictly enforced and fines are hefty. Traffic moves fast on the autoroutes and toll roads with speed limits of 130 kph (81 mph). On the secondary highways the speed limit is 90 kph (56 mph). The speed limit within city and town limits is usually 60 kph (38 mph).

Charges on toll roads are assessed according to the distance travelled. A travel ticket is issued on entry and the toll is paid on leaving the autoroute. The ticket will outline costs for distance travelled for various types of vehicles. It is expensive to travel on toll roads, so weigh the advantage of time versus cost carefully. If you have unlimited time and a limited budget you may prefer the smaller freeways and country roads. A suggestion would be to use the autoroutes to navigate in and out of, or bypass, large cities and then return to the country roads. At toll booths French francs are the only acceptable currency and travellers' checks of any kind are not accepted for payment.

*ROAD SIGNS*: Before starting on the road, prepare yourself by learning the international driving signs so that you can obey all the rules of the road and avoid the embarrassment of heading the wrong way down a small street or parking in a forbidden area. There are several basic sign shapes. The triangular signs warn that there is danger ahead. The circular signs indicate compulsory rules and information. The square signs give information concerning telephones, parking, camping, etc.

# HOTELS

*DESCRIPTIONS*:   In the second section of this guide is a selective listing of hotels that are referenced alphabetically by town.   Included are only hotels that I have visited during the past couple of years.   It is impossible to revisit them all on one trip as there are always new regions and hotels to investigate as well, but on each successive journey I try to revisit as many as possible.   I also rely on feedback from readers and try to follow up on any complaints and eliminate any hotels that are not maintaining their quality of service, accommodation and welcome.   This book is designed for travellers who want to see the French at home, who are willing to conquer their inhibitions and to speak a few French phrases and who prefer antiques and charm to a modern plumbing system.   People who want to add personal experiences to their list of overnight stops will remember the country inns and chateau-hotels included in this book.   The hotels might range from luxurious to country-cozy, but they are all charming, quaint and typically French.

For some of you, cost will not be a factor if the hotel is outstanding; for others, budget will guide your choice.   The appeal of a little inn with simple furnishings will beckon some, while the glamor of ornate ballrooms dressed with crystal chandeliers and gilt mirrors will appeal to others.   I have tried to describe as clearly and accurately as possible what a hotel and its setting have to offer so that you can make the choice to suit your own preferences.

*RATES AND INFORMATION*:   As of January 1988 the French Government is no longer involved in the regulation of hotel rates in France.   For the first time, hoteliers themselves will determine and set their prices.   Therefore, this year, instead of all hotels increasing their rates by approximately the same percentage, some owners have opted to maintain 1987 prices, while others have opted to lower and still others have opted to increase rates.   Due to the fluctuating exchange rate and the range of prices available at each hotel, giving travellers an accurate idea of cost continues to be a problem.   Quoting rates in dollars or ranges proved inaccurate from the moment previous books went to press. With this edition, in the hopes of providing more accurate information, we quote published 1988 rates or those learned by phoning the hotel. Most hotels have an intricate system of rates. There are winter prices and summer prices and "in between season" prices. There are rooms without private baths and luxury two-bedroom suites or apartments. There are special weekly bargains and holiday surcharges. There is not space to give you each and every price for each hotel accurately. The rates given are for the LEAST expensive single room and the MOST expensive double room inclusive of tax and breakfast. Not all hotels conform so where dinner is included it is stated in the listing. If you travel off season and ask for a room without a private bath you will secure a room for less money than published. One of the best travel values in Europe is what is called "map" or "demi-pension" - this means two meals a day included with your room rate. To take advantage of demi-pension you usually need to book into the hotel for at least three nights. Please ALWAYS CHECK prices and terms with hotels when making bookings.

*RESERVATIONS*: People often ask, "Do I need a hotel reservation?" The answer really depends on how flexible you want to be, how tight your schedule is, which season you are travelling, and how disappointed you would be if your first choice is unavailable.

It is not unusual for the major tourist cities to be completely sold out during the peak season of June to September. Hotel space in the cities is especially crowded, particularly during annually scheduled events. So unless you don't mind taking your chances on a last-minute cancellation, staying in larger hotel properties or on the outskirts of a town, make a reservation. Space in the countryside is a little easier. However, if you have your heart set on some special little inn, you certainly should reserve as soon as travel dates are firm.

Reservations are confining and lock you into a solid framework. Most hotels will want a deposit to hold your room and frequently refunds are difficult should you change your plans - especially at the last minute.

For those who like the security blanket of each night pre-planned so that once you leave home you do not have to worry about where to rest your head each evening, there are several options for making reservations which we have listed below and on the following pages.

*Letter*:  If you start early, you can write to the hotels directly for your reservations. There are certainly many benefits to this in that you can be specific as to your exact preferences.  The important point, because of the language difference, is to be brief in your request.  Although most hotels can understand a letter written in English, on page 333 we have provided a reservation request letter written in French with an English translation.

*Telephone*:  One of the most satisfactory ways to make a reservation is to call long distance: the cost is minimal if you dial direct and you can have your answer immediately.  If space is not available, you can then decide on an alternative or adjust your dates based on availability.  Ask your local operator about the best time to call for the lowest rates.  Consider the time difference between the United States and France and try to avoid the hectic morning hours when guests are leaving or during the dinner hour when the chef, who is often also the owner/manager, is occupied with the evening meal.

To phone France, dial 011, then 33, France's international code, and then the local number.  The telephone numbers appear as they should be dialed in the hotel description section of this book.  For information on how to dial within France, please see the Post Offices section for telephone services that the French Post Office offers.

*Telex*:  If you have access to a telex machine, this is another efficient way to reach a hotel.  When a hotel has a telex, the number is included under the hotel listings. Be specific as to your arrival and departure dates, number in your party, and what type of room you want and include your telex number for their response.

*Travel Agent*:   A travel agent can be of great assistance - particularly if your own time is valuable.   A knowledgeable agent can handle the details of your holiday and "tie" it all together for you in a neat little package including hotel reservations, airline tickets, boat tickets, train reservations, ferry schedules, opera tickets, etc. To cover their costs, travel agencies often charge for special travel arrangements. Talk with your local agent, discuss your budget and ask exactly what the agency can do for you and what the charges will be.   Although the travel agency in your town might not be familiar with all the little places in this guide, since many are so tiny that they appear in no other major sources, lend them your book - it is written as a guide for travel agents as well as for individual travellers.   (Note for travel agents who read this guide· most of the small inns in this guide pay no commission.)

*U.S. Representative*:   Hotels that are represented by a United States reservations office will appear in listings by representatives at the end of the hotel descriptions section, beginning on page 321.   Contacting a representative is an extremely convenient way to secure a reservation.   However, the majority of representatives charge for their services, often reserve only the more expensive rooms, or quote a higher price to protect themselves against currency fluctuations. Ask the individual representatives to detail their charges and then decide if the additional cost is worth your time saved.


## ITINERARIES

I have divided France into sections: Normandy, Brittany, the Chateau Country, Dordogne, Gorges du Tarn (Tarn Canyon), Provence, Cote D'Azur, Gorges du Verdon (Verdon Canyon), a Gourmet Itinerary, Alsace and Le Lot.   For each of these sections I have organized four- to six-day itineraries.   The itineraries can easily be joined together, enabling you to extend your journey into another region if you have the time.   These itineraries should be used as guidelines; depending on your own preference, you might choose to establish yourself at one inn as opposed to three or four in a specific region.  From the numerous hotels recommended on each itinerary it would perhaps be more restful to establish yourself at one, use it as a base, and branch out from there.  Checking in and out, packing and unpacking can be time consuming and tiresome.

Covering the highlights of the regions, these itineraries are set up for touring France by car.  You should be able to find an itinerary, or section of an itinerary, to fit your exact time frame and suit your own particular interests.  You can tailor-make your own holiday by combining segments of itineraries or using two "back to back".  I cannot help, however, adding a recommendation: do not rush.  Allow sufficient time to settle into a hotel properly and absorb the special ambiance each has to offer.

Please note that although a hotel is suggested for each destination in an itinerary, the hotel is just that - a SUGGESTION.  Perhaps the hotel seems over your budget, or too fancy, or too simple.  Or just not "you".  If this is the case, review the itinerary maps.  Stars indicate locations of alternate hotels and descriptions of each can be found, alphabetically sequenced by town, in the second section of the book.

## MAPS

With each itinerary there is a map showing the routing, overnight hotel locations, alternate hotel locations and suggested places of interest along the way. These are an artist's renderings and are not intended to replace a good commercial map. To supplement the routings you will need a set of detailed maps which will indicate all of the highway numbers, autoroutes, alternative little roads, autoroute access points, exact mileages, etc. Our suggestion would be to purchase a comprehensive selection of both city maps and regional maps before your departure. The Michelin maps are exceptionally good: one reason being that if you want to deviate from an itinerary to explore on your own, Michelin marks in green the most scenic or interesting roads. Michelin maps also tie in with their excellent Green Guide province series, which is an outstanding reference for sightseeing, background and museum times.

Before the Paris and Countryside Hotel Descriptions, there is a map outlining the "arrondissements" of Paris and four section maps of France: Maps I, II, III, IV, that detail by numbered circles all the towns in which hotels are recommended. A list of the numbered circles, their corresponding towns and hotels and the pages on which they are described are referenced on a facing page. The numbers flow across the map to aid you in quickly finding alternative hotels in the area should your first choice be unavailable. Which map a town and hotel appear on is cross-referenced in the hotel description section and in the index.

## MONEY

The unit of currency is the French franc, abbreviated to F (1F = 100 centimes). It is generally best to cash ordinary travellers' checks at a bank with a "bureau de change" desk - remember to take your passport for identification. There can be quite large variations in the exchange rates and service charges offered by banks even in the same street. "Bureaux de change" are open twenty-four hours at the

Paris Charles de Gaulle, Le Bourget and Orly airports, and normally open from 7:30AM to midnight at major railway stations.

*Banks*: Banking hours vary, but in most large towns and cities banks are open Monday to Friday, 9:00AM to 4:30PM. Banks close at midday on a day prior to a national holiday and all day on a Monday if a holiday falls on a Tuesday. In small towns banks are often closed on Mondays instead of on Saturdays.

## POST OFFICES

Post Offices are open in most towns from 8:00AM to 7:00PM Monday to Friday and from 8:00AM to midday on Saturdays. The address of the Paris post office which is open twenty-four hours a day is 52, Rue du Louvre, 75001 Paris. Traditionally we think of post offices as related to mail service. In France the post offices do of course perform all of the standard expected services, but in addition telephone calls can be efficiently and relatively inexpensively placed at most post offices. The procedure is customarily to give the telephone number to one of the attendants who will then assign you a booth, place the call and pass it through to your booth. Payment is made after you hang up. Depending on the destination of your call, a deposit is sometimes required. There are also telephone booths where you can place local calls without the assistance of an attendant. Dial the number and wait for the phone to ring. (Sometimes when dialing within France, but outside a region or district, it is necessary to first compose an area code. Information will be posted in the booth or available from the operator.) When your call is answered, there will be a beeping sound to indicate that you should insert either coin or card. Almost all French public phones are now operated, like those in the United States, either with coins or cards. The old-style apparatus requiring tokens or "jetons" is virtually phased out.

# RESTAURANTS

French cuisine is incomparable in art and price. It is not uncommon to pay more for dinner than for a room. There are ways to save both your money and your appetite for a memorable dinner: fruit and croissants for breakfast; bread, cheese and wine for lunch and an occasional pastry in the afternoon are anything but a sacrifice and can be purchased in grocery stores and patisseries along the way. One word of caution, however: stores customarily close from 12:00 midday to 2:00PM every afternoon, and in small towns from 12:00 midday to 4:00PM. On Mondays most stores are closed all day and only a few are open until midday. However, food stores such as bakeries, fruit stands, cheese shops and butchers open as early as 8:30AM and are even open on Sunday mornings.

Almost all restaurants have a tourist menu or menu of the day. These are set meals which usually include specialities of the house and are quite good and reasonable. Sundays, however, only a few restaurants remain open and rarely do they offer a tourist menu, as French families still regard Sunday dinner as a special outing. Restaurants known for their gourmet cuisine, often offer a "menu degustation", so that a sampling of the chef's many artful creations can be enjoyed by one-time guests.

If you want a quick snack, stop at a bar advertising itself as a "brasserie". Here an omelette, a crepe, various salads or a "croque monsieur" (a ham sandwich toasted with cheese), are normally available, tasty and inexpensive.

Many hotels during their high season prefer overnight guests to dine at their restaurant. Also, some hotels were restaurants first and now offer rooms as a convenience for their restaurant patrons. Such "restaurants with rooms", understandably want to reserve rooms for guests of their dining room. To avoid misunderstandings inquire about a hotel's dining policy when making your room reservation.

The French are known for and justifiably proud of their wine. Each region produces its own special wine, a result of the climate and soil conditions which influence the variety and characteristics of the local grapes. The food specialties of each region are selected to complement the local wine. Without writing another book, it would be impossible to detail all the wines available in France. Do, however, sample the wines of a particular region as you travel it. One can select from a region's most famous and expensive labels or, better still, ask the "sommelier" (wine steward) for his suggestion of a good, local wine.

## TOURIST INFORMATION

Syndicat d'Initiative is the name for the tourist offices found in all larger towns and resorts in France (their offices are usually indicated by a sign with a large "I" - for information). These tourist offices are pleased to give advice on local events, timetables for local trains, buses and boats, and often have maps and brochures on the region's points of interests. The main tourist office in Paris is located at 127, Avenue Champs Elysees, 75008 Paris (near the Georg V metro stop, open Monday to Sunday from 9:00AM to 10:00PM).

A further contact for information concerning your travels in France can be obtained from the "Accueil de France", welcome office. The Accueil de France will book hotel reservations within their area for the same night or twenty-four hours in advance (no group or agency requests). As a special bonus, 1990 has been designated as "The Year of the French Provinces", and to assist travellers while exploring the countryside, more than 1,000 Welcome Centers throughout France are established with English-speaking staff. They are located in principal railroad stations, regional and city tourist offices, car rental offices, hotels and principal points of contact for travellers and offer assistance, information and documentation in English. Also new in 1990, visitors to France are able to secure last minute information in English simply by dialing the French toll-free "Green Number" 05.21.12.02.

Information can be obtained before you leave for France from the French Government Tourist Office located at 610 Fifth Street, New York, New York 10020, telephone (212) 757-1125; 9454 Wilshire Boulevard, Beverly Hills, California 90212, telephone: (213) 271-6665; 645 North Michigan Avenue, Chicago, Illinois 60611-2836, telephone: (312) 337-6301, or 2305 Cedar Spring Road, Dallas, Texas 75201, telephone: (214) 720-4010. Information can now also be obtained by dialing 1-900-420-2003 (9 a.m. to 7 p.m. EST Monday through Friday). Callers will pay 50 cents per minute for the service and will receive additional, detailed information by mail.

Visas are no longer required for Americans who wish to travel in France.


## TRAINS

France has an excellent train system that serves major towns and cities. However, it is often necessary to supplement your travel arrangements with either taxi or car rental to reach the small countryside hamlets and isolated inns. Depending on the number of people in your travel party it can be more economical to travel by train than by private car, but perhaps not as convenient. Review your travel plans and select the best mode of travel based on your objectives and budget. If you decide to travel by train, in addition to point-to-point tickets, there are some unlimited travel passes available to you. Information, reservations and tickets can be obtained through offices of the French National Railroad.

# NORMANDY

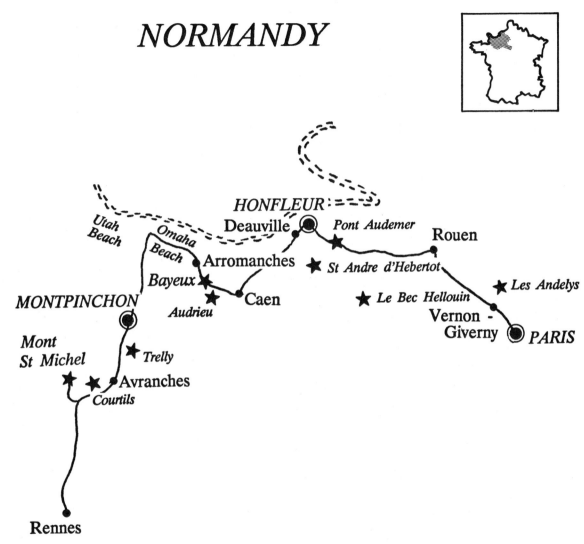

Utah Beach

Omaha Beach

Deauville

HONFLEUR

Pont Audemer

Rouen

Arromanches

St Andre d'Hebertot

Bayeux

MONTPINCHON

Caen

Audrieu

Le Bec Hellouin

Les Andelys

Vernon - Giverny

PARIS

Mont St Michel

Trelly

Avranches

Courtils

Rennes

# *Normandy*

This itinerary takes you to the well-known D-Day beaches where on June 6, 1944 American and British troops landed in a major and dramatic attempt to change the pace of World War II. Decades have passed since then, but pill boxes, although abandoned, remain strategically positioned along the deserted beaches and many vivid memories and tragic losses have yet to be forgotten. Normandy also calls to mind the Vikings and their invasions, as well as William the Conqueror and his. Normandy is also dairies, isolated and beautiful stud farms, mile after mile of rolling green pastures and picturesque resort areas. This itinerary will travel the breadth of Normandy, following the coastline, then progress inland through farmland before returning to the coast to visit the picturesque island of Mont St Michel.

*Honfleur*

Begin your day with what might well prove the highlight of your trip.  Follow the Seine north out of Paris to VERNON and GIVERNY, Monet's beautifully restored house, studio, greenhouse and gardens.  Here Monet lived and created masterpieces.  Walk the gardens and discover the enchantment of the lilypads ... all to understand what inspired the brilliance of the artist.  Pack a lunch and take advantage of the fact that for a small fee you can linger and enjoy one of the world's most magnificent spots.

It is not a long drive from Paris to the capital and heart of Normandy, the city of ROUEN, one of the most important tourist centers of northern France.  William the Conqueror died here in 1087 and Joan of Arc was burned at the stake in the Place du Vieux Marche in 1431.  Although the city was practically destroyed during World War II, it still has many interesting museums and its famous cathedral, so well known to many from Monet's paintings.

Not far from Rouen, deep in the Normandy countryside, is the tanners' town of PONT AUDEMER.  It is also the town that the father of William the Conqueror stormed.  In spite of World War II destruction, the town managed to salvage a number of old timbered houses which line the Rue de la Licorne.  Pont Audemer is also the location of a cozy, timbered inn, L'AUBERGE DU VIEUX PUITS, owned by the kind couple, Monsieur and Madame Jacques Foltz.  If the hour is approaching midday, you might consider stopping here for lunch.

The next and final destination for today is the picturesque harbor town of HONFLEUR.  The narrow, seventeenth-century harbor with its many colorful boats with their flapping sails is lined by numerous, well-preserved old timbered houses.  Cafes hug the docks and with the promise of a warm day their tables and umbrellas are set outside, so that customers can enjoy the sun and the picturesque location.　Honfleur is the birthplace of the humorist Alphonse Allais, the musician Erik Satie and the painter Eugene Boudin.　There is a unique wooden church and the house of the King's lieutenant, all that is left of a sixteenth-century chateau. Wander and explore the streets of this enchanting town.　In addition to having a number of quaint shops and inviting restaurants, Honfleur is still a haven for artists and there are a number of galleries to visit.　For a delightful fish restaurant, the first choice with locals is L'ANCRAGE, located on a street just off the port: 12, Rue Montpensier, tel: 31.89.00.70.

Not more than a mile around the peninsula from Honfleur is a typical Norman timbered farmhouse colored with overflowing flowerboxes at each window, LA FERME ST SIMEON.　It was purchased not too many years ago by a young couple, the Boelens, who strive to meet your every need.

*La Ferme St Simeon*
*Honfleur*

La Ferme St Simeon is an excellent hotel and you should consider it "home" for the time you anchor on the Normandy coast. The dining room is cheerful with yellow walls, bright yellow tablecloths and colorful flower arrangements. The cuisine is plentiful and delicious, although expensive. Everything is a la carte. The hotel has recently expanded its accommodation to thirty-five rooms, every one handsomely decorated with fine antiques. Reservations are a must and should be made long in advance. (Note: a moderately priced alternative would be the Hotel l'Ecrin, located in a residential section of Honfleur.)

With La Ferme St Simeon as your base, be sure to take the time to enjoy Honfleur. It is particularly scenic in the soft light of early morning or in the subtle colors of sunset. There are also other attractive seaside resorts to visit, all within an easy drive of Honfleur. The beachside towns were popular with and inspired many Impressionist artists, especially Monet and Renoir. You might feel as if you have already seen this particular stretch of Normandy coastline if you have spent any time in the Musee D'Orsay in Paris.

TROUVILLE has set the pace on the "Cote de Fleurie" since 1852. A stretch of water divides it from its very close neighbor, DEAUVILLE, perhaps the most elegant resort of them all. Internationally popular, dazzling and luxurious, every variety of entertainment is to be found here. The casinos are a hub of activity and if you visit in the late summer, you will experience the excitement and sophistication of a major summer playground for the rich and famous. For a few weeks each August there is the allure of the race tracks, polo fields, glamorous luncheons and black tie dinners. Celebrities and the wealthy international set come here to cheer their prize thoroughbreds on. Get a relaxed glimpse of these million-dollar babies as they "limber up" with an early morning stretch along Deauville's glorious expanse of sandy beach.

To devote an entire day to exploring the landing beaches, depart early from La Ferme St Simeon.   The first stop is CAEN, situated on the banks of the Orne, which lost nearly all of its ten thousand buildings in the Allied invasion of 1944.   A large port, it is also the city that William the Conqueror made his seat of government.   Northwest of Caen is BAYEUX, an ancient Roman metropolis. Once a capital of ancient Gaul, this city was successfully invaded by the Bretons, the Saxons and the Vikings but somehow escaped the Allied invasions which brought with them so much destruction.   As a result, the town still possesses Norman timbered houses, stone mansions and cobblestoned streets.   It is also where the Bayeux tapestry is displayed.   Commissioned in England, this tapestry portrays in fifty-eight dramatic scenes the Battle of Hastings in 1066.   Bayeux is also referred to as a center of lace-making.   In the nineteenth century the craft monopolized the efforts of the village and neighboring towns.   Over five thousand artisans were located here and produced a lace known as bobbin lace.   This kind of lace is made by intertwining and manipulating numerous threads, each from different bobbins. Today the five thousand craft centers have been reduced to ten and they are all associated with a center devoted to the preservation of the lace-making heritage of Normandy.   You can visit the Norman Bobbin Lace-Making Center at 5, Place aux Pommes both to view the masters at work and buy samples of their craft.   From Bayeux, the road intersects with the route that winds along the coast following its curves and the beaches of the D-day landings.

The little fishing port of ARROMANCHES LES BAINS, at the center of the British sector, "Gold Beach", was designated to receive the fantastic artificial harbor "Mulberry B" for the disembarkation of ammunitions and supplies. ("Mulberry A" was to be installed on "Omaha Beach", a few miles west at ST LAURENT, VIERVILLE SUR MER and COLLEVILLE, to supply American units.)   The Mulberries, designed by British Admiralty engineers, were comprised of massive concrete caissons, floating pier-heads and ten miles of floating pier "roads", towed across the Channel. Landing at nearby Asnelles and Ver sur Mer, the British Fiftieth Division captured Arromanches in the afternoon of June 6, 1944. By the end of August five hundred thousand tons of material had been landed at Mulberry B; half-submerged remnants of the harbor can still be seen. (Mulberry B was destroyed by a freak storm on June 19, 1944.)

Among other displays, the Arromanches Museum shows a film of the 1944 landings which will set the mood for your visit to the beaches. Note: if you are travelling off-season be sure to ask for the headphones with the English commentary.

*Chateau de la Salle*
*Montpinchon*

The traces of war's devastation are a jarring reminder of the fierce and tragic reality of our history. The D-Day beaches stir many emotions. With thoughts, visions and memories, leave the coastline and drive inland across farmland to MONTPINCHON and the CHATEAU DE LA SALLE. Once a private estate, this lovely stone mansion is set deep in the Normandy countryside and enjoys the peace and quiet that location has to offer. The Chateau de la Salle has only ten bedchambers. Each room is large, handsomely decorated and either with bath or shower. The restaurant is intimate with a few heavy wooden tables positioned before a warming fire. The accommodation, the cuisine and the salon warmed by a burning log fire will tempt you to linger at this delightful estate.


## DESTINATION III    MONT ST MICHEL    Hotel Mere Poulard

From Montpinchon travel south in the direction of AVRANCHES. It was here on July 30, 1944 that General Patton began his attack against the German Panzer counter-offensive from Mortain.

From Avranches cross into Brittany to the famous French town of MONT ST MICHEL. One of France's proudest possessions, Mont St Michel is unique, dramatic and definitely a site to visit. The magnificent town is built on a rock two hundred thirty-five feet high and, depending on the tide, is either surrounded by water or by exposed quicksand. Wander up the narrow cobblestoned streets to the crowning twelfth-century abbey and visit the remarkable Gothic and Romanesque complex, culminating in the glories of the "Merveille" (Marvel) - the group of buildings on the north side of the Mount. St Michael, the militant archangel, is the appropriate saint for the beaches you have just seen. On the left as you enter under the city gates of Mont St Michel is the entrance to the restaurant of the

**HOTEL MERE POULARD.** You will be tempted inside by the smell and cooking display of the famous Mere Poulard omelette. The preparation of the omelette can be seen from the street and is an attraction in itself. The eggs are whisked at a tempo and beat set by the chef and then cooked in copper pans over an open fire. You can stay overnight at the Hotel Mere Poulard, enabling you to experience the town without the midday crowds and tours. Note: the guest rooms at the Hotel Mere Poulard are very simple, but there are no deluxe hotels on this tiny island.

From Mont St Michel it is approximately an hour's drive south to the city of RENNES. From here you can easily return to Paris or, if tempted, journey on into the region of Brittany. Mont St Michel is also the first destination for the following Brittany itinerary.

*Hotel Mere Poulard*
*Mont St Michel*

Mont St Michel

*Normandy*

# BRITTANY

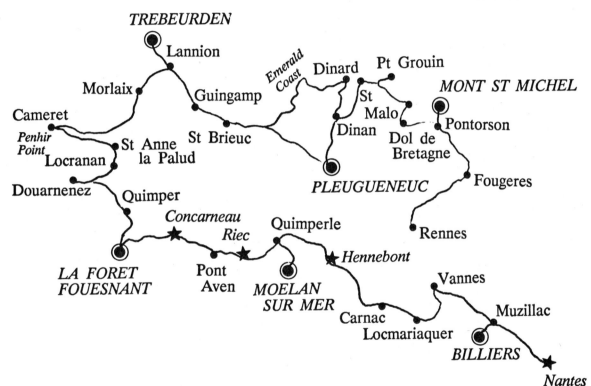

TREBEURDEN

Lannion

Morlaix

Emerald Coast

Dinard

Pt Grouin

MONT ST MICHEL

Cameret

Guingamp

St
Malo

Pontorson

Penhir
Point

St Anne
la Palud

St Brieuc

Dinan

Dol de
Bretagne

Locranan

Fougeres

Douarnenez

Quimper

PLEUGUENEUC

Rennes

Concarneau
Riec

Quimperle

LA FORET
FOUESNANT

Pont
Aven

Hennebont

MOELAN
SUR MER

Vannes

Muzillac

Carnac

Locmariaquer

BILLIERS

Nantes

# *Brittany*

Brittany is a region of beautiful forests bounded by nearly one thousand miles of coastline.  This peninsula, jutting out from the northwest side of France, is culturally different from the rest of the country.   The regional language is Breton and traditional costumes are proudly worn by the inhabitants.   Crepes or galettes, which are crepes without sugar, filled with ham, eggs or cheese, fish and cider are Brittany's culinary specialities.   Most of the houses are fresh white stucco with angled blue-grey roofs.   Windmills pop up every so often on the crest of a hill.  The people are friendly and their French carries a distinctive accent.   This itinerary traces Brittany's coastline from Mont St Michel to Nantes.   Each town along the coast is too fascinating to miss.   The wooded interior, although not emphasized on this particular itinerary, is also very beautiful and should not be overlooked especially if camping, riding or walking interest you.

Your tour begins at RENNES, the administrative and cultural capital of Brittany. It is a large commercial city but Vieux Rennes, or the old part of town, is composed of quaint narrow streets which are lined by dignified old timbered houses. From Rennes drive north to FOUGERES which has a magnificent feudal castle with thirteen large towers isolated on an island.

MONT ST MICHEL crests the coastal skyline approximately sixty-six kilometers from the city of Rennes. The mount has been photographed by millions. This is the militant Archangel Michael's domain. The fantastic two hundred thirty-five-foot high church is built on a rock. The distant appearance of the town is that of a child's sand castle, with narrow, cobblestoned streets winding up to the twelfth century abbey at the top in the center of the town. Mont St Michel is famous for the extreme tide levels which occur every day: at different intervals, according to the type of tide, the city is either completely surrounded by water or by patches of quicksand. Access to the island is across an old causeway that is covered at high tide. Check the tide schedule and then choose a restaurant where you can enjoy a meal or snack and watch the waters surround the island.

The home of Monsieur and Madame Bernard Heyraud is also the HOTEL MERE POULARD, enabling you to stretch out your stay in this island town. The rooms, although not very large, are comfortable though simply furnished. The hotel also has a cheery and bright restaurant which is famous for its Poulard omelette. Please note: although the restaurant of the hotel is perhaps the best on the island, it does not look out across the water.

*Hotel Mere Poulard*
*Mont St Michel*

| DESTINATION II | PLEUGUENEUC | La Motte Beaumanoir |
|---|---|---|

For miles after departing Mont St Michel you will find yourself glancing back at the spectacular citadel until it finally fades on the horizon. From Mont St Michel drive south to PONTORSON and DOL DE BRETAGNE, the capital of the marshland, and then east along the coastline. Heading for St Malo you pass through VIVIER, a large mussel producing area, CANCALE, a picturesque seaside resort, and POINT GROUIN where you enjoy a sweeping panorama from CAP FREHEL across to Mont St Michel. It is here at Point Grouin that the beautiful EMERALD COASTLINE begins.

ST MALO, known as the city of Corsairs, was once the lair of pirates. Its setting is beautiful and it has become an important tourist center. The city was destroyed by a Nazi fire in 1944, but the thirteenth- and fourteenth-century ramparts that surround the town have since been restored. It is a wonderful city to explore: the narrow streets at the city center house a number of interesting shops and small restaurants. Linger at lunch time and sample the local crepes (sweet pancakes) filled with butter, sugar, chocolate or jam or the gallettes (wheat crepes) enhanced with cheese, ham, onions or mushrooms and the local, surprisingly potent "cidre". South of St Malo is the walled town of DINAN. Once fortified by the Dukes of Brittany, the town is very old. Dinan is known for its houses built on stilts over the streets and the remnants of its once fortified chateau. DINARD lies only twenty-two miles north of Dinan. A popular resort, Dinard is a lovely town with many safe and protected beaches. The Emerald Coast between Dinard and Cap Frehel is impressive, jagged and beautiful.

*Chateau de la Motte Beaumanoir*
*Pleugueneuc*

Not far from this wild coastline is another equally beautiful attraction: the CHATEAU DE LA MOTTE BEAUMANOIR. This lovely and spectacular stone manor house is located just four hundred meters south of the town of PLEUGUENEUC which is located on Route 137, forty kilometers west of Rennes. The owners, Charles and Jacqueline Bernard, and their son, Eric, are your warm and gracious hosts.    They moved here from Belgium and it is truly the result of one man's, Charles Bernard's, dream and his personal sense of artistry and labor, that this manor is such an exceptional home and now hotel.    The Bernards accurately describe their home as a dramatic, five hundred-year-old castle, isolated by vast acres of forest.    On the property they have just completed work on a man-made lake and stables are available for guests who wish to board their horses.    The Bernards have eight bedrooms, all with private bath, to offer guests.    Handsomely decorated with wall coverings and materials to match the style and period of the castle, six of the rooms face onto the lake and two overlook the grounds at the back. Although the chateau does not have a formal restaurant, meals will gladly be prepared for guests when requested and served with silver and candlelight in the elegant dining room.

## DESTINATION III        TREBEURDEN                    Ti Al-Lannec

When you leave Pleugueneuc it is approximately forty-five kilometers to ST BRIEUC, one of the most important industrial centers of the region, located on a bay.    You navigate your way into the town to discover that there are many pretty walks to take, old mansions and majestic townhouses.    Do not miss the fortified cathedral of St Stephen and the fifteenth-century fountain.

The drive continues on to TREBEURDEN, one of the northernmost tips of the Breton coastline.    This small town is a very popular and lovely seaside resort set on the hills above the coast, with striking views out to the Grande Molene and Milliau islands on a clear day.    Yachts anchor off the scattered stretches of sandy beach and shops on the main shopping streets cater to the summer holidaymakers.    Let the season and weather determine your length of stay.

*Ti Al-Lannec*
*Trebeurden*

But regardless of whether or not the sun shines, your destination is the charming hotel perched on a point that is convenient to the beaches in warm weather and cozy on a dreary, dark, grey day - the TI AL-LANNEC. The Ti Al-Lannec achieves a feeling of "home away from home", from the smell of croissants baking to the personal touches in the decor. The restaurant is lovely and opens onto glorious views of the coast. The public rooms have been thoughtfully equipped to accommodate the hobbies of the guests and the unpredictable moods of the weather. There are jigsaw puzzles, books and games, in addition to a swing on the lawn and an outdoor, knee-high chess set. Gerard and Danielle Jouanny are responsible for the careful renovation of this once private home and Madame Jouanny's feminine touch is apparent in the sweet choice of prints that decorate the majority of rooms. The bedrooms are all extremely comfortable and invite extended stays. Most of the rooms look out to sea. This is a perfect hotel for families on holiday.

When it is time to leave Trebeurden, backtrack to Lannion and head south to take the road which follows the coastline out to the very tip of the peninsula and the lobster port of CAMARET.   In the area there are many scenic peninsulas and the most beautiful of all is PENHIR POINT.   Pass through STE ANNE LA PALUD, one of the most frequented pilgrimage centers in Brittany, to the quaint village LOCRANAN.   Now known for its woodcarvers, it once was called the "city of weavers" when three hundred workers gathered here to weave sails for the British navy. Located on the square is a group of lovely Renaissance houses. DOUARNENEZ, a lively sardine fishing port, lies to the west of Locranan and QUIMPER, a city famous for its pottery, lies to the south.

*Manoir du Stang*
*La Foret Fouesnant*

From Quimper it is only sixteen kilometers farther south to LA FORET FOUESNANT and the marvellous sixteenth-century manor house, MANOIR DU STANG. This private home is handsomely inviting, the food is always hearty and good and the owners are very accommodating. The manor is surrounded by flower gardens, a small lake, woods and acres of farmland. The furnishings retain the feeling of a private estate, yet the rooms have all the modern conveniences and comforts. The Louis XV-styled dining room is as romantic as the rest of the hotel, superbly decorated with antiques and waitresses adorned in Breton costume add an air of festivity. The owner requests that you dine at the hotel for either lunch or dinner.

## DESTINATION V     MOELAN SUR MER     Les Moulins du Duc

The next destination, Moelan sur Mer, and recommended hotel, Les Moulins du Duc, are a short distance further west of La Foret Fouesnant, travelling the southern coastline of Brittany, and the inn is as charming as the Manoir du Stang is stately. En route you will first pass through CONCARNEAU. An old port, this walled town has houses dating from the fourteenth century. As with almost all Breton seaside villages, Concarneau also has its share of white sandy beaches. Continuing on through the peaceful market village of PONT AVEN, it is a short distance to the small town RIEC SUR BELON where flat-shelled oysters and the charming HOTEL CHEZ MELANIE are found. You might want to lunch or dine here; the seafood specialties are superb.

Driving further, you arrive in the village of QUIMPERLE. This pretty town is divided by the Laita and Elle rivers. The upper town is centered around the church of Our Lady of the Assumption and in the lower section some interesting old dwellings are grouped around the former Abbey of Ste Croix.

LES MOULINS DU DUC, tonight's destination, is located about ten kilometers south of Quimperle at MOELAN SUR MER, alongside a small lake with lily pads, ducks and a few colorful rowing boats. Dating from the sixteenth century, this charming mill once belonged to the Dukes of Brittany. In a beamed ceilinged restaurant of Les Moulins du Duc, the dining is exquisite: both the atmosphere and specialities provide the ingredients for a perfect evening. The owner, Monsieur Quistrebert, is ever-present, providing charming, refined service. The various bedrooms are tucked away in small buildings along a babbling stream. The accommodation is all modern, not quite as cozy as the interior of the main building, but offering a comfortable bed where you can sleep well after a delicious dinner.

*Les Moulins du Duc
Moelan Sur Mer*

*Domaine de Rochevilaine*
*Muzillac*

From Moelan sur Mer return to Quimperle and then travel further to the once fortified town of HENNEBONT.   Continue on to the small town of CARNAC, a seaside resort famous for its field of megaliths.   Similar to Stonehenge, these huge stones are an important prehistoric find and yet they appear scattered and abandoned in an open field.   There are no fences to restrict your exploration nor stands with postcards and mementos.   At the far end of the site is a cafe where you can sample some of the Breton galettes, crepes and cider.   A short distance away at LOCMARIAQUER are two additional prehistoric stones: the Merchant's Table and its Great Menhir.

Return to the main road between Vannes and Nantes.   At MUZILLAC take the road that leads you to the tip of the Pen-lan peninsula and the small village of BILLIERS. Here on a rocky promontory is a hotel that will leave you with a lasting impression of Brittany. In 1982 Monsieur Patrick Gasnier and "sa brigade" took charge of the DOMAINE DE ROCHEVILAINE and the hotel has dramatically improved under his care and supervision. The bedrooms are handsomely furnished and beautifully appointed. Lovely Oriental carpets adorn hardwood floors and on sunny days breakfast is enjoyed in the well kept gardens that are protected from salt-water breezes by whitewashed walls.

The vast windows in the dining room of the Domaine de Rochevilaine overlook rocky cliffs, and there is a distinct sensation of being shipboard ... all you see from the table is the wild open sea.

The Domaine de Rochevilaine is dramatically positioned on Brittany's jagged and rocky coastline. The views from the hotel are stupendous with the sun shining on the glistening sea; or on a stormy day with the wind whipping the waves as they crash against the rocks so near your bedroom window. The setting of this hotel exaggerates Brittany's most spectacular feature - its coastline, and it is a perfect choice for this itinerary's final destination.

Return to the main road and it is a direct route to either VANNES or NANTES. Vannes, the capital city, was constructed around the Cathedral of St Peter and consists largely of ancient houses within thirteenth- and fifteenth-century ramparts. It is a straight line from Vannes to Nantes where your tour of Brittany ends. Nantes was Brittany's capital from the tenth to the fifteenth centuries. It has a beautiful old quarter, Duke's Palace, and Cathedral of St Peter and of St Paul.

*Brittany*

# CHATEAU COUNTRY

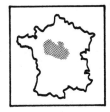

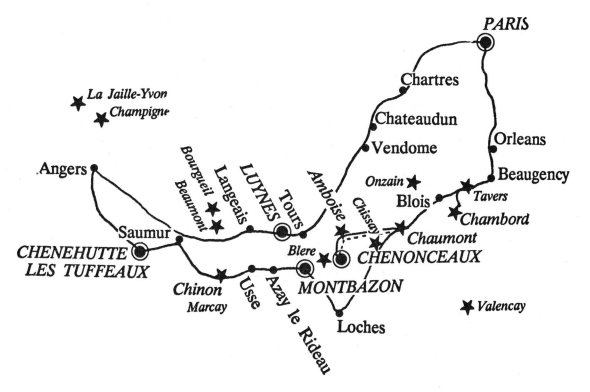

La Jaille-Yvon
Champigne

Angers

Bourgueil
Langeais
Beaumont
LUYNES
Tours
Amboise
Saumur
Chissay
CHENEHUTTE
LES TUFFEAUX
Blere
Chinon
Marcay
Usse
Azay le Rideau
MONTBAZON
Loches

Chartres

Chateaudun

Vendome

Orleans

Onzain
Blois
Beaugency
Tavers
Chambord
Chaumont
CHENONCEAUX

Valencay

PARIS

# CHATEAU COUNTRY

A highlight of any holiday in France is a visit to her elegant chateaux nestled along the banks of the Loire. Also known as the "garden of France", the chateau region conjures up the grandeur and excitement of life at the French Court. This itinerary suggests a route that circles the region and uses a different hotel for each destination. However, the distances are short enough that you can also select just one hotel and use it as a base for exploring the numerous castles.

*Chateau de Chambord*

*Chateau Country*

An hour southwest of Paris is the city of CHARTRES with its magnificent cathedral. Monopolizing the horizon, the Gothic cathedral is dedicated to Mary, the Holy Mother. Its feminine qualities are best evidenced by its amazing stained-glass windows dappling the church with color and light. The cathedral is considered by many to be the greatest achievement of the Middle Ages, a "stone

*Domaine de Beauvois*
*Luynes*

testament" of that period. On most days you find Mr Malcolm Miller describing the history and design of this marvelous cathedral, his knowledge of Chartres giving an added dimension to any visit. Very British, he is based in Chartres and if you would like to arrange a personal tour, you can write to him care of the cathedral or Chartres' tourist office. From Chartres continue south to TOURS. Located at the junction of the Cher and Loire rivers, Tours has played an important role in history.

Drive west along the north bank of the Loire to the small town of LUYNES and the

DOMAINE DE BEAUVOIS.   Here you can go one step beyond just visiting your first chateau on the Loire; you may stay here for the night.   This fifteenth-century chateau with its seventeenth-century "improvements" is surrounded by a wooded two hundred-acre estate and has forty attractive rooms and a heated pool.   Spoil yourself as did the lords and ladies who flocked to the Loire Valley in ages past; enjoy the luxury of the chateau's accommodation and savor the splendors of its restaurant.   The Domaine de Beauvois offers an enchanting setting.


## DESTINATION II      CHENEHUTTE LES TUFFEAUX  Le Prieure

Begin your adventures in the Loire Valley by a visit to CHATEAU DE LANGEAIS.   Although one of the smaller chateaux in this region, it is beautifully furnished and well worth a visit.   A recent addition to commemorate the royal wedding of Charles VIII and Anne of Brittany that took place on a cold December morning in 1491 is authentically portrayed by a scene staged by wax characters. Built in the fifteenth century, Langeais was completed in a period of four to five years and since then has remained intact.   On a nearby ridge stand the ruins of a tenth-century stone "donjon" or keep, one of Europe's first.   It was a stronghold of the notorious Fulk Nerra ("the Black"), Count of Anjou.

Drive further east to the town of SAUMUR which lies directly on the river's edge. The captivating CHATEAU DE SAUMUR is strategically located above the town overlooking the Loire.   The town is very picturesque, set in a region of vineyards famous for their "mousseux" or sparkling wines.

Extending over both banks of the Maine on the outskirts of the chateau region is ANGERS, the former capital of the Dukes of Anjou.   The first castle, built by Fulk Nerra, was replaced under the thirteenth-century king, Louis IX.   During the sixteenth century many of the seventeen massive towers were dismantled, on royal command, to the level of the wall-walk.

LE PRIEURE in CHENEHUTTE LES TUFFEAUX is the next destination.   This is a dramatic hotel, set high on the hillside, offering a fantastic forty-mile-wide panorama of the Loire Valley.   The bedrooms located in the castle proper are very regal in their decor.   (However, be aware that there is also a motel-like annex found near the pool.)   Enjoy the early evening on the castle terrace overlooking the Loire and make your selections from the enticing menu.   The dining room is very elegant and service quite formal.

*Le Prieure*
*Chenehutte les Tuffeaux*

## DESTINATION III       MONTBAZON       Domaine de la Tortiniere

This morning continue west but this time follow the road along the south bank of the Loire.   The first stop is CHINON, one of the oldest castles in France whose fortress straddles the skyline of the town. It is interesting to see the skeleton of the castle, but be prepared to fill in large chunks of the interior with your imagination. The castle is made up of three distinct fortresses: Fort Saint Georges, Chateau de Milieu, and Chateau du Coudray, each separated by a deep moat. In 1429, Chinon witnessed the historic encounter between Joan of Arc and Charles the Dauphin. Later that year, inspired by her, he was crowned at Reims as Charles VII, defying the English Henry VI who held Paris as "King of France".

USSE is the next destination. The Castle of Usse, located in the dark forest of Chinon overlooking the Indre, is everything you would expect a castle to be: it has steeples, turrets, towers, chimneys, dormers and enchantment. It is believed to be the castle that inspired Perault to write "Sleeping Beauty".

*Domaine de la Tortiniere*
*Montbazon*

AZAY LE RIDEAU and its elegant Renaissance chateau are not far from Usse. The Chateau Azay le Rideau is situated on a small island in the Indre and was so beautifully designed and built in 1518 by Gilles Berthelot, a financial adviser of Francois I, that the King himself took possession. The memory of this ornate chateau reflecting in the water and framed by wispy trees will linger.

DOMAINE DE LA TORTINIERE in Montbazon equals if not surpasses any of the chateaux seen today and serves as an ideally located hotel for touring the region. The chateau has a fine intricate structure, a lovely pool, grounds designed for romantic strolls, elegant, comfortable bedrooms and a superb restaurant. Each evening a delicious menu is created by the chef in addition to the "a la carte" selection. Mme Denise Olivereau Capron is your hostess and manages this delightful castle hotel with the help of her three children.


## DESTINATION IV    CHENONCEAUX    Hotel du Bon Laboureur

Southeast of Montbazon is the town of LOCHES, found in the hills along the banks of the Indre, and referred to as the "City of Kings". The ancient castle is the "Acropolis of the Loire", the buildings around it form what is called "Haute Ville". It was a favorite retreat of King Charles VII and here you will find a copy of the proceedings of Joan of Arc's trial. The king's mistress, Agnes Sorel, was buried in the tower and her portrait is in one of the rooms.

From Loches drive northeast to the lovely CHATEAU DE CHAUMONT SUR LOIRE which was built by Charles D'Amboise during the reign of Louis XII. Later the castle was owned by Henry II. After his death, Diane de Poitiers, his mistress, was given the chateau by his jealous wife, Catherine de Medicis, in exchange for the more beautiful Chenonceaux. Surrounded by a spacious park, the castle has a lovely position overlooking the Loire.

Just a few miles to the west of Chaumont sur Loire is another beautiful castle, the CHATEAU D'AMBOISE. During the reign of Francois I court life relished and thrived upon the festivals, masquerades and flourish of the Italian Renaissance. The King finished the wing of the castle begun by Louis XII in an architectural style inspired by the period. He also extended an invitation to Leonardo da Vinci who came to spend his last years at the castle and is buried here. A tour of the castle will also unveil details of its bloody past. The Amboise Conspiracy of 1560 involved a group of Protestant reformers who followed the royal court from Blois to the Chateau d'Amboise under the pretense of asking the King for permission to practise their religion. However, their plot was betrayed and upon arrival many were hung from the castle battlements, beheaded and quartered or thrown in sacks down to the Loire.

*Chateau de Chenonceaux*

A trip to the Loire Valley would lose all significance if the CHATEAU DE CHENONCEAUX, only a few miles south of Amboise, were omitted from the itinerary. It gracefully spans the lazy Cher and is known as the "Chateau of the Six Women": Catherine Briconnet, the builder; Diane de Poitiers, the ever-beautiful; Catherine de Medici, the magnificent; Louise de Lorraine, the inconsolable; Madame Dupin, lover of letters; and Madame Peolouze, lover of antiquity. The chateau achieved a new dimension with each of its six female occupants. The rooms and bedchambers, elegantly and lavishly furnished, are fun to wander through slowly to avoid missing even the smallest detail.

Chenonceaux merits a leisurely visit and the lovely small HOTEL DU BON LABOUREUR ET DU CHATEAU, located in the town, enables you to linger over the charm and enchantment of the most elegant chateau on the Loire. A friendly welcome has become a tradition for the Jeudi family. The gastronomic splendors of their table and the comfort and calm of their simply decorated rooms will convince you that they know how to provide the delights one associates with a French country inn.

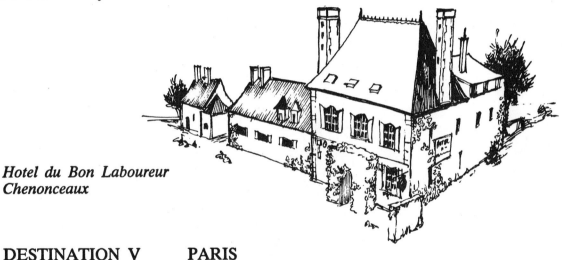

*Hotel du Bon Laboureur*
*Chenonceaux*

## DESTINATION V        PARIS

From Chenonceaux retrace a path northeast past Amboise and Chaumont sur Loire and continue on to BLOIS. The castle of Blois is a thirteenth-century chateau constructed by the royal Orleans family. Highlights of this chateau are the magnificent Francois I stairway; Catherine de Medici's bedchamber with its many secret wall panels (used, in the true Medici tradition, to hide jewels, documents and poisons) and the King's bedchamber, where the murder of the Duc de Guise occurred.

The largest of the chateaux, CHAMBORD, is just a short distance further north from Blois. Although almost bare of furniture, it retains its grandeur and enchantment, especially at sunset or shrouded in the morning mist.

The last stretch along the Loire before turning north towards Paris takes you through BEAUGENCY and then ORLEANS. Beaugency is an ancient town noted for its Notre Dame church. Orleans is famous as the scene of Joan of Arc's greatest triumph, when she raised the English siege in 1429. From Orleans drive back to Paris. the fabulous city that both begins and ends this itinerary.

*Azay le Rideau*

# DORDOGNE

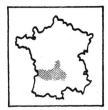

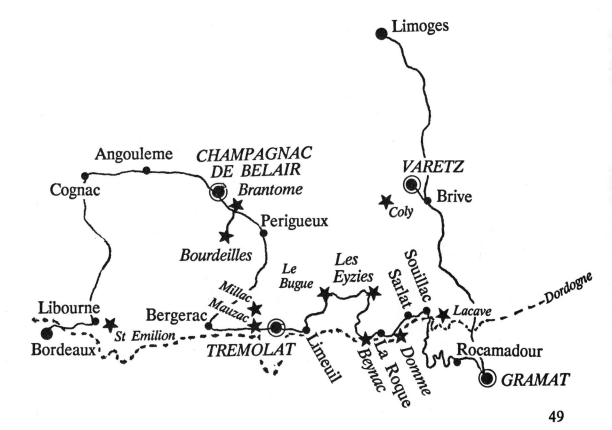

Limoges

Angouleme  CHAMPAGNAC
DE BELAIR

Cognac  Brantome

VARETZ

Coly  Brive

Perigueux

Bourdeilles

Les
Eyzies

Le
Bugue

Souillac

Sarlat

Dordogne

Libourne  Millac  Lacave

Bergerac  Mauzac

Bordeaux  St Emilion  TREMOLAT  Limeuil  Beynac  La Roque  Domme  Rocamadour

GRAMAT

# *Dordogne*

The Loire Valley is famous.  South of the Loire Valley is a lesser known but equally beautiful valley, the Dordogne.  Here you will find sleepy country roads, rolling green hills, mountains dressed with vineyards and magnificent chateaux - as one chateau fades from sight, another seems magically to appear on the horizon. Groves of aspen and birch blaze in the sunlight along the lazy Dordogne as it winds its way through this spendid region of France.  This itinerary takes advantage of the Bordeaux wine region and then follows the Dordogne, passing through romantic little villages along the way.

*Beynac*

The starting point for this itinerary is the beautiful city of BORDEAUX. An important port, the old section is jammed with shops and decorated with ornate fountains and old churches. The name Bordeaux is synonymous with the largest fine wine district on earth: the red wine districts to the north, the Medoc immediately to the south, and all of the country along the north bank of the Dordogne and facing the Medoc across the Gironde. Most of the white wine is grown in the region between the two rivers, an area called "entre deux mers".

This is a region to explore, to visit its marvellous chateaux and their cellars. Leave Bordeaux for LIBOURNE, the center for the wines of ST EMILION, POMEROL and FRONSAC. If wine pleases your palate, there are many cellars in the vicinity to sample. Chateau Videlot lies between Libourne and St Emilion: it is a beautiful house and the owner, Monsieur Jean Pierre Moueix is a true wine connoisseur. The hilltop village of St Emilion is definitely worth a visit and its medieval streets house a number of fine cellars where a selection of regional wines are beautifully displayed and convenient for purchase. It is also in St Emilion, in late September, that the festivities to commemorate the "vendage" or beginning of the harvest are enjoyed in the grandest splendor and tradition. Neighboring the town of St Emilion are two noteworthy chateaux. Chateau Ausone is the more famous, where you can walk into a ground-floor cellar with a ceiling of vines. Chateau Cheval Blanc, painted a refreshing cream color, produces some of the most splendid full-bodied red wines. It is generally agreed that Chateau Petrus, another vineyard, is one of the most outstanding of the Pomerol district.

COGNAC is the name of both a small town and the brandy distilled from grape wine. The Charente Vineyards, now given over exclusively to cognac, originally produced inferior wines sold to seamen from Britain and the Low Countries who ventured here to buy salt. It was only in the seventeenth century that some of these immigrants began "burning" the wine, and once the experiment had been made the word quickly spread. In and around Cognac there are a number of distilleries and warehouses: those of Hennessy and Martell are two of the best known. From Cognac continue east towards ANGOULEME, founded by the Romans. The upper part of the city is surrounded by ramparts.

LE MOULIN DU ROC awaits you only a short distance from Angouleme. Tucked off a small country road on the outskirts of CHAMPAGNAC DE BELAIR is a small seventeenth- and eighteenth-century stone mill, one of France's most splendid little inns. The twelve rooms, although not large, are each enchanting. Windows throughout the mill overlook the lazy Dronne river, the gardens and the beautiful birch-lined pastures: the waterside setting is peaceful and relaxing. Under dark, heavy beams, the dining room is intimate and the atmosphere is captivating. Madame Gardillou is responsible for the kitchen and the superb cuisine. Monsieur Gardillou serves as a most gracious and charming host. Le Moulin du Roc is a gem.

*Le Moulin du Roc*
*Champagnac de Belair*

From Champagnac de Belair country roads will direct you to the heart of the Dordogne.   Tucked along the banks of the Dronne are the charming villages of BRANTOME and its neighbor BOURDEILLES.  Bounded by the Dronne, Brantome is a very pretty village with its ancient abbey enhancing the picture. Founded by Charlemagne in 769, the abbey was reconstructed in the eleventh century after it was ransacked by the Normans.  The church and adjoining buildings were constructed and modified between the fourteenth and eighteenth centuries.   Follow the valley of the Dronne just a few miles further to Bourdeilles. Crowned by its twelfth-century castle, Bourdeilles bridges the river and is a small and picturesque town to explore.   Should you wish to lunch in the area there are many outstanding choices.   Two suggestions are: in Brantome, MOULIN DE L'ABBAYE, a converted mill on the water's edge with a gorgeous outlook, and in Bourdeilles, HOTEL DES GRIFFONS, a delightful restaurant where the chef is flattered when you request regional specialities.

From Brantome continue on to PERIGUEUX, an interesting old city, and then on to BERGERAC, a town directly on the Dordogne and reputedly Cyrano's home. From here the road runs alongside the Dordogne; as it nears TREMOLAT the valley becomes more gentle and lush.

LE VIEUX LOGIS ET SES LOGIS DES CHAMPS is an ideal base from which to explore one of France's loveliest regions.   The character of Le Vieux Logis matches the beauty of the valley.   Opening up on one side to farmland, this charming hotel also has its own little back garden with a small stream and various small bridges.   The rooms, recently redone, are perfectly color coordinated down to the smallest detail.   In room ten everything is in large red and white checks: the duvets, the pillows, the curtains, the canopy on the four-poster bed.   The restaurant is in the barn where the tables are cleverly positioned within each of the stalls.   Take a stroll after dinner and wander through the sleepy tobacco growing village of Tremolat.   The large doors of the lofty barns lie open and hang heavy with tobacco.   The town's church is one of the oldest in the area and has a lovely stained glass window.

*Le Vieux Logis*
*Tremolat*

Linger in this region for as many days as your itinerary allows; use Tremolat as your base and let the river be your guide.   Discover the beauty of the Dordogne by driving along the quiet roads and simply happening upon the peaceful riverside villages.   However, a few suggestions of what not to overlook follow.

From Tremolat, which is located at the "Cingle de Tremolat" (a loop in the path of the river), it is easy to follow the lazy curves of the beautiful Dordogne.   When the sun shines you might want to pick out a picnic spot as you drive through LIMEUIL, a neighboring village of Tremolat at the juncture of two rivers.   Limeuil is a pretty hamlet with some picnic tables set on the grassy river banks.

In addition to just driving and absorbing the beauty of the Dordogne, you should stop at LES EYZIES DE TAYAC, known as the prehistoric capital, where the Cro-Magnon skull was unearthed. A national prehistoric museum is installed in the ancient castle of the Barons of Beynac. But most impressive are the caves just outside the town at the GROTTO DE FONT DE GAUME. On the cave walls are incredibly well preserved prehistoric drawings, the colors still so rich that it is hard to comprehend the actual passage of time. The caves are well worth a visit but the hours are limited and the caves a bit damp and dark. To avoid disappointment, please check the opening times with the tourist office.

BEYNAC ET CAZENAC is a beautiful little village on a wide bend of the Dordogne; a castle looming above further enhances its picturesque setting. In the summer months a number of people negotiate the river by boat and Beynac, with its wide grassy banks, proves to be a popular resting spot. Beynac castle can be reached by climbing up the narrow streets or by car along a back road. The furnishings are sparse but the castle is interesting to explore and its dominating position provides some spectacular views of the valley. Beynac also offers one of the loveliest settings for lunch. On the water's edge the HOTEL BONNET is an excellent choice and it is a memorable treat to dine under vine covered trellises on the riverside terrace. This lovely restaurant-hotel has been operated for generations by the Bonnet family.

LA ROQUE GAGEAC, an extremely colorful medieval town, clings to the hillside above the Dordogne. Be sure to have your cameras ready as the road rounds a bend of the Dordogne on the western approach to town because the town, framed by lacey trees, is a photographer's dream. At La Roque Gageac there is a grassy area along the river bank with a few picnic tables.

It is only a short drive to the medieval hilltop village of DOMME, which, although a bit touristy at the height of the season, guards a position fifteen hundred feet above the river and commands views of the valley that cannot be challenged. Domme also has access to some interesting stalactite and stagmite grottos.

CHATEAU DE MONTFORT, down the river from Domme, is definitely worth a visit. Built by one of the region's most powerful barons, this majestic castle rises out of a rocky ledge. The Chateau de Montfort, not massive and overpowering, but rather, small and intimate, is a private residence, with its rooms elaborately furnished and renovated.

Also stop in SARLAT, which has an atmospheric old quarter with narrow cobbled streets that wind through a maze of magnificent gourmet shops. On Saturday mornings there is a colorful market in the town square.

## DESTINATION III    GRAMAT    Chateau de Roumegouse

Travel east along the Dordogne and then south in order to see the " Mont St Michel of the south", ROCAMADOUR. The road approaching the village is small, twisting and picturesque. Dominated by its church, the town of Rocamadour grips the steep and rugged walls of the Alxon Valley. It is a spectacular sight and has long been a popular pilgrimage spot.

Not far from Rocamadour is GRAMAT, a small village possessing a lovely chateau hotel. As you travel through, watch for signs directing you to the CHATEAU DE ROUMEGOUSE. Large majestic towers will emerge, peering above the treetops, revealing the chateau. Monsieur and Madame Lauwaert retired five years ago but the management of the hotel is now in the capable hands of their daughter and her husband, Monsieur and Madame Laine. Elegant furnishings, in keeping with the mood of the castle, are found throughout. The bedroom suites are extremely handsome. The dining room is in Louis XV decor; in summer, dinner is served on the terrace overlooking the valley. The Laines request that overnight guests lunch or dine at the hotel.

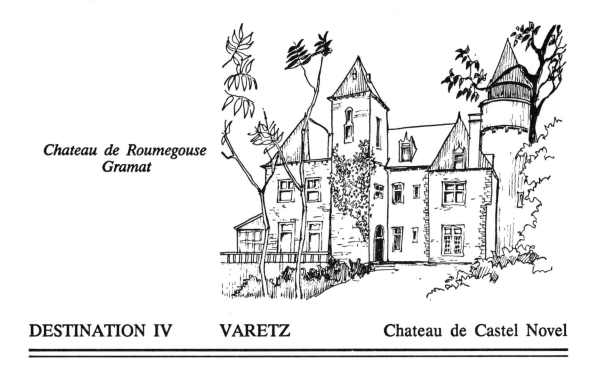

*Chateau de Roumegouse*
*Gramat*

## DESTINATION IV      VARETZ      Chateau de Castel Novel

If time allows, you might want to consider continuing south from the Dordogne to the region of the Lot Valley. The Lot runs parallel to the Dordogne and is equally as spectacular in its scenic beauty. An itinerary for the Lot follows this one. The next destination, however, is suggested for those journeying to Paris or travelling north to tour the castles of the Loire. (See Chateau Country itinerary.)

VARETZ is located to the north of the Dordogne just a few miles outside the city of BRIVE. Follow a winding country road up to the magnificent, turreted CHATEAU DE CASTEL NOVEL, managed graciously and professionally by the Parveaux family. This is a suberb hotel that will surpass all your expectations. The bedrooms are individual in their decor: spend the night in a wooden canopy bed looking out over the back garden or secluded in one of the castle's turrets. The elegant dining room and highly praised menu guarantee a memorable evening. The Chateau de Castel Novel will prove the highlight of any trip and serves as an ideal place to conclude this itinerary.

*Chateau de Castel Novel*
*Varetz*

LIMOGES, famous for its porcelain, is only ninety-one kilometers north of Varetz. A wonderful exhibition of ancient and modern ceramics from all over the world is at the national Adrien-Dubonche Museum.   One can also make arrangements to visit Haviland, one of Limoges' renowned porcelain factories.   Limoges is a large city and from here transportation and connections to other destinations in France are easy and frequent.

# LE LOT

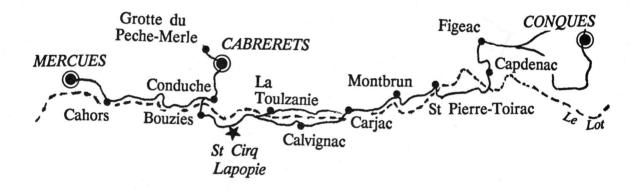

# Le Lot

This itinerary proposes a section of the Lot Valley that travels perhaps the most stunning fifty-one-kilometer stretch in France. The Lot Valley rivals the Dordogne and yet remains relatively undiscovered and less travelled. The road winds along the curves of the wide, calm river, aggressively cutting into the sides of the chalky canyon walls. At some stretches the route follows the level of the river and at others it straddles the cliff tops. Vistas are dramatic at every turn although the restricting narrow roads will frustrate the eye of any photographer - there is rarely a place to stop.

*St Cirq Lapopie*

*Le Lot*

Your adventure begins at CAHORS, a lovely city at the heart of a flourishing wine district.    Of particular interest is the Valentre Bridge with its three impressive towers spanning the Lot.

Just a few miles from the city of CAHORS is the CHATEAU DE MERCUES perched high on the hills above the Lot in the small village of Mercues.    For almost twelve centuries the chateau was a palace of the count-bishops of Cahors, whose names are recorded on plaques in the chapel.    Possession of the Chateau de Mercues was taken by the State during the revolution.    However, in this century the chambers of this magnificent castle are being offered as hotel rooms.    Under new ownership, the Chateau de Mercues maintains its standards as one of France's finest hotels and the chateau alone would warrant a visit to this region.

Most of the luxuriously furnished rooms in the chateau look out through thick castle walls to sweeping vistas of the serene and undeveloped valley.    (Note that a newly constructed wing of rooms has been added.    They are less expensive and principally built to accommodate seminars and conferences.)    The dining room is outstanding.    Elegantly set with china that displays the family crest of the current owners, the tables are positioned in front of windows that frame the valley through majestic thick stone walls.

The valley is planted with vineyards which yield some of the finest grapes in the region.    Under its owners, the Vigouroux family, the Chateau de Mercues exports a good deal of its wine.    As a whole, the region is noted for its deep-colored and full-bodied reds, the impressive "black wines" of Cahors which have become more and more widely available in the United States since the mid-1980s.

*Chateau de Mercues*
*Mercues*

## DESTINATION II    CABRERETS    Hotel La Pescalerie

From Cahors the Lot travels under the Valentre Bridge along a route whose beauty remains unchallenged.   The short stretch of river mapped out on this itinerary can be encompassed by car in a day, but try to stretch your stay.   This is a region to be roamed at a lazy pace in order fully to appreciate its character and charms.

Each turn presents a new interest.   There are castles, villages whose houses are built into the cliff face, grottos and glorious scenery.   Just two kilometers from the town of CABRERETS is LA PESCALERIE, the family home of Monsieur Belcour and a spectacular hotel, managed by Helene Combette, that does justice to the region. La Pescalerie is a magnificent weathered-stone manor house in a lovely riverside setting. Ten handsomely appointed bedrooms are divided between two levels and open onto the garden through thick sixteenth- and seventeenth-century walls. The rooms are pleasingly different, yet each is an attractive melange of modern furniture and cherished antiques. The top-floor rooms are set under the beams of the house with delightful dormer windows, and a few have lofts ideal for children with a sense of adventure. La Pescalerie also has a bar and intimate restaurant. Opened less than a decade ago, La Pescalerie ideally accommodates those who have the time to linger in this striking valley.

Cabrerets is a pretty village and the nearby GROTTE DE PECH MERLE is a definite attraction. Discovered by two fourteen-year-old boys, the vast caverns of this grotto are painted with prehistoric designs (mammoths, bison, hands, horses) and contain stalagmite columns.

Set your own pace and simply let the river be your guide. Towns and vistas are enchanting. When travelling the road from Cahors, cross the river just before Cabrerets to the village of BOUZIES. Take a moment to look back across the bridge and see the medieval buildings constructed into the walls of the canyon above the small tunnel. Just outside Bouzies, the road climbs and winds to some spectacular vistas of the very picturesque ST CIRQ LAPOPIE. Clinging to sheer canyon walls, this village is a perched cluster of soft ochre and tile-roof buildings. St Cirq Lapopie dominates a strategic position on a wide bend of the Lot and has certainly one of the prettiest settings in the region.

As the river guides you further, it presents a number of lovely towns and with each turn reveals another angle and view of the valley. LA TOULZANIE is a small village nestled into a bend of the river, pretty and interesting because of the houses built into the hillside. CALVIGNAC is an ancient village whose fortress clings to a spur on the left bank. On a rocky promontory, the village of MONTBRUN is dressed with the ruins of its fortified castle and looks across to the "SAUT DE LA MOUNINE". Translated roughly as the "Jump of the Monkey", this dramatic cliff face offers incredible views and a legend of romance.

*Hotel La Pescalerie*
*Cabrerets*

It seems that to punish his daughter for falling in love with the son of an opposing baron, a father ordered her thrown from the cliffs to her death. Dressed in the clothes of a woman, a blind monkey fell to its death instead and the sadness and regret that the father felt for his extreme punishment was erased by joy when he discovered the substitution and that his daughter was still alive. Set on a plateau, the CHATEAU DE LARROQUE TOIRAC is open to visitors and makes an impressive silhouette against the chalky cliffs and the town of ST PIERRE TOIRAC.

CONQUES is a bonus to this itinerary but requires that you journey a short distance beyond the Lot.   Unfortunately, after FIGEAC the idyllic scenery of the Lot Valley is interrupted by larger towns and traffic, but quiet prevails once again as you detour up a narrow river canyon in the direction of Conques.

*Hotel Ste Foy*
*Conques*

The medieval village of Conques has a dramatic position overlooking the Dourdou Canyon.   Tucked a considerable distance off the beaten track, it is a delightful, unspoilt village to explore - especially glorious in the gentle light of evening or in the mist of early day.  Conques' pride is a classic eleventh-century abbey.

Directly across from the church is a simple but charming hotel, the STE FOY. Some of the shuttered windows of the rooms open onto the quiet cobbled village streets, others open onto the hotel's inner courtyard or look up to the church steeples. Wake in the morning to the melodious church bells that warm the silence of the village and ring out to the surrounding hills. The decor of the Ste Foy is neat and attractive and one can't improve upon its location. Dinner is served family-style on a sheltered courtyard terrace. The menu offers a number of regional specialities and is very reasonable in price. The hotel's finest feature is Madame Cannes, whose charm, welcoming smile and eagerness to please create the wonderful atmosphere of the Ste Foy. It is easy to settle happily here and Conques serves as a delightful conclusion to this itinerary.

*Conques*

# GORGES DU TARN

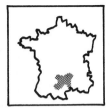

# Gorges Du Tarn

This itinerary follows the truly spectacular River Tarn as it winds back and forth along the Tarn Gorge. With each turn the drive becomes more beautiful, never monotonous. The canyon is at its most glorious in early autumn - a perfect time to visit. The French will be back to work or in school again and you will have the autumn beauty to yourself. In autumn the grass carpeting the mountains and hillsides is lush, all shades of green, and the trees blaze gold, red and orange in the sunlight. But whatever time of year, the Gorges du Tarn is incredibly lovely. Drive, walk and picnic your way through the Tarn Canyon or, if you prefer to savor the beauty from the water, there is an approximate one hour and fifteen minute boat trip originating in La Malene (the price includes a return taxi trip back to La Malene). This itinerary begins at Montpellier, follows the canyon of the Tarn, includes a visit to the walled city of Carcassonne and concludes in the city of Toulouse.

*Gorges du Tarn*

MONTPELLIER, a university town since the seventeenth century, can be considered the "Oxford" and "Cambridge" of France. Capital of the Languedoc, the city's pace is lively and happy - a perfect town for window-shopping or sipping coffee on the Place de la Comedie. A highlight, Montpellier's museum, "Le Musee Fabre", is the home for one of France's most impressive collection of European seventeenth-, eighteenth- and nineteenth-century painters.

*Demeure des Brousses*
*Montpellier*

At night, if you want to leave the noise behind, the DEMEURE DES BROUSSES is everything you could wish for in a small hotel. Located on the outskirts of Montpellier, this is a marvelous old chateau removed from the noise and tension of the city. Spacious and grand, the manor is beautifully furnished. The rooms, all with bath, are lovely: room sixteen is the most expensive, but also the nicest, with its own balcony and splendid views. The Demeure des Brousses serves a country breakfast and delightful dinners are served in the restaurant, L'Orangerie.

From Montpellier travel approximately fifty kilometers to the famous "GROTTO DES DESMOISELLES"; discovered in 1770, this is one of the most dramatic grottos to visit.

*Chateau d'Ayres*
*Meyrueis*

From the grotto it is a lovely drive to MEYRUEIS.   Overpowered by the towering Jonte Canyon walls, the picturesque buildings of Meyrueis huddle together along the banks of the Jonte.  A farm road's distance from this quaint village is the enchanting CHATEAU D'AYRES.   Hidden behind a high stone wall, this superb hotel has managed to preserve and protect its special atmosphere, beauty and peacefulness.

The chateau was built in the twelfth century as a Benedictine monastery.   In its colorful past the chateau has been burned, ravaged and at one time was owned by Nogaret, an ancestor of the Rockefellers, who arrested Pope Boniface VIII at Anagni. The Chateau D'Ayres came into the possession of the Teyssier du Cros family when the senior Monsieur Teyssier du Cros came to the chateau to ask for the hand of his wife and recognized the grounds as those where he had played as a child. The Teyssier du Cros family operated the Chateau d'Ayres for a number of years until they sold it in the late 1970s to an enthusiastic couple, Jean Francois and Chantal de Montjou. It is under their care and devotion that the hotel is managed today. Now there are twenty-three beautiful bedchambers instead of the original two, and a superb kitchen where works of art are created daily. The Chateau d'Ayres, which has a character formed by so many events and personalities, is a lovely and attractive hotel. It will serve as an ideal beginning to an excursion into the Tarn Canyon.

## DESTINATION III    LA MALENE (La Caze)      Chateau de la Caze

From Meyrueis drive northeast to the town of FLORAC, the starting point of the canyon. From Florac continue north in the direction of Mende but at the town of Biesset head west. The Ispagnac Basin, located at the entrance to the canyon, is filled with fruit trees, vineyards and strawberries. Here towns are scattered artistically about; chateaux and ruins appear often enough to add enchantment. STE ENIMIE is a pretty town caught in the bend of the canyon. An old attractive bridge arches across the river and a church wedged into the mountainside piques the curiosity.

A short distance south of Ste Enimie, majestically positioned above the Tarn is a fairytale castle, the CHATEAU DE LA CAZE, converted to a marvellous hotel. You can settle here at the heart of the canyon and pursue your explorations at your own pace and whim.   There are many quaint towns to visit:   LA MALENE, LES VIGNES, LA MUSE (HOTEL DE LA MUSE has a lovely restaurant with a panoramic view), POINT SUBLIME.   Then, at the end of each day, you can return to the Chateau de la Caze and be royally pampered by Madame Roux.

*Chateau de la Caze*
*La Malene*

Although each room at the chateau is like a king's bedchamber, room number six is the most beautiful of all.   It has a large wooden canopied bed and an entire wall of windows overlooking the Tarn and canyon.   It was the apartment of Sonbeyrane Alamand, a niece of the Prior Francois Alamand: she chose the location and had the chateau built in 1489 to serve as her honeymoon haven.   There are paintings on the ceiling of the eight sisters who later inherited the chateau.   These eight sisters, according to legend, were very beautiful and had secret rendezvous each night with their lovers in the castle garden.   The restaurant in the chateau has several house specialities; for dinner you might choose "caneton Chateau de la Caze" or "les filets de fruit sombeyrane".

When you eventually decide to leave the Tarn Canyon and the Chateau de la Caze, the scheduled drive will demand an early start.  The only disappointment about MILLAU is sadly that it marks the end of the canyon.  This agreeable town is known for its leather goods, particularly gloves.  MONTPELLIER LE VIEUX is an intriguing rock formation northeast of Millau and southeast is ROQUEFORT SUR SOLZON, the town which is home to the distinctive Roquefort cheese.  If this regional speciality appeals, you might enjoy a tour of one of the cheese cellars.

*Hotel du Grand Ecuyer*
*Cordes*

ALBI is about a two-hour drive through farmland from Roquefort.  With its cathedral dominating the entire city, Albi, mostly built of brick, is also referred to as "Albi the red".  The Toulouse Lautrec Museum is one of its more interesting attractions.

From Albi it is another half-hour drive to the medieval town of CORDES. Perched watching over the Cerou Valley, Cordes has been given the poetic title of "Cordes in the Heavens". It is an enchanting hilltop village, a treasure that will prove a highlight of any itinerary. Known for its leather goods and handwoven fabrics, Cordes offers many "ateliers" or craft shops along its cobblestoned streets. Found at the heart of Cordes is the HOTEL DU GRAND ECUYER which is filled with antiques and charm from the ground entrance to the slanting upper levels. The rooms are impressive with their large old beds, often a fireplace and magnificent views of the velvet green valley below. The hotel has a good restaurant which reflects the expertise of Monsieur Yves Thuries. His specialty is desserts and they are divine in taste as well as presentation.

## DESTINATION V      PONT DE LARN      Chateau de Montledier

It is an undemanding drive south from Cordes to PONT DE LARN where, tucked away into the beauty and quiet of the Black Mountains, you will find the spectacular CHATEAU DE MONTLEDIER. Here you will develop a taste for the splendor and elegance of a castle hotel.

The ten rooms of the Chateau de Montledier are magnificent; "Raymond" is the loveliest room of all, with two stunning antique canopied beds and a spacious, modern bathroom. The restaurant, in the cellar, is quite intimate. The cuisine is marvellous and the service impressive; everything is done to perfection and with taste. This is one place where the specialities outnumber the rooms.

Located just a few miles south of Pont de Larn is CARCASSONNE, Europe's largest medieval fortress and a highlight of this itinerary. Carcassonne rises above the vineyards at the foot of the Cevennes and Pyrenees. The massive protecting walls were first raised by the Romans in the first century BC. Never conquered in battle, the mighty city was lost to nature's weathering elements but has been restored. It looks as it did when constructed centuries ago. Stroll through the powerful gates and wander back into history.

*Chateau de Montledier*
*Pont de Larn*

As you drive on from Carcassonne, glance back at the city with its impressive towers and walls. From Carcassonne continue on to TOULOUSE, known for its pink stone buildings. Located in the midst of a rich agricultural district, Toulouse has become a very important industrial center with electronics and aerospace research as principal interests. Toulouse is also a large artistic center and has many sights worth seeing such as the beautiful Church Basilique St Sermin, picturesque old homes and various museums. In Toulouse your journey ends.

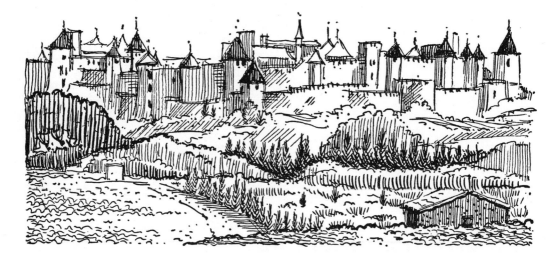

*Carcassonne*

*Gorges du Tarn*

# PROVENCE

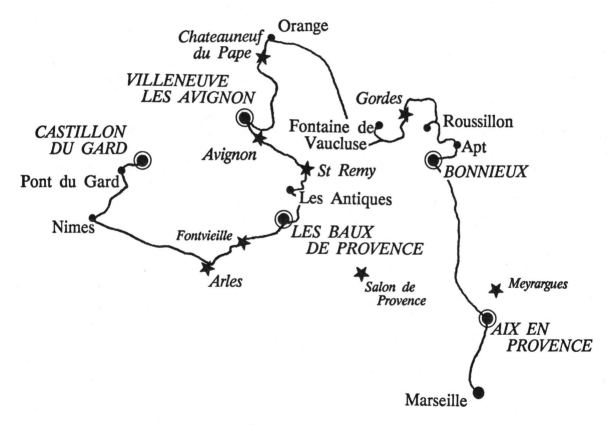

# *Provence*

Provence, settled by the Romans around 120 BC, is a region of contrasts and colors. This delightful region of the French "Midi" ("the South") is associated with warm breezes, a mild climate and rolling hillsides covered in the grey washes of olive trees.   Some of the world's most popular wines are produced here and complement the regional cuisine.   The romance and beauty of Provence has inspired artists and writers for generations.

Gordes

MARSEILLE is the second largest city in France. Settled as a Phoenician colony, this major Mediterranean port with twenty-five centuries of history is where this tour of Provence begins. Apart from the Roman docks and fortified church of St Victor, there are few monuments within the city to its past. However, you must see La Canebiere, a major boulevard which captures the activity, gaiety and pace of Marseille. The old port has a number of museums to draw your interest; the Grobet-Labadie Museum has a beautiful collection of tapestries, furniture, paintings, musical instruments, pottery and sculpture.

*Hotel Le Pigonnet*
*Aix en Provence*

From Marseille drive north to AIX EN PROVENCE, a cheerful city that deserves time to be visited properly. Aix was once the capital of Provence and a great art center under "Good King Rene" (1470s). There are a number of impressive fountains, hidden squares, charming little back streets lined with shops and majestic avenues. The beckoning cobblestone streets of the old quarter are intriguing to wander at night and the illuminated tree-lined Boulevard Mirabeau is enchanting - a bit reminiscent of Paris with its many sidewalk cafes.  From the fountain it is just a fifteen-minute walk to the very professionally run and attractive HOTEL LE PIGONNET.  A road shaded by trees leads you to this hotel away from the noise and traffic of the city.  Here you will find an abundance of flowers, cozy sitting rooms, a heated swimming pool, a fine restaurant and pleasant bedrooms.

While in Aix en Provence, with Le Pigonnet as your base and weather permitting, you can stroll down the old streets or join the crowd having coffee in one of the many cafes on the Boulevard Mirabeau.  Nineteen seventeenth-century tapestries from Beauvois are on display in the Museum of Tapestries.  Another fifteen Flemish tapestries can be found in the Cathedral St Sauveur.  Aix is the city where Paul Cezanne studied with Emile Zola and traces of his past can be seen throughout the city.

## DESTINATION II     BONNIEUX     Hostellerie du Prieure

From Aix en Provence travel north on country roads through groves of olive trees and acres of vineyards to the hilltowns of Provence.  Less travelled, the medieval perched villages of this region are delightful and intriguing to explore. BONNIEUX is a marvelous town.  Guarding a picturesque setting on a plateau above the Luberon Valley, it affords a convenient location to settle as well as accommodation at one of France's loveliest hotels. HOSTELLERIE DU PRIEURE is absolutely charming because of the owner and the enchanting decor of the inn.  It may surprise you to discover a hotel of such superior quality tucked away in this small hillside village until you learn that the owner, Monsieur Chapotin, is a member of a family long responsible for some of France's finest and most prestigious hotels.  Having recently left a financial career behind in Paris,

Monsieur Chapotin has chosen this small seventeenth-century Catholic abbey as his new venture and second home. You will discover wonderful antiques in a setting of luxurious calm. Hostellerie du Prieure has a superb restaurant with specialities all too impossible to resist. A list to tempt even the most disciplined: "cassolette de ris de veau a l'orange", "pigeon roti au gigondas" and "gateau au chocolat fondant".

*Hostellerie du Prieure*
*Bonnieux*

Hostellerie du Prieure's restaurant is a gorgeous place to linger in the evening. It is decorated with pale pink tablecloths, fresh flowers and soft lighting. On warmer evenings, meals are served in the shade of the garden. The traditionally beautiful bedrooms have handsome furnishings. It is hard not to take special notice of the magnificent works of art and paintings found throughout the inn. Monsieur Chapotin has a great appreciation of art and has plans to turn the adjoining chapel into a gallery. Under the care and direction of Monsieur Chapotin and Charlotte Keller, Hostellerie du Prieure will most certainly enhance your travels in Provence.

Include the two neighboring towns of ROUSSILLON and GORDES in your explorations. Roussillon is a maze of narrow streets, small shops and restaurants that climb to the town's summit. In various shades of ochres, Roussillon is an enchanting village, especially on a clear day when the sun warms and intensifies the colors. Gordes, perched at one end of the Vaucluse Plateau and dominating the Imergue Valley, is dressed in tones of grey - a wonderful town to explore.

Known for its surrounding fields producing delicious melons, CAVILLON is another village to include should your schedule permit. From Cavillon continue north to the amazing FONTAINE DE VAUCLUSE. In the late afternoon as the sun begins its descent, walk around the celebrated natural fountain: at certain times of the year the shooting water is so powerful that it becomes dangerous and the fountain is closed to observers. The most dramatic seasons to visit are either winter or spring.


## DESTINATION III     VILLENEUVE LES AVIGNON     Le Prieure

From Bonnieux continue on toward ORANGE. The drive is an easy one and takes approximately an hour and a half. The city has character and the antique theater and commemorative arch, improperly named the "Arc de Triomphe", are worth seeing.

Just south of the city of Orange, travel the wine road of some of the world's most treasured labels. The grapes of CHATEAUNEUF DU PAPE were first planted to fill the reserve of the Papal city of Avignon. Watch for the signs to the chateau. Although it has been in ruins since the religious wars, its skeleton still secures a fabulous hilltop position and offers sweeping views of the region. The chateau would serve as a spectacular picnic spot or for a more elaborate feast consider the excellent dining room of the HOSTELLERIE FINES ROCHES. It seems only appropriate that in an area producing some of the finest wines is also the location for an outstanding restaurant-hotel. Monsieur Estevenin is a gracious host to some very famous guests and although he still oversees the kitchen, his son is now in charge as the chef. The Hostellerie Fines Roches is just off the wine route and its turrets are easy to spot.

*Le Prieure*
*Villeneuve les Avignon*

In the fourteenth century AVIGNON was the seat of the Papacy. The Palace of the Popes is grand and dwarfs the rest of the city. Devote the majority of your time to visiting this feudal structure, but if you have time to spare, journey out to the Pont St Benezet (constructed with pedestrians and horsemen in mind) and to the Calvet Museum which has a rich collection of artifacts and paintings from the School of Avignon. Avignon remains one of the most interesting and beautiful of the medieval walled cities of Europe.

VILLENEUVE LES AVIGNON is separated from Avignon by the Rhone. It is a stronghold which has retained several military buildings including the Philippe le

Bel Tower (where the caretaker will tell you all the historic facts he feels you lack) and the Fort St Andre. If you walk up to the fort you will discover a wonderful view across the Rhone to Avignon and the Popes' Palace.

A highlight of Villeneuve les Avignon is its thirteenth-century priory. LE PRIEURE was constructed by order of Cardinal Arnaud de Via and was purchased and transformed into a first-class hotel in 1943 by Monsieur Mille. The rooms of Le Prieure are bursting at the seams with charm. Be sure to take advantage of the beautiful pool and lovely gardens.

## DESTINATION IV    LES BAUX DE PROVENCE    L'Oustau Baumaniere

From Avignon it is a very pleasant drive south along a lazy, tree-lined road to ST REMY EN PROVENCE. Of interest is the priory where Van Gogh was nursed, a Romanesque church, Renaissance houses and a busy public square.

*L'Oustau Baumaniere*
*Les Baux de Provence*

Just a mile or so beyond the outskirts of St Remy are LES ANTIQUES, the site of the excavations of an ancient Glanum, an arch and a mausoleum.

The next destination for this particular stretch of the itinerary is LES BAUX DE PROVENCE in the hills of the Alpilles just a few miles southeast of St Remy. The mineral bauxite derives its name from the town, being first discovered here. Les Baux de Provence is interesting to explore as it has retained its Provencal charm. The ruins appear to be a continuation of the rocky spur from which they rise. There are a number of craft shops and inviting creperies tucked away. From Les Baux you will not only have splendid views of the area but also of a marvelous hotel nestled in its shadow.

L'OUSTAU BAUMANIERE is considered one of France's finest hotels. Set among flowers, trees and gardens, the hotel has a lovely pool, an outstanding restaurant and bedrooms and service that deserve only praise.


## DESTINATION V      CASTILLON DU GARD      Le Vieux Castillon

The distance to be covered after departing from Les Baux is relatively short but the sights to be seen are very interesting. ARLES is a city abounding in character, a truly lovely city whose growth is governed by the banks and curves of the Rhone. It is a Roman-influenced port city, glorified because of its magnificent Gallo-Roman arenas and theaters.

NIMES lies approximately thirty-five kilometers west of Arles. A Gallic capital, it was also popular with the Romans who built its monuments. Without fail you should see the amphitheater that once held twenty-one thousand spectators, the arenas, Maison Carre, and the magnificent fountain gardens.

Twenty kilometers or so north of Nimes the spectacular PONT DU GARD aqueduct bridges the River Gard. Still intact, three tiers of stone arches tower more than one hundred twenty feet across the valley. Built by Roman engineers about 20 BC as part of a fifty-kilometer-long system bringing water from Uzes to Nimes, the aqueduct remains one of the world's marvels.

*Le Vieux Castillon*
*Castillon du Gard*

The village of CASTILLON DU GARD sits on a knoll surrounded by grey-green olive trees and stretches of vineyard just a few miles from Pont du Gard. Housed within its medieval walls, the hotel LE VIEUX CASTILLON runs the length of one small street in this village of sienna-tiled, sunwashed houses, so typical of Provence. The style here is one of Mediterranean elegance and leisure. Le Vieux Castillon is a remarkable accomplishment: eight years were spent to renovate a complex of village homes into this luxurious hotel. Care was taken to retain the character of the original buildings and, amazingly, stones were preserved, cleaned and reset within the renovated walls. The restaurant overlooks the pool that is staged magnificently against a backdrop of the town ruins with vistas that sweep out over the countryside. Le Vieux Castillon is a perfect place to conclude any travels.

# GORGES DU VERDON

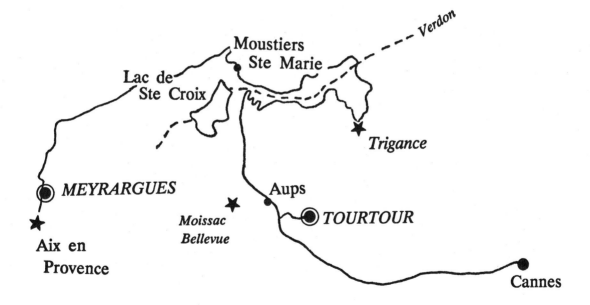

# Georges du Verdon

The Gorges du Verdon is the French equivalent of the Grand Canyon, but with an even greater variety of colors. The River Verdon has carved through the limestone plateaux and created the magnificent canyons of Haute Provence. The river then plunges into the dramatic trench-like Gorges du Verdon and is enclosed within its steep jagged walls. This area is convenient to visit when travelling from the Cote d'Azur towards central Provence; a few days spent in this region will prove memorable.

*Gorges du Verdon*

With an early departure from the cosmopolitan city of CANNES, you can take either the coastal route, a bit more demanding in time, or the autoroute through the mountains in the direction of Aix en Provence. The coastal route sets off in the direction of St Raphael. The coastline between La Napoule and St Raphael is rugged and has been called the "Corniche d'Or" (golden mountain road). The road is a chain of spectacular views: everywhere the fire-red mountains contrast dramatically with the dark blue sea. ST RAPHAEL is a small commercial port

*Bastide de Tourtour*
*Tourtour*

with a pleasant beach frequented by tourists throughout the year. Leaving St Raphael, the road leads towards ST TROPEZ along the Massif des Maures. En route are dozens of small ports and beaches, but St Tropez, an active port where each fisherman sorts and displays his catch, is easily the most enchanting of all. Drive inland at Ste Maxime along a scenic mountain road that connects with N7 at

LE MUY.   Cross the N7 and continue north in the direction of DRAGUIGNAN and watch for signs to TOURTOUR.   The drive, along a quiet country road weaving between mountains and through vineyards, is beautiful.   On the approach to Tourtour the small road climbs high to a city referred to as the "city in the heaven".   The BASTIDE DE TOURTOUR is a dramatically situated hotel on the outskirts of Tourtour.   The Provencal-styled rooms all have a private bath and twelve have terraces.   Located on one of the highest points in Provence, the hotel provides panoramic views of the region.   From the swimming pool area or in the grand restaurant you can relax and watch evening fall on the valley below.   The chef prepares divine cuisine - there is an outdoor grill for summer.   Although on our last visit we found the Bastide in need of some fresh paint, it is still a very pleasant hotel, one of the best that the region has to offer.


DESTINATION II        MEYRARGUES           Chateau de Meyrargues


It is best to depart early from Tourtour to enable you to take a leisurely tour of the Verdon Canyon.   Travelling both roads encircling the ravine, you are able to view every aspect and angle of the impressive canyon.

North of AUPS on D957, the road soon connects with D19, the CORNICHE SUBLIME.   Along this two-hour drive, the most startling and magnificent views are exposed. Just past LA COURNERELLE head north towards LA TRIGANCE, a convenient half-way point.   The chateau here is a wonderful place to stop for lunch, if you have not already packed a picnic.   The cellar restaurant of CHATEAU DE LA TRIGANCE and its delicacies have attracted gourmets from all over France.   If you want to extend your stay and perhaps walk the canyon, the Chateau de la Trigance would prove an ideal place to stay.

Continue now on D955 winding through the valley and at PONT DE SOLEILS pass once again through the jagged mouth of the Verdon Canyon. Every second the drive is spectacular. The canyon is almost overpowering: its sides plunge down to depths far below where the river forges a path through narrow stretches and then slows and calms in wider sections, pausing to create glistening, dark green pools. A spectacular journey.

*Chateau de Meyrargues*
*Meyrargues*

The road veers away from the edge at points and rolls past beautiful green meadows dotted by a few mountain cabins and hamlets. There are many ideal picnic spots, so many that it will be difficult to choose one. Wild flowers bloom everywhere. It is impossible to describe the beauty of the region. The road gradually returns to the valley, and at the end is the quaint village of MOUSTIERS STE MARIE, famous for its pottery. Considering its size, it is hard to believe, but the workshops of Moustiers Ste Marie fulfil requests from all over the world for their hand-painted faience or pottery.

Leaving the canyon behind, drive towards MEYRARGUES, a small town approximately twenty-five kilometers from Aix en Provence. A tiny road winds up from the little town to the CHATEAU DE MEYRARGUES, which dominates the area. Once a stronghold for the mightiest lords of Provence, the chateau became a hotel in 1952 and is still today majestic and fit for nobility. The building, in the shape of a U, shelters a peaceful terrace where you can enjoy a delicious breakfast and vistas that stretch for miles. All of the rooms are beautiful, some truly exceptional: "Napoleon", with a large canopied bed with red velvet curtains tied to each corner, appears unchanged from the day the titled inhabitants departed. The cuisine is first rate.

From Meyrargues drive south to AIX EN PROVENCE, where you can connect with other transportation or continue on to explore the region of Provence.

*Gorges du Verdon*

# COTE D'AZUR

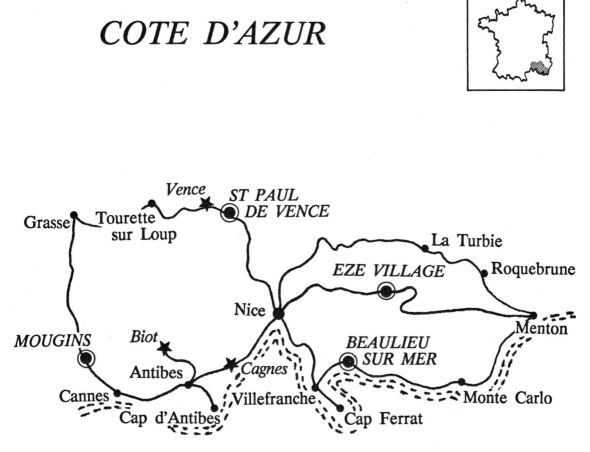

Vence
ST PAUL
DE VENCE
Grasse
Tourette
sur Loup
La Turbie
Roquebrune
EZE VILLAGE
Nice
Menton
MOUGINS
Biot
BEAULIEU
SUR MER
Antibes
Cagnes
Cannes
Villefranche
Monte Carlo
Cap d'Antibes
Cap Ferrat

# Cote d'Azur

The Cote d'Azur is known for its continuous stretch of beaches, clear blue water, warm sunshine and the habits of the wealthy international jet-setters who make this their playground. Now filled with millions of tourists, or rather sun-worshippers, the coastal towns are always bustling and guarantee excitement. In the mountains overlooking the Mediterranean are a number of smaller, "perched" towns, removed from the continuous activity of the Riviera and offering a beautiful, yet, peaceful setting.

*Cote d'Azur*

The French Riviera or the Cote d'Azur is actually the area between Menton and Nice.   Even the French say the "Nicoise" are not typically French: they are more gentle and agreeable.   This itinerary begins at its capital, NICE, "Queen of the Riviera".   Nice is colorful, elegant and always a bustle of activity.

*La Colombe d'Or*
*St Paul de Vence*

Nice is a large city with an old and a new section: the old quarter is quite picturesque with its flower market and magnificent Baroque churches; the new section is a mecca for tourists with its Promenade des Anglais which runs along the seashore lined with elegant hotels and casinos.   Lighted at night, the promenade is a romantic place to stroll.

LA COLOMBE D'OR is located opposite the main square at the gates to the fortified town of ST PAUL DE VENCE.   The hotel has many attractive salons, a refreshing pool and rustic decor. The restaurant of La Colombe d'Or is both excellent and attractive. Dine either in the intimacy of a room warmed by a cozy fire or on the patio whose stone walls are draped with ivy at tables set under the shade of cream umbrellas. The hotel boasts a fantastic collection of art. In the past a number of now famous painters paid for their meals with their talents - and now the reputation of the inn dictates that one complements the other.

Settle in your room and then stop for a drink at the outdoor terrace-bar of the neighboring Cafe de la Paix. It is an ideal place to relax and you will be entertained by the locals playing "boules". The fortified town of St Paul de Vence is a picturesque mountain stronghold which once guarded the ancient Var Frontier. Cars are forbidden inside the old town and so it is necessary to go on foot beyond the ramparts to enjoy its feudal atmosphere. The town is a cluster of galleries and tourist shops, cobbled streets and walls from which there are panoramic views of the ever-expanding hilltowns of the Riviera.

Just outside the walled town of St Paul de Vence is the MAEGHT FOUNDATION. This is a private museum that sponsors and hosts numerous collections of works of some of the world's finest contemporary artists.


## DESTINATION II     MOUGINS     Le Moulin de Mougins

Just a short distance north of St Paul de Vence is another mountain town, VENCE. Here there are dozens of back streets with interesting shops to discover and little cafes where you can sample regional pastries. Leave Vence in the direction of Grasse along a narrow mountain road that is popular with cyclists who take advantage of the lovely weather and quiet shady roads.

On the way to Grasse you will pass through a few more towns, each consisting of a cluster of medieval buildings and winding, narrow streets that, without exception, encircle a towering church and its steeple.  TOURETTES SUR LOUP is just one of the perched towns.  After World War II it became active again in the textile market as it had been in the Middle Ages: now it is one of the top "tissage a main" (hand weaving) centers in the world.  The workshops and stores are open to the public and fascinating to visit.

Road signs are not necessary: you will know by the sweet fragrance of flowers when you have arrived in the perfume center of GRASSE.  No longer a country village, the town is constantly growing but the old section is fun to wander through.  A tour of one of the perfume factories - Fragonard or Molinard - is interesting and the views of the valley below are stunning.

*Le Moulin de Mougins*
*Mougins*

This region of lavender, roses, carnations, violets, jasmine, olives and oranges is too enchanting to hurry through so continue on to explore the fortified town of MOUGINS, about twelve kilometers south of Grasse.  It is characteristic of many of the medieval towns and can be seen only on foot, which luckily preserves the atmosphere that horns and motors all too often obliterate.   Located in the center of Mougins is a small courtyard decorated with a fountain and flowers and shaded by trees.   Here you will discover a few small cafes where local inhabitants meet to gossip about society, life and politics.

On the outskirts of Mougins in the direction of Cannes is a marvellous inn, LE MOULIN DE MOUGINS.   It is actually a sixteenth-century mill that was still producing oil as recently as 1960.   Tucked off the busy road to Cannes, the inn is sheltered from the activity of the Riviera by the beauty and calm of its setting. Each of the rooms is charmingly comfortable and the personal attention you will receive during your stay will delight you.   The superb cuisine is prepared by the owner himself, Monsieur Roger Verge.   All of his courses are universally known, particularly his "pate de sole en croute sauce grilott" and his "supreme de loup Auguste Escoffier".


## DESTINATION III        BEAULIEU SUR MER        La Reserve

From Mougins return to the coast and the cosmopolitan city of CANNES. Located on the Golfe de Napoule, Cannes is the center for many festivals, most famous being the Cannes Film Festival held annually in May.   The Boulevard de la Croissette is a wide street bordered by palm trees separating the beach from the elaborate grand hotels and apartment buildings.   The Le Suquet quarter at the west end of the popular boulevard appears as if from the past and has a superior view of the colorful port.

Around the bend from Cannes (about twelve kilometers in the direction of Nice) is the small elite town of CAP D'ANTIBES whose sparkling harbor shelters many boats.   Their image, reflected in the calm blue water, forms a perfect picture with the old Fort Carre of Antibes on a small peninsula in the background.

A few miles farther along near the coast is a small village, BIOT, where glassware has been made for only just under two decades and yet has already won high acclaim and a valued reputation.   A visit to a glass factory to see the assortment of styles and types of glassware available is quite interesting.   They vary from the usual types to the Provencal "caleres" or "ponons-bottles" that have two long necks and are used for drinking.   The medieval village of small narrow streets, lovely little squares and a maze of galleries and shops is a gem.

*La Reserve*
*Beaulieu sur Mer*

Driving further you will discover yourself at CAGNES SUR MER, located only a few kilometers south of St Paul de Vence; this is a port town struggling to resemble the other coastal centers.   HAUT DE CAGNES, an old section located on the hill, has charm and character.   The Chateau Grimaldi was built by Raynier Grimaldi,

Sovereign of Monaco and a French Admiral in 1309. Also of interest is the house, now the Musee Renoir, where Renoir spent his last days. LE CAGNARD, a hotel-restaurant, is tucked away in the old village and its terrace dining is both atmospheric and excellent.

Continuing for a few kilometers you arrive again at the exciting city of NICE. Travel round the peninsula of Nice on the low road and discover the picturesque ancient port tucked around its sheltered harbor. The old city is colorful and contrasts with the new.

Leaving Nice in the direction of Menton, you not only have a choice between the "high" road and the "low" road, but also of the "middle" road, or you can switch off and on among the three. The roads all run somewhat parallel to each other following the contours of the coast. The Grand Corniche or "high" road was built by Napoleon and passes through two picturesque towns, ROQUEBRUNE and LA TURBIE. The Moyenne Corniche or "middle" road is a lovely, wide, modern road. The Corniche Inferieure or "low" road was built in the eighteenth century by the Prince of Monaco and enables you to visit ST JEAN CAP FERRAT, the wealthy community of BEAULIEU and the small state of MONACO. Take the "low" road out of Nice and you will discover what many have already claimed for their luxurious hideaways - the peninsula of St Jean Cap Ferrat. Drive through this residential district and scout out the villas and the celebrities and then wind down to the coastal village of Beaulieu sur Mer and your luxurious hotel.

To appreciate fully the luxury and grandeur of the Riviera, let yourself be pampered at LA RESERVE. Set right on the Mediterranean with a magnificent terrace restaurant, it is one of the Riviera's highlights. The restaurant of La Reserve was founded by the Lottier family in 1894 and it is a most elegant "restaurant with rooms".

Its reputation as one of the country's most accredited restaurants is now established and acknowledged by celebrities and royalty. You will be expertly catered to both in the dining room and hotel. The restaurant, with floor to ceiling windows overlooking the salt-water pool and sea, is bordered by an outside terrace where lunch and dinner are served in the balmy summer months. The pool is heated in the winter and is surrounded by a private dock where yachts are moored while guests dine. There are fifty bedrooms (each traditionally furnished) and three apartments (each with a sitting room and a private balcony).

## DESTINATION IV     EZE VILLAGE     Chateau de la Chevre d'Or

*Chateau de la Chevre d'Or*
*Eze Village*

*Cote d'Azur*

As the road leaves Beaulieu sur Mer in the direction of MONACO, it hugs the mountain and tunnels through the cliff-face just above the Mediterranean. MENTON is a bustling but charming port town on the Italian border. Return in the direction of Nice via the "middle" road which affords magnificent views and winds past the medieval village of ROQUEBRUNE and on to the village of EZE.

Of all the perched villages, Eze remains a favorite. It is a quaint medieval place with cobblestoned streets overlooking the sea. (Park your car where you can below the village and leave your luggage to be collected by porters.) Walk into this enchanting medieval village and you will discover the fabulous CHATEAU DE LA CHEVRE D'OR.

For more than a thousand years this chateau has soaked up the sun and looked down upon the beautiful blue water associated with the Cote d'Azur. With restorations, the additions of antiques and touches to decorate the walls, the chateau came alive once again as the magnificent Hotel de la Chevre d'Or. The attractive rooms, attentive service, superb cuisine, glorious views and lovely pool wedged into the hillside make the chateau a hotel which will be hard to leave and delightful to return to.

Stationed at Eze and the Chateau de la Chevre d'Or, you can choose your own time to explore the three corniches and all the port towns. Take advantage of the beautiful beaches and warm blue waters, gamble at the casino in Monaco, enjoy the night life of the cities and sample the many tempting restaurants.

Eze Village is conveniently located just twenty minutes by the Autoroute to the international airport at Nice.

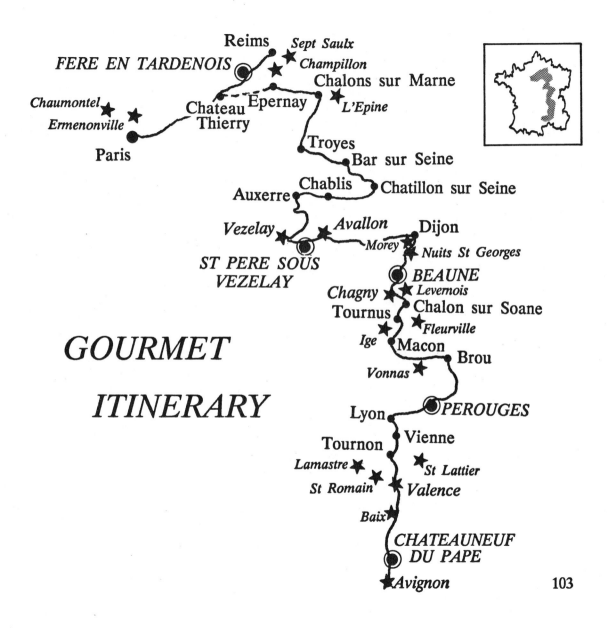

# GOURMET ITINERARY

Reims

*Sept Saulx*

*FERE EN TARDENOIS*

*Champillon*

Chalons sur Marne

*Chaumontel*

*Ermenonville*

Chateau Thierry

Epernay

*L'Epine*

Paris

Troyes

Bar sur Seine

Chablis

Chatillon sur Seine

Auxerre

*Vezelay*

*Avallon*

Dijon

*Morey*

*Nuits St Georges*

*ST PERE SOUS VEZELAY*

*BEAUNE*

*Chagny*

*Levernois*

Tournus

Chalon sur Soane

*Fleurville*

*Ige*

Macon

Brou

*Vonnas*

Lyon

*PEROUGES*

Tournon

Vienne

*Lamastre*

*St Lattier*

*St Romain*

*Valence*

*Baix*

*CHATEAUNEUF DU PAPE*

*Avignon*

103

# Gourmet Itinerary

Wine and dine your way through the "gastronomique" areas of France. Travel through the regions of Champagne and Burgundy and down the Rhone Valley. The wines are plentiful and delicious; the cuisine of Burgundy is considered to be the best in all France. Enjoy the luxury of visiting the wine cellars and selecting your own vintage. I will suggest some specific "caves" of the different proprietors ("vignerons") wherever possible. Most of the chateaux are private residences, but although you might not find their name listed on a tourist pamphlet, if a sign "degustation" (wine tasting) is posted, you will always be more than welcome. The families are dependent on selling wine and they are delighted to have you sample theirs. Experience their style of life, if only for an afternoon: join them in the fields, pick some ripe grapes and learn how they make the wine.

*Gourmet Itinerary*

Leave Paris for the Champagne district.  En route is the town of CHATEAU THIERRY.  Beautifully set on the Marne against a lovely wooded backdrop, Chateau Thierry has played an important role in many historic battles.  The English claimed it as theirs in 1421, then Joan of Arc recaptured it for France. The gates through which she entered the city still stand - Porte St Pierre. Napoleon defended the city against Russian and Prussian troops in 1814.

The Champagne region, whose soil and climate are important factors in making champagne such a delicious wine, is about one hundred sixty-five kilometers northeast of Paris.  This region centers around a small range of hills rising from a plain of chalk and divided by the winding Marne.  Unlike Burgundy, the quality of Champagne is not derived solely from the area but also from the manufacturing process.  It is the dose of sugar or "bead" that makes the bubbles, and the smaller the bead, the better the champagne: the quantity of sugar is sometimes increased to cover the poorer qualities of the wine.  The essence of champagne is the blending of several different grapes; a branded wine, it is known by the maker and not by the vineyard.  There are three distinct zones for the fifty-five thousand acres in Champagne:  the "Montagne de Reims", the "Vallee de la Marne" and "Cote des Blancs".  Each produces a characteristic essential to the classic champagne blend.

The old cathedral city of REIMS was the traditional coronation city of the French kings; it remains the provincial capital of the Champagne region, situated high on a steep hillside.  The views from the medieval ramparts are magnificent.  Although Reims is not blanketed with vineyards, it is in the district of the "Montagne de Reims" and its underground chalk tunnels serve as a storage place for bottles of sparkling wine.  Take advantage of the many renowned Champagne cellars by visiting and sampling their creations.  A few of the cellars require letters of introduction and prearranged appointments.  However, there are others that conduct tours daily. One of the most famous, Mumm, is located at 34, Rue de Champ de Mars and escorts a forty-five-minute tour. There are a number of cellars in the Champ de Mars quarter and at the end of St Nicaise - chalk cellars.

*Hostellerie du Chateau*
*Fere en Tardenois*

Further details and names of other cellars can be obtained from the tourist office near the railway station; they will be able to supply you with information as to which winery will allow you to visit on that day. Also, before leaving Reims be sure to see the famous Gothic cathedral of Notre Dame, the exceptional twelfth-century monument where most of the French kings were crowned.

Champagne is associated with celebrations and celebrate is exactly what you should do upon arrival at the lovely hotel HOSTELLERIE DU CHATEAU. Tucked away beside the ruins of a castle, the location is peaceful and the views are splendid. The restaurant has an excellent menu (with delicacies such as "turbot au Champagne" and "ecrevisses fine Champagne", and the pastries and fruit tarts are too tempting to resist. There are twenty individually decorated and appealing bedrooms with beautiful fabrics covering the walls. The beds are large and comfortable and even the bathrooms are spacious. It is hard to narrow a selection of favorite rooms down to a few; however, Rooms twenty-nine, thirty and twelve are exceptional. The latter two are large, lovely apartments, and twenty-nine is a tower that dates back to 1527. There are windows on two sides wedged between thick walls and overlooking the valley.

## DESTINATION II     ST PERE SOUS VEZELAY                    L'Esperance

From Fere en Tardenois head in the direction of EPERNAY, which is in the old province of Champagne, now the second of the distinct Champagne zones, the "Vallee de la Marne". Epernay is located thirty-two kilometers south of Reims on the southern banks of the Marne. It is a small town surrounded by vineyards, the best of which are to the south of Epernay and produce the white Chardonnay grape. The cellars to visit here are all familiar labels. With the largest cellars in the world and over thirty kilometers of aging wine, Moet et Chandon is located at 18, Avenue de Champagne. Mercier, at 75, Avenue de Champagne, has in addition to its cellars, twenty kilometers of galleries, a display of wine presses and the largest wine cask in the world (built in 1889 - having a capacity for two hundred thousand bottles of wine). The cellars of De Castellane are found at 57, Rue de Verdun. Also interesting to include in a tour of Epernay is a visit to its Museum of Champagne in the ancient Perrier chateau.

From Epernay drive southeast towards CHALONS SUR MARNE, through the third zone, the "Cote des Blancs". Then continue south through the major city of TROYES and from Troyes follow the path of the Seine on to other major champagne towns, BAR SUR SEINE followed by CHATILLON SUR SEINE.

From Chatillon sur Seine, it is a lovely drive to the region and town of CHABLIS. For a town whose name is almost a generic term for "white wine", Chablis is a quiet place whose homes are nestled on the banks of the Serein at the base of seven small vineyards. In this serene country town, wine can be tasted from an appropriate "tastevin" (a small shallow silver dish that exposes the qualities and characteristics of the wine). Dauvissat and Servin are particularly good wines to sample at the Chablisien "caves" or cellars.

From Chablis continue on to AUXERRE and then head south to AVALLON and the famous HOSTELLERIE DE LA POSTE. This ancient post house now serves some of the finest cuisine in France. Here you can order lunch and have your first taste of what the Burgundy kitchens offer. Every dish here is considered a speciality but best of all are "timbale d'homard gourmande" and "pintadeau roti".

Just a few kilometers from Avallon is the walled, hilltop village of VEZELAY. One of France's most picturesque villages, Vezelay is a "must" today just as it was in the Middle Ages when it was considered an important pilgrimage stop. Perched on the hillside overlooking the romantic valley of the Cousin, Vezelay is a wonderful place to spend the afternoon, enjoy a countryside picnic or, if afforded the luxury of time, to linger and spend the early evening in the confines of this medieval village with its splendid views.

Three kilometers southeast of Vezelay, retracing steps in the direction of Avallon, is the small village of ST PERE SOUS VEZELAY and the wonderful hotel and gourmet restaurant, L'ESPERANCE. The Meneaus are your hosts and dining in the care of Marc Meneau is truly a memorable experience. Shadowed by his devoted Doberman, Marc Meneau, a tall and handsome man, sports a tie under his chef's white and is ever present to welcome guests before attending to his culinary creations. His lovely wife, Francoise, graciously supervises the attentive, professional staff of waiters. The dining room is casual yet quietly elegant and looks out onto the garden through floor-to-ceiling windows. Tables are set with soft pastel linen, stunning flower arrangements, elegant crystal and silver. As dining at L'Esperance is an entire evening's entertainment, it is a fortunate few who are able to secure a room reservation. The hotel has thirteen beautifully appointed bedrooms located upstairs, traditional in furnishings. There are an additional three suites and five bedrooms, lovely and more rustic in decor, situated in a renovated mill just three hundred meters from the reception area. L'Eperance is a charming hotel and its gourmet restaurant makes it an ideal stopover for this itinerary.

*L'Esperance*
*St Pere sous Vezelay*

## DESTINATION III     BEAUNE                    Hotel le Cep

The routing from St Pere sous Vezelay marks the end of the Champagne and Chablis regions and the beginning of the Burgundy. Within the area titled "Burgundy" there are a number of distinct wines; the region produces a variety of white, red, and rose wines. Burgundies vary: the soil, the grape, the climate, and the individual vineyards which produce them are all responsible for the distinctions. "Burgundy" is a misused term and there are many imitations unjustly claiming the title: this wine can only come from the true Burgundy region where conditions are unique. The "real" Burgundy wine is not plentiful but it is truly great. Leave the isolated region of Chablis and drive towards the heart of Burgundy known as the

*Hotel Dieu*
*Beaune*

COTE D'OR which begins at Dijon and ends at Chagny and produces Burgundy's finest wines. Today this "Cote d'Or" or "golden slope" is divided in two: three-quarters of the great red wines are produced in the northern Cote de Nuits; the remainder of the reds and the great white wines are from the southern Cote de Beaune. From Chagny almost to Lyon is an area more generally known for the wines of southern Burgundy which are divided into three districts: Cote de Chalonnais, Cote de Maconnais and Cote de Beaujolais.

*Gourmet Itinerary*

Retrace your path from St Pere sous Vezelay to Avallon and then head for DIJON on the tip of the Cote de Nuits. Very prosperous, Dijon is known for its wine as well as for its mustard. It was the ancient capital of the Dukes of Burgundy, and some of its old streets twist and wind with a character and atmosphere of old. Traces of history are also glimpsed in the Palace of Charles de Valois whose museum, the Beaux Arts, displays some wonderful old wood carvings and paintings. While in France you will most likely be offered an aperitif called Kir, and it is interesting to note that it originated here in Dijon. Kir is made from a mixture of cassis and wine, Kir Royal made from champagne and cassis: Dijon produces eighty-five per cent of France's cassis. Kir was named for a mayor, Canon Kir, who made the drink of cassis and wine popular. If your travels are in November, visit the superb Gastronomic Fair in Dijon.

South of Dijon is the colorful old city of BEAUNE and stretching between the two is a wine route dotted with some of the region's most impressive vineyards. GEVREY CHAMBERTIN'S origin was Clos de Beze and was first produced by the monks of Beze Abbey. The label changed to Chambertin when Bertin purchased the neighboring field and now Charmes Chambertin is the principal wine bottled. The vineyards of CHAMBOLLE MUSSIGNY produce a wine that rivals Chambertin. The hillsides of VOUGEOT were first planted by Cistercian monks in the fourteenth century and a stone wall was built to encircle the vineyards and protect them from raiders in the One Hundred Years' War. Now recognized worldwide, an organisation called "Chevaliers du Tastevin" chose Vougeot's sixteenth-century chateau in 1944 as a base from which to publicize Burgundy wines. The chateau is open to the public, except when the Chevaliers du Tastevin are in session. NUITS ST GEORGE is a small version of Beaune and boasts some highly praised wines. The vineyards of ALOXE CORTON have hung heavy with grapes since the time of Charlemagne. Legend states that Aloxe Corton is known for both its red and white wines because during the time that Charlemagne owned the vineyards, his wife claimed that red wine stained his white beard and so he ordered the production of white wines too.

BEAUNE is the wine capital of Burgundy, and some say of the world.   Beaune was the residence of the Dukes of Burgundy installed in their fifteenth-century house which now contains a marvelous museum on the history and cultivation of Burgundy wines.   Take time also to visit the Hospice and Hotel Dieu - both hospitals that date from the Middle Ages.   Supported by proceeds from an annual sale of their wines, the hospitals contain some lovely tapestries and art.   A walk along the town's ramparts affords a leisurely view and tour of Beaune.

*Hotel Le Cep*
*Beaune*

HOTEL LE CEP is a wood-framed building blending easily with the character of the walled town.   It is a small hotel but can play a large part in establishing wonderful memories for your trip in and around Beaune.   The rooms are all decorated with well-chosen antiques.   There are old beamed ceilings throughout the hotel and even the winding staircase creaks every so often to add to its authentic yet relaxed atmosphere.   Simple meals will be prepared on request and served in the vaulted cellar where one large table constitutes the restaurant.

POMMARD, MEURSAULT and PULIGNY MONTRACHET are charming and important wine towns which lie between Beaune and Chagny. These three wine growing communities produce the greatest white Burgundies. Wine tasting is hosted daily at the Domaine du Chateau de Meursault. CHAGNY has a marvelous hotel-restaurant, the LAMELOISE. If you have stopped at every wine cellar en route it might be best that you take a break. The Lameloise restaurant is a fine choice.

*Ostellerie du Vieux Perouges*
*Perouges*

South from Chagny lie the vineyards of the "Cote de Chalonnaise". The drive, now bordered with crops as well as vineyards, continues south through the town of CHALON and weaves alongside the path of the Saone. The route passes through the medieval town of TOURNUS with its Romanesque abbey of St Philibert, then on into the region of "Maconnais" and on to the seventeenth-century town of MACON. Between the towns of Tournus and Macon, a wine that bears the simple appellation of Macon or Macon Villages is produced. Some of the communities involved are VIRE, IGE and LA ROCHE LES VINEUSE. Detour south of Macon along a steep road that explores little villages and some of the world's most treasured vineyards: POUILLY, FUISSE, ST VERAND.

At Macon, leave the Saone and drive east. At the town of BROU, with its great monastery and church, begin the drive south. VIEUX PEROUGES, a medieval village, has cobblestoned streets (explore the character of the village on Place du Tilleul and along Rue des Rondes), art and pottery workshops and boutiques.

OSTELLERIE DU VIEUX PEROUGES and its excellent restaurant are comfortable and attractive, located in one of Perouges' many old, wood-timbered homes that no longer stand erect, but rather lean out over the narrow streets. The hotel has twenty-five rooms in two separate buildings; fifteen are furnished with antiques, and the others are more simple, yet still inviting.


## DESTINATION V    CHATEAUNEUF DU PAPE    Hostellerie Fines Roches

Return to the Saone and continue south as the road leads to the metropolitan city of LYON and back to the wine valley. Lyon is the home of the silk industry and has a museum on the history of fabrics. Its restaurants are some of the best in the world, and, depending on your mood, you might want to visit the old Gallo-Roman quarter and have lunch here, or you might prefer to continue south back to the quiet country along the Rhone. Geographically, Lyon is where the Saone valley ends and the Rhone wine valley begins.

Along the course of the Rhone the countryside changes from oak forest to the herbal scrub and olive groves so characteristic of Provence. The wine regions of the Rhone fall into two groups: northern and southern. In the north, the COTE DE ROTIE and CONDRIEU are the two principal vineyards, and in the south the wine generally falls under the title of the Cote du Rhone. The first great vineyards lie about forty kilometers south of Lyon across the river from the old Roman town of VIENNE. In the span of just a few short kilometers

*Hostellerie Fines Roches*
*Chateauneuf du Pape*

between Vienne and Valence are the CROZES HERMITAGE, the HERMITAGE, the TAIN, the CORNAS and ST PERAY vineyards whose sun-burnt slopes and granite terrain produce some extremely splendid and full-bodied wines. The town of VALENCE, built on terraces overlooking the Rhone, has a number of Roman monuments and is the location of the famous restaurant PIC, where you might want to have lunch if you did not stop at Lyon.

As the Rhone flows into Provence the best of climate and soil combine to produce ideal conditions and some of the world's finest vineyards: RASTEAU, TAVAL and

CHATEAUNEUF DU PAPE.   It seems only appropriate that a region of France's finest wines is also the location of a superior chateau-hotel with an outstanding restaurant, the HOSTELLERIE FINES ROCHES.   Just south of Orange, with an imposing position on a hillside surrounded by vineyards, this castle hotel has surprisingly few rooms.   The seven suites are handsomely furnished and spacious. Monsieur Estevenin is a gracious host and although he still oversees the kitchen, his son is in charge as chef.   Some specialities include "filets de rougets" and a magnificent assortment of desserts.   If the weather is nice you might want to consider packing a picnic and enjoying lunch and the view from the ruins of the Chateauneuf du Pape castle.

Now, a few pounds heavier and imbued with grander knowledge of wine (or perhaps just with wine imbibed), your "wine and dine" tour comes to an end. Please refer to the Provence Itinerary beginning on page 77 for more detailed information on the region should you wish to extend your stay here.

Marlenheim

Molsheim

Rosheim

Obernai

*Itterswiller*

Barr

Andlau

*Colroy*

Chartenois

*Ribeauville*

Riquewihr

*Kayersberg*

*Strasbourg*

Selestat

Turckheim

Colmar

*ALSACE*

*Munster Valley*

Hohneck

Pt Ballon

*ROUFFACH*

Vieil

Quebwiller

*Route des Cretes*

Cernay

Mulhouse

117

# *Alsace*

The Alsatian region borders Germany and as a result the language has a definite German accent, the people tend to be physically broad and tall, the homes resemble those of the Tyrol and the wine is definitely similar to German in its fruity bouquet (although made in the French manner). Rooftops ornamented with storks dot the horizon. Beginning in March, tens of thousands of storks break their journey to the African continent in Alsace. Then, or any time, Alsace has character: the region is dramatically beautiful and a visit is rewarding.

| DESTINATION | ROUFFACH | Chateau d'Isenbourg |
|---|---|---|

Depart from MULHOUSE, a fairly large industrial city. The first few hours in Alsace will be spent following the Route des Cretes which winds along the Vosges and through its valleys. Strategically located, this road was constructed by the

French during World War I to ensure communications between the different valleys. Thirty thousand German and French soldiers died on the ledges of VIEIL ARMAND during this tragic war. There are splendid views and many sad memories.

GRAND BALLON, the Vosges' highest peak, deserves a hike. From its summit the Vosges range, the Black Forest and - on a clear day - the Jura and the Alps can be seen.

HOHNECK is perhaps one of the most celebrated summits of the Vosges. Again, the panorama is splendid. From Hohneck this itinerary veers towards the Alsace wine road. En route you will pass through the Munster Valley where the farmland is fenced by the mountains themselves.

*Chateau d'Isenbourg*
*Rouffach*

Reaching the wine road, N83, drive south to CHATEAU D'ISENBOURG in ROUFFACH, an outstanding hotel set on a hillside laced with vineyards. This is an ideal spot to unpack and settle while you make excursions to the colorful small Alsatian towns and visit their wine cellars. During the Middle Ages the Chateau d'Isenbourg was the cherished home of the prince bishops of Strasbourg and more recently it was owned by wealthy wine growers. On the hillside above the town of Rouffach, the chateau is still surrounded by its own vineyards. You can savor your delicious meal and fine Alsatian wines in the vaulted wine cellars which now serve as a very pleasant restaurant. There are forty bedrooms, a number of which are exceptionally elegant with impressive, handpainted ceilings. The chateau has a large swimming pool.

The wine road follows the base of the mountains which are dressed with vineyards. In the stretch between Rouffach and Obernai, you will find wine is king, dominating and affecting the character and personality of each town and the lifestyle of the people. In the northern section from Obernai to Marlenheim neither tradition nor culture has suffered in the least; costumes are predominant and festivals and holidays are still adhered to. At intervals buildings group together forming towns, each town a charming stroll. Of these OBERNAI is said to be the prettiest, then RIBEAUVILLE, RIQUEWIHR, KAYERSBERG, TURKHEIM and EQUISHEIM not far behind. COLMAR is a larger but attractive town on the River Luach. The heart of Colmar, with its old houses, still maintains the charm of a small Alsatian village.

STRASBOURG, on France's border with Germany, is a beautiful city and a convenient point to end your trip. The walls of Strasbourg's Gothic cathedral absorbed much of the city's history. A walk through the old city will take you back to another era. The Rue du Bain aux Plantes is bordered by many sixteenth- and seventeenth-century homes of the Alsatian Renaissance; this quarter is where the craftsmen gathered and left their mark in the best preserved section of Strasbourg, referred to as "La Petite France".

Take your time visiting the region, enjoying the wines, the life and culture Ideally, plan your visit during autumn to coincide with the wine festivals.

# PARIS

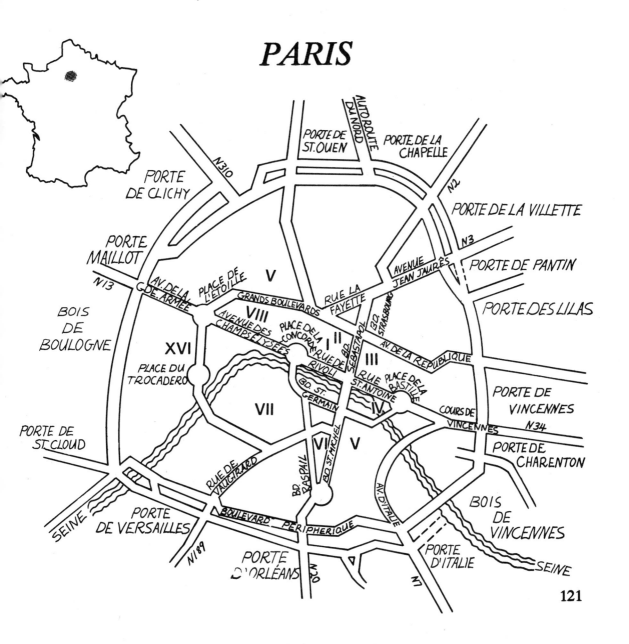

PORTE DE ST.OUEN

AUTOROUTE DU NORD

PORTE DE LA CHAPELLE

N310

PORTE DE CLICHY

N2

PORTE DE LA VILLETTE

PORTE MAILLOT

N3

AVENUE JEAN JAURÈS

PORTE DE PANTIN

N13

AV. DE LA G.DE. ARMÉE

PLACE DE L'ETOILE

V

RUE LA FAYETTE

PORTE DES LILAS

BOIS DE BOULOGNE

GRANDS BOULEVARDS

VIII

AVENUE DES CHAMPS ELYSÉES

PLACE DE LA CONCORDE

II

BD. DE STRASBOURG

BD. SEBASTOPOL

AV. DE LA RÉPUBLIQUE

XVI

I

RUE DE RIVOLI

III

PLACE DU TROCADERO

BD. ST. GERMAIN

RUE ST. ANTOINE

PLACE DE LA BASTILLE

PORTE DE VINCENNES

VII

IV

COURS DE VINCENNES

N34

PORTE DE ST. CLOUD

VII

V

PORTE DE CHARENTON

RUE DE VAUGIRARD

BD. RASPAIL

BD. ST. MICHEL

AV. D'ITALIE

BOIS DE VINCENNES

SEINE

PORTE DE VERSAILLES

BOULEVARD PERIPHERIQUE

SEINE

N189

PORTE D'ORLÉANS

N20

N7

PORTE D'ITALIE

# PARIS

Paris, beautiful and sophisticated, lives up to her reputation. Sectioned off by "arrondissements", there is not just one interesting area to visit, but many. Each arrondissement has its own character, flavor and style. It is almost as if "Paris" were a name given to a group of clustering villages. Depending on the reason for your trip or the number of times you've been to Paris, each arrondissement will have its own appeal and attraction.

Included are descriptions of selected arrondissements and a few small hotels found within each. The arrondissements chosen are especially interesting and have some charming, almost country hotels to recommend. Included in this edition are a few old favorites and some exciting new discoveries. To avoid disappointment, hotel reservations should be made as far in advance as possible.

## First Arrondissement

The FIRST ARRONDISSEMENT is an ideal location for "first-timers" in Paris. As the heart of the city, many of the major tourist attractions are situated here: the Place de la Concorde, Rue de Rivoli, the Madeleine, elegant and expensive shops along the well-known Rue du Faubourg Saint Honore, the Tuileries and the Louvre.

Find a hotel here and you will never have to deal with the Metro or taxi drivers. You can take romantic walks along the Seine or in the Tuileries Gardens. Excitement was born on the Champs Elysees, a wide boulevard that runs from the Place de la Concorde to the Arc de Triomphe at the Place de L'Etoile, officially known as the Place Charles de Gaulle. In the First Arrondissement it is possible to see and experience so many of the different aspects of the city that if you have not spent time in Paris before, this is the only place to begin.

## FAMILY HOTEL                                     First Arrondissement

This a budget hotel whose location alone could demand a higher price. On the Rue Cambon, just a few blocks off the Rue de Rivoli, the Family Hotel offers very simple accommodation. With the exception of one ground floor apartment, the twenty-five rooms of the hotel are basic in their decor, not all have private bath, but are clean and adequate. This hotel's greatest attributes are its location, price, clean accommodation and personal management.

*FAMILY HOTEL*
*35, Rue Cambon, 75001 Paris*
*Tel: (1) 42.61.54.84, Open: All year*
*25 Rooms - Sgl from 250F, Dbl to 500F, Credit cards: Unknown*

## HOTEL MAYFAIR                                     First Arrondissement

On a small street just off the Rue de Rivoli is a lovely hotel combining modern comforts with elegance. The rooms are pleasing in their decor and service is attentive. The bedrooms are not consistent in size, but all have private bath, direct dial phones and mini-bar. The Mayfair does not have a restaurant, which might prove to be more fortunate than not, for Paris already has numerous restaurants from which to choose. The Hotel does have a comfortable salon-bar.

HOTEL MAYFAIR
*3, Rue Rouget de L'Isle, 75001 Paris*
*Tel: .(1) 42.60.38.14, Telex: 240037, Open: All year*
*53 Rooms - Sgl from 700F Dbl to 1068F, Credit cards: All major*

## HOTEL VENDOME                              First Arrondissement

The Hotel Vendome is a small distinguished hotel, located on the Place Vendome, a neighbor of the famous Ritz Hotel, designer shops and prestigious financial offices. The varying sizes of the bedrooms are reflected in their price, but all are attractive and comfortable. On the first floor is a bar and simple restaurant, modern in their decor. The foyer of the hotel is small but is the base for the delightful receptionist and very accommodating concierge. Service at the Vendome is very professional, yet friendly and personal.

HOTEL VENDOME
*Hotelier: M Andre, 1, Place Vendome, 75001 Paris*
*Tel: (1) 42.60.32.84, Telex: 680403, Open: All year*
*35 Rooms - Sgl from 800F Dbl to 1350F, Credit cards: AX*

## *Third and Fourth Arrondissements*

The highlight of the THIRD ARRONDISSEMENT is the picturesque Place des Vosges and the focus of the FOURTH ARRONDISSEMENT is the Ile de St Louis. The Place des Vosges is a tranquil park, shaded by trees and echoing with the sound of children at play. The Ile de St Louis is a charming island neighboring the Ile de la Cite with many enticing antique and craft shops. Crossing the bridge in either direction, it is a short walk along the "quai" to the Latin Quarter or a pleasant stroll to the Louvre. The hotels are quaint and inviting.

## PAVILLON DE LA REINE                    Third Arrondissement

Recently opened, this charming hotel offers visitors to Paris a wonderful location on the beautiful square and park, the Place des Vosges. The Pavillon de la Reine, owned and operated by the same management as the very popular Relais Christine, benefits from the same trademarks of tasteful furnishings and, most importantly, the same pride and excellence of service. Set back off the Place, fronted by its own flowered courtyard, the Pavillon de la Reine was built on the site of an old monastery. With every modern convenience the hotel offers luxurious comfort but a warm decor of beamed ceilings, antiques, handsome reproductions, beautiful art and paintings. Accommodations are offered as standard double rooms, two level duplexes and two bedroom suites. The hotel does not have a restaurant, but a lovely salon, and breakfast is served under the vaulted ceilings of the old cellar.

*HOTEL PAVILLON DE LA REINE*
*Hotelier: M. Sudre, 28, Place des Vosges, 75003 Paris*
*Tel: (1) 42.77.96.40, Telex: 216 160, Open: All year*
*50 Rooms - Dbl 910F, Duplex 1360F to 1610F, Suite 1850, Credit cards: All major*

## HOTEL DEUX ILES Fourth Arrondissement

The quaint and charming Hotel Deux Iles is converted from a seventeenth-century house. Interior decorator Roland Buffat, responsible for the already popular Hotel de Lutece, has employed cheerful prints, bamboo and reed in the furnishings; made an open fireplace an obvious reason and focal point for a cozy retreat or rendezvous and expanded a central area into a garden of plants and flowers. The result, an unusual and harmonious blend of color, furnishings and an inviting atmosphere. Paris has once again profited from the talents of Roland Buffat.

*HOTEL DEUX ILES*
*Hotelier: M Buffat, 59 Rue St Louis en L'Ile, 75004 Paris*
*Tel: (1) 43.26.13.35, Open: All year*
*17 Rooms - Sgl from 425F Dbl to 585F, Credit cards: None*

## GRAND HOTEL JEANNE D'ARC Fourth Arrondissement

This is another hotel chosen as a budget entry. The Grand Hotel Jeanne d'Arc is tucked off a small side street near the Place des Vosges. It is a clean, simple hotel run by a +ovely couple and their lounging dog. A pretty salon and breakfast room are found just off the hotel's narrow entry hall. In the public areas the furnishings are decorative, lace curtains soften the windows and plants are an attractive backdrop. The upstairs bedrooms are basic in their decor and comforts, all have private bath or shower.

*GRAND HOTEL JEANNE D'ARC*
*3, Rue Jarente, 75004 Paris*
*Tel: (1) 48.87.62.11, Open: All year*
*38 Rooms - Dbl from 250F to 290F, Credit cards: Unknown*

The charm of the Ile de St Louis has penetrated the walls of the Hotel de Lutece. It is obvious from the moment you are welcomed into the foyer with its log-burning fire, flowers, antiques and central, tropical garden. The rooms are all comfortable and inviting. Provincial fabric prints cheerfully complement the bedroom decor whether its furnishings are the light and airy rattan or the more traditional wood. Bedrooms vary in size which is reflected in their price.

*HOTEL DE LUTECE*
*Hotelier: M Buffat, 65, Rue St Louis en L'Ile, 75004 Paris*
*Tel: (1) 43.26.23.52, Open: All year*
*23 Rooms - Dbl Room 650F, Credit cards: None*

## HOTEL ST LOUIS
Fourth Arrondissement

This is a small hotel with atmosphere located on the Ile de St Louis, near antique and pastry shops. The rooms are not large, but they are simple and nicely furnished. A few choice accommodations: rooms fifty-one and fifty-two are doubles with bath and fifty-three is a double with shower. Mme Record describes her hotel "as if in another era ... fifty years behind - no TV, no telephone, no lift!". Guests leave only praises in the register with vows to return. The presence of the Records is a welcome advantage as they are efficient and very caring of their guests. Their hospitality far exceeds any other on the island.

*HOTEL SAINT LOUIS*
*Hotelier: Andree & Guy Record, 75, Rue St Louis en L'Ile, 75004 Paris*
*Tel: (1) 46.34.04.08, Open: All year*
*25 Rooms - Dbl from 450F Dbl to 700F, Credit cards: None*

# *Fifth, Sixth and Seventh Arrondissements*

All three, the FIFTH, SIXTH AND SEVENTH, are the ARRONDISSEMENTS which comprise the ever-popular Latin Quarter. Here you will find activity and companionship abound. There are creperies, sidewalk cafes, food stands, the Sorbonne and its students, antique shops and art galleries, and so many restaurants, all promising "favorites" to be discovered. At night many of the small streets are blocked off and the Latin Quarter takes on a very special ambiance. The left bank of the Latin Quarter is separated from the right bank by the Seine and the Ile de la Cite. The grandeur of Notre Dame is overpowering when illuminated at night. Do not overlook the Ste Chapelle and its praised stained-glass windows. Along the "quai" are many secondhand book stalls. Housed in the grand old train station, the recently opened Musee d'Orsay houses an exhibition of Paris's greatest collection of Impressionist art. In the Latin Quarter there is a constant wave of activity, but although it is a bustling area there are several hotels where you can find a room and close out the noise.

HOTEL COLBERT                                    Fifth Arrondissement

Hotel Colbert is a real find: a charming and quiet hotel at the hub of the Latin Quarter. Located on a street of the same name, Rue Hotel Colbert, it enjoys a secluded location on a small side street.    A private courtyard leads to the entrance and adds to the hotel's peaceful setting.    Recent renovation has left the bedrooms with a much more spacious feeling and modernized all the baths, while retaining the old-fashioned French character.    The top floor now houses two apartments, one a luxurious two-bedroom, two-bath suite connected by a sitting area and the second a two-bedroom, one-bath, both of which afford spectacular views of Notre Dame. Of the forty rooms, ten enjoy glimpses of Notre Dame, and many of the others enjoy the quiet tranquility of the courtyard view. An inviting bar just to the left of the reception area is a welcome spot to relax after long Parisian walks.    The management of the hotel is very personal and caring, catering to individual travellers as opposed to businessmen, see many return visitors, and both welcome and appreciate American clientele.

*HOTEL COLBERT*
*Hotelier: M J. Canteloup, 7, Rue de l'Hotel Colbert, 75005 Paris*
*Tel: (1) 43.25.85.65, Telex: 260690, Open: All year*
*40 Rooms - Sgl from 470F Dbl to 730F, Apt 1060F Credit cards: AX, VS*


## HOTEL DES GRANDS HOMMES                    Fifth Arrondissement

Facing onto the Place du Pantheon, the Hotel des Grands Hommes is a haven in Paris.    Small and quiet, the lobby abounds with fresh flower arrangements, has an interior court garden and inviting leather couches and chairs adorning its marble floors.    A delicious "cafe complet" can be savored at small wooden tables paired with tapestry chairs all set under the light stone arches of the house's original cellar. The bedrooms are found up a spiral staircase (or elevator) and are beautiful in their decor of warm colors, fabrics, antiques and exposed beams.    The beds are firm and the bathrooms lovely and modern.    This is a delightful hotel, a bargain for its price, owned and managed by a very gracious and attentive Madame Brethous. She and her staff are friendly and speak wonderful English, yet they are courteous if you would like to practice your French.    No restaurant.

*HOTEL DES GRANDS HOMMES*
*Hotelier: Mme Brethous, 17, Place du Pantheon, 75005 Paris*
*Tel: (1) 46.34.19.60 Telex: 200 185, Open: All year*
*32 Rooms - Sgl from 485F Dbl to 650F, Credit cards: All major*

## RESIDENCE DU PANTHEON                Fifth Arrondissement

This hotel is located next door to the Hotel des Grands Hommes and is also owned and managed by Madame Brethous. Identical in feeling and decor, both eighteenth-century houses have been attractively converted and the Pantheon's thirty-four bedrooms all profit from Madame's excellent taste and are furnished in period style. Although there is no restaurant, the vaulted basement cellar is now used as a breakfast room or you can enjoy morning coffee and croissants in the privacy of your own room looking out to the Pantheon.

*RESIDENCE DU PANTHEON*
*Hotelier, Mme Brethous, 19, Place du Pantheon, 75005 Paris*
*Tel: (1) 43.54.32.95 Telex: 206 435, Open: All year*
*34 Rooms - Sgl from 485F Dbl to 650F, Credit cards: All major*

## HOTEL ABBAYE ST GERMAIN                Sixth Arrondissement

Suggested by readers on numerous occasions, the Hotel Abbaye St Germain is definitely a hotel deserving of recommendation. Madame Lafortune has achieved a delightful countryside ambiance utilizing her tasteful decorating choices to accent the charm and character of this restored eighteenth-century residence. Serviced by a lift, the bedrooms, if not large, are pleasantly appointed and each is equipped with private bath and may overlook a tranquil courtyard or bordering garden. Breakfast or refreshments can be enjoyed in the serene setting of a central patio-garden.

HOTEL ABBAYE ST GERMAIN
Hotelier: M & Mme Lafortune, 10, Rue Cassette, 75006 Paris
Tel: (1) 45.44.38.11, Open: All year
45 Rooms - Sgl from 500F Dbl to 630F, Credit cards: None


## L'HOTEL                                      Sixth Arrondissement

L'Hotel is a colorful and glamorous hotel whose expensive lodgings attract many celebrities.   Its presence, on a small side street in the heart of the Latin Quarter, is barely noticeable: a small door and name plaque are the only clues.   Inside, the hotel is graced by a beautiful open rotunda and displayed about are fountains, plants and birds.   Although expensive, this hotel's ornately decorated rooms draw many appreciative guests.   There are two spectacular suites with kitchenettes that occupy the top two floors and look out across the rooftops of Paris.   The Oscar Wilde chamber boasts its own terrace and is always reserved well in advance.   For dining the restaurant is popular with a sophisticated, late-night crowd.   The piano bar opens at 6:00PM and in the restaurant the last order is accepted at 1:00AM.

L'HOTEL
Directeur: J.F. Grand, 13, Rue des Beaux Arts, 75006 Paris
Tel: (1) 43.25.27.22, Telex: 270870, Open: All year
27 Rooms - Sgl from 930F, Dbl to 1840F, Credit cards: All major


## RELAIS CHRISTINE                            Sixth Arrondissement

The Relais Christine achieves a countryside ambiance at the heart of Paris's Latin Quarter.   A large, flowering courtyard buffers the hotel from any noise and a beautiful wood-panelled lobby ornamented with antiques, Oriental rugs and distinguished portraits is your introduction to this delightful hotel.   The Relais Christine is privately owned and now managed by Jean Jacques Regnault who for many years so successfully directed the Lancaster Hotel. A converted monastery, the hotel underwent complete restoration and modernization in 1979. Fully air conditioned, there are thirty-five double rooms whose beds easily convert to twin beds. There are two-level and single-level accommodations, all individual in their decor - ranging from attractive contemporary to a dramatic Louis XIII. A few of the bedrooms overlook a small back street, but the majority open onto the garden or front courtyard. The Relais also has sixteen beautiful suites, of which four on the ground floor open directly onto a sheltered garden. The Relais Christine is an outstanding hotel and the only property on the left-bank to offer secure, underground parking.

*RELAIS CHRISTINE*
*Hotelier: Jean-Jacques Regnault, 3, Rue Christine, 75006 Paris*
*Tel: (1) 43.26.71.80 Telex: 202 606, Open: All year*
*51 Rooms - Dbl from 950F Suite to 1770F, Credit cards: All major*

## HOTEL DES SAINTS PERES                    Sixth Arrondissement

This is a delightful left-bank hotel whose forty commodious rooms are set back off the main road and overlook a quiet, central courtyard. Located at the heart of the St Germain des Pres quarter, the Hotel des Saints Peres is converted from a private seventeenth-century residence. The hotel has a very peaceful, central courtyard hung heavy with vines where one can enjoy breakfast or afternoon tea. A comfortable salon-bar is also found off the main lobby. Bedrooms are found up a stairway with a dramatic wooden banister. There is one exceptional suite with floor to ceiling windows, a gorgeous, raised handpainted ceiling and an ultra modern bathroom with sunken tub. The other bedrooms are charmingly individual in their decor and comfortable.

*HOTEL DES SAINTS PERES*
*65, Rue des Saints Peres, 75006 Paris*
*Tel: (1) 45.44.50.00 Telex: 205 424, Open: All year*
*40 Rooms - Sgl from 550F Dbl to 900F, Apt 1100F, Credit cards: VS, MC*

## HOTEL SAINT SIMON                     Seventh Arrondissement

Hotel Saint Simon is a quaint hotel where all the personnel speak English due to the many British and American guests. The bedrooms are cheerful and sweet in their decor. Some have private balconies and others overlook the small courtyard and garden in the back. The largest and best double rooms are twenty-four, twenty-five and fourteen, and forty-two, a twin-bedded room, has its own terrace. The hallways are spotlessly clean, hung with nice prints, and the delightful foyer is welcoming and brightened by geraniums. I was pleased to discover that both day and night you are away from the noises of the city.

*HOTEL SAINT SIMON*
*Hotelier: M Lalisse, 14, Rue St Simon, 75007 Paris*
*Tel: (1) 45.48.35.66, No credit cards accepted*
*34 Rooms - Sgl from 580F Dbl to 960F*

The Hotel de Varenne is recommended as a budget, left-bank property. A long, narrow courtyard leads to the hotel's entry. The reception is friendly and off the lobby are two comfortable sitting areas. A stairway (no elevator) leads up to the Hotel de Varenne's very simple, but clean rooms. Furnishings are sparse, but colors used in the decor are tasteful - soft colors and delicate prints, no loud colors. The Hotel de Varenne has only twenty-four rooms, and its attraction is a quiet setting, clean accommodation and inexpensive prices.

*HOTEL DE VARENNE*
*44, Rue de Bourgogne, 75007 Paris*
*Tel: (1) 551.45.55 Open: All year*
*24 Rooms - Sgl from 310F Dbl to 550F, Credit cards: VS, AX*

# *Eighth Arrondissement*

Crowned by the Arc de Triomphe and graced by the Champs Elysees, the EIGHTH ARRONDISSEMENT is a bustle of activity. There are shops, pavement cafes, nightclubs, cinemas and opportunities for endless people-watching.

Hotel Lancaster is one of the truly elegant and luxurious hotels of Paris.   Prices are high but reflect the magnificence of the rooms.   A beautiful entry hall graced with antiques and bountiful flower arrangements envelops you with the traditional atmosphere of this hotel.   Lovely public rooms are found off the lobby as well as a tranquil garden.   The restaurant is intimate and the service discreet and personal. The Lancaster offers first class accommodation, with bedrooms and suites all modeled after an elegant Parisian townhouse.   This is a beautiful hotel found on a small side street just off the Champs Elysees.

*HOTEL LANCASTER*
*Hotelier: M J. Sinclair, 7, Rue Berri, 75008 Paris*
*Tel: (1) 43.59.90.43, Telex: 640891, Credit cards: All major*
*58 Rooms - Sgl from 1385F Dbl to 1970F*

Bright, overflowing windowboxes hung heavy with red geraniums caught my eye and tempted me down a small side street just off the Place de Madeleine to the Hotel Lido.   My small detour was greatly rewarded.   The Hotel Lido is a "gem". Tapestries warm the heavy stone walls and Oriental rugs adorn the tile floors. Copper pieces are set about and wooden antiques dominate the furnishings in the entry lobby, an intimate sitting area and cozy bar.   Downstairs breakfast is served under the cellar's stone arches.   The hotel was full, but we were able to see what was described as one of the more basic rooms, yet we found it to be extremely charming with a delicate lace bedspread and inviting antique decor.

*HOTEL LIDO*
*Hotelier: M & Mme Teil, Tel: (1) 42.66.27.37*
*4, Passage de la Madeleine, 75008 Paris, Open: All year*
*32 Rooms - Sgl from 460F Dbl to 630F, Credit cards: AX, VS*


## HOTEL SAN REGIS                    Eighth Arrondissement

Small, traditional and intimate, the San Regis was once a fashionable townhouse. With exclusive boutiques and embassies as its sophisticated neighbors, the hotel maintains an air of simple yet authentic elegance. It is easy to pass this marvellous hotel by: a small sign is the only thing that advertises its presence. Beyond the small foyer is a comfortable lounge area and small dining room, where one can enjoy a quiet drink and/or an often-welcome light meal (soups, salads, sandwiches). The bedrooms are large, handsomely furnished, and the bathrooms are very modern and thoughtfully stocked. Huge double doors buffer sounds from other rooms. The rooms that front the Rue Jean Goujon are favored with a view across to the tip of the imposing Eiffel Tower, but rooms on the courtyard are sheltered from any street noise and quieter.

*HOTEL SAN REGIS*
*Hotelier: M Maurice George,  12, Rue Jean Goujon, 75008 Paris*
*Tel: (1) 43.59.41.90, Telex: 643637, Open: All year*
*42 Rooms - Sgl from 1015F Dbl to 1865F, Credit cards: All major*


# *Sixteenth Arrondissement*

The SIXTEENTH ARRONDISSEMENT is Paris's elite residential district. It is a quiet area, characterized by stately elegant apartment buildings, lovely shopping streets and corner markets ... and by people who are walking their dogs. The Rue de la Pompe and the Avenue Victor Hugo are two well-known avenues lined with beautiful and expensive shops. The Sixteenth Arrondissement is bordered on one side by the Bois de Boulogne, a scenic park where people walk, cycle, run, play soccer and unwind.

## HOTEL ALEXANDER                    Sixteenth Arrondissement

Tucked amongst the elegant designer boutiques of the Avenue Victor Hugo, the Hotel Alexander is highly spoken of by many who return time after time. The rooms are stylishly decorated and extremely comfortable and the entrance and sitting area are attractive. The hotel is popular with American travellers, and English is spoken by all the employees. Hotel Alexander is a lovely hotel that offers consistently comfortable accommodation and a friendly welcome.

*HOTEL ALEXANDER*
*102, Avenue Victor Hugo, 75116 Paris*
*Tel: (1) 45.53.64.65, Telex: 610373, Open: All year*
*60 Rooms - Sgl from 500F Dbl to 780F, Credit cards: AX, VS*

## THE ST JAMES CLUB                    Sixteenth Arrondissement

The exclusive St James Club with properties in London, Antigua and Los Angeles has recently selected the prestigious residential district, the sixteenth, for its Paris location. It is not required that one be a full-time member in order to stay at the St James as temporary membership is included in the cost of renting a room. An imposing arched entry frames the elegant stone manor that is set back behind a lovely large fountain and circular drive. A proper British taxi (for guests' use) and a cherry red phone booth are present on the grounds and claim the heritage of the club. The interior of the club is quite grand in its spaciousness and furnishings.

The famous interior decorator, Putnam, has established a fresh, clean, albeit somewhat modern, theme to the decor. The bedrooms are equipped with every imaginable comfort from exterior blinds that open and close at the touch of a switch found within reach of the bed to a coffee table that rises to accommodate a morning breakfast tray. The traditional roof of this mansion has been replaced with a glass dome to benefit the four top suites. A wide central corridor is a maze of ivy-covered lattice work that sections off individual garden patios for each suite. As every British club should, this has a handsome, richly decorated library bar and the basement sports a billiard table, sauna and exercise room. The dining room is elegant, with soft rose drapes and an abundance of crystal and china.

*THE ST JAMES CLUB*
*Director: Kenneth Boone, 5, Place Chancelier Adenauer, 75116 Paris*
*Tel: (1) 47.04.29.29, Telex: 643850, Credit cards: All major*
*48 Rooms - Dbl from 1500F to 2500F, Suites to 4000F*

# Countryside
# Hotel Descriptions

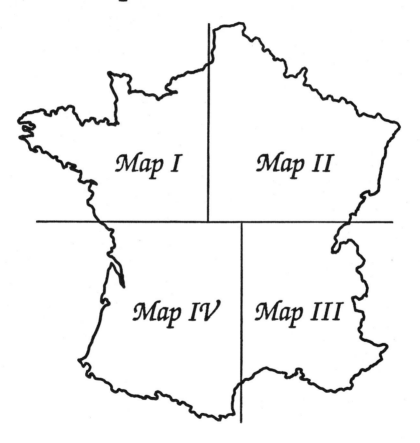

# MAP I

## NORMANDY:

## BRITTANY·

## LOIRE VALLEY:

# Map I

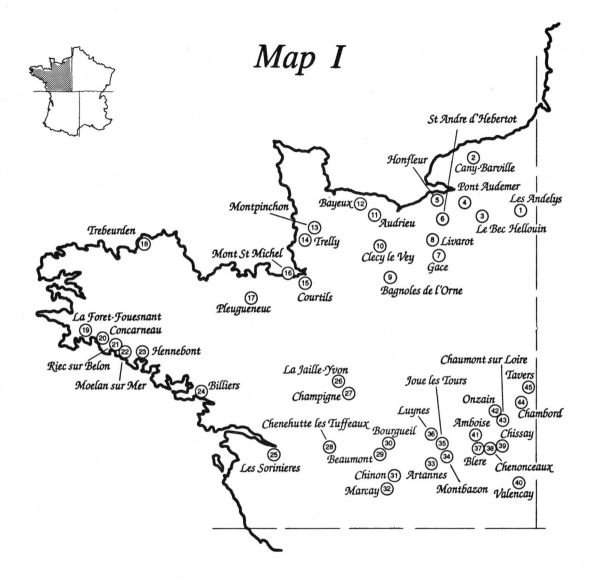

St Andre d'Hebertot

Honfleur

Cany-Barville ②

Pont Audemer

Bayeux ⑫

Montpinchon

⑬

⑭ Trelly

Mont St Michel

Trebeurden

⑱

⑯

⑮ Courtils

⑰

Pleugueneuc

Audrieu ⑪

Livarot ⑧

Clecy le Vey ⑩

Gace ⑦

Bagnoles de l'Orne ⑨

Les Andelys ①

④

③ Le Bec Hellouin

⑤

⑥

La Foret-Fouesnant ⑲

Concarneau ⑳

㉑

㉒ ㉓ Hennebont

Riec sur Belon

Moelan sur Mer

㉔ Billiers

La Jaille-Yvon ㉖

Champigne ㉗

Chenehutte les Tuffeaux ㉘

Beaumont ㉙

㉚ Bourgueil

Chinon ㉛

Marcay ㉜

Les Sorinieres ㉕

㉝ Artannes

Luynes

Joue les Tours

㊱ ㉟

㉞ Montbazon

Chaumont sur Loire

Tavers ㊺

Onzain ㊷

㊸ Chambord

㊸

Amboise ㊶

㊲ ㊳ ㊴ Chissay

Blere ㊳㊸

Chenonceaux

⑨ Valencay ㊵

Map I Showing Hotel Locations    **141**

# MAP II

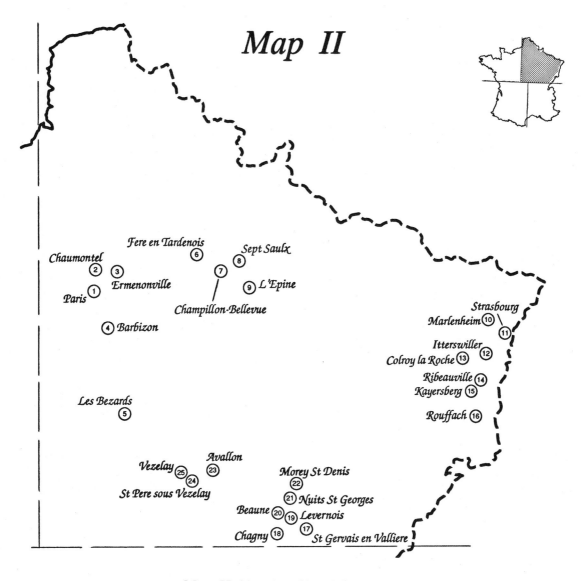

# Map II

Chaumontel
② ③
Ermenonville
Paris ①

Fere en Tardenois
⑥
⑦
Sept Saulx
⑧
⑨ L'Epine
Champillon-Bellevue

④ Barbizon

Marlenheim
Strasbourg
⑩
⑪
Itterswiller
⑫
Colroy la Roche ⑬
Ribeauville ⑭
Kayersberg ⑮
Rouffach ⑯

Les Bezards
⑤

Vezelay
⑤ ⑳⑤
②④
St Pere sous Vezelay

Avallon
㉓

Morey St Denis
㉒
㉑ Nuits St Georges
Beaune ⑳⑲ Levernois
⑰
Chagny ⑱
St Gervais en Valliere

**Map II Showing Hotel Locations**     143

# MAP III

## RHONE VALLEY:

1  Fleurville,  *Chateau de Fleurville, p218*
2  Ige,  *Chateau d'Ige, p230*
3  Vonnas,  *Hotel-Restaurant Georges Blanc, p313*
4  Perouges,  *Ostellerie du Vieux Perouges, p114, 264*
5  Talloires,  *L'Auberge du Pere Bise, p295*
6  St Lattier,  *Le Lievre Amoureux, p280*
7  Valence,  *Hotel-Restaurant Pic, p304*
8  St Romain de Lerps,  *Chateau de Besset, p287*
9  Lamastre,  *Chateau d'Urbilhac, p238*
10  Baix,  *La Cardinale et Sa Residence, p160*

## TARN:

11  La Malene,  *Chateau de la Caze, p71, 242*
11  La Malene,  *Manoir de Montesquiou, p243*
12  Meyrueis,  *Chateau d'Ayres, p70, 249*

## PROVENCE:

13  Montpellier,  *Demeure des Brousses, p69, 255*
14  Castillon du Gard,  *Le Vieux Castillon, p86, 188*
15  Chateauneuf du Pape, *Hostel. Fines Roches, p82, 116, 196*
16  Villeneuve les Avignon,  *L'Atelier, p311*
16  Villeneuve les Avignon,  *Le Prieure, p84, 312*
17  Avignon,  *Hotel d'Europe, p158*
18  Gordes,  *Les Bories, p222*
18  Gordes,  *Domaine de l'Enclos, p223*
18  Gordes,  *La Mayanelle, p224*
19  Bonnieux,  *Hostellerie du Prieure, p80, 177*
20  St Remy,  *Chateau des Alpilles, p286*

21  Les Baux de Provence, *L'Auberge de la Benvengudo, 162*
21  Les Baux de Provence,  *La Cabro d'Or, p163*
21  Les Baux de Provence, *L'Oustau Baumaniere, p85, 164*
22  Fontvieille,  *La Regalido, p219*
23  Arles,  *Hotel d'Arlatan, p151*
23  Arles,  *Hotel Jules Cesar, p152*
24  Salon de Provence,  *L'Abbaye de Ste Croix, p289*
25  Aix en Provence,  *Hotel le Pigonnet, p80, 143*
26  Meyrargues,  *Chateau de Meyrargues, p92, 248*

## HAUTE PROVENCE:

27  Chateau Arnoux,  *La Bonne Etape, p195*
28  Moissac-Bellevue,  *Hotel le Calalou, p252*
29  Tourtour,  *Bastide de Tourtour, p90, 297*
30  Trigance,  *Chateau de la Trigance, p90, 302*

## RIVIERA:

31  Mougins,  *Le Moulin de Mougins, p98, 260*
32  Biot,  *Hotel Galerie des Arcades, p175*
33  Cagnes sur Mer,  *Le Cagnard, p184*
34  St Paul de Vence,  *Hotel la Colombe d'Or, p95, 282*
34  St Paul de Vence,  *Le Hameau, p283*
34  St Paul de Vence,  *Les Orangers, p284*
35  Vence, *L'Auberge des Seigneurs et du Lion d'Or, 306*
35  Vence,  *Chateau St Martin, p307*
36  Beaulieu sur Mer,  *Hotel la Reserve, p100, 166*
37  Eze Village,  *Chateau de la Chevre d'Or, p102, 215*
37  Eze Village,  *Chateau Eza, p216*

# Map III

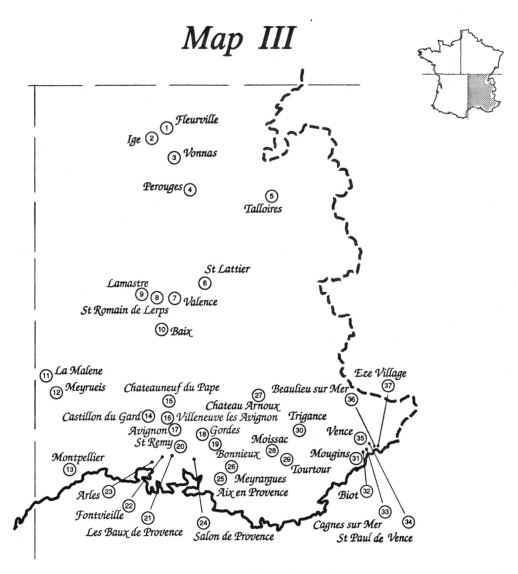

Fleurville 1
Ige 2
Vonnas 3
Perouges 4
Talloires 5
St Lattier 6
Lamastre 9 8 7 Valence
St Romain de Lerps
Baix 10
La Malene 11
Meyrueis 12
Chateauneuf du Pape
Beaulieu sur Mer 27
Eze Village 37
36
Chateau Arnoux
Castillon du Gard 14 16 Villeneuve les Avignon
Trigance
Vence 35
Avignon 17
Gordes 18
Moissac
St Remy 20 19
Bonnieux 28
Mougins 31
Montpellier 13
26
Tourtour 29
25 Meyrargues
Biot 32
Arles 23
Aix en Provence
33
Fontvieille 22
21
34
Les Baux de Provence 24 Salon de Provence
Cagnes sur Mer
St Paul de Vence

**Map III Showing Hotel Locations**

# MAP IV

# Map IV

Nieuil ㉚    ㉙ *St Martin du Fault*

Champagnac de Belair ㉗    ㉘ *La Roche L'Abeille*

Brantome ㉖

Bourdeilles ㉕

Coly  ⑫ *Varetz*

St Amand de Vergt  *Le Bugue*  ⑬

㉒  *Les Eyzies de Tayac* ⑭

St Emilion ㉔  ⑱

Millac ㉑ ⑲  ⑮ *Vezac*

Mauzac ⑳  ⑯  ⑰ *Domme*

*Beynac*

Tremolat  ⑪  ⑩ *Gramat*

Monviel  *Lacave*  ⑧ *Cabrerets*  ⑥ *Conques*

㉓  Mercues ⑨  ⑦

*St Cirq Lapopie*

⑤

Cordes  ④ *Salles Curan*

St Jean de Luz

㉛ *Segos*

㉝ ㉜ *Lac de Brindos*  Pont de Larn ③

㉞ *Sare*

*Peyriac Minervois*

② ①

Carcassonne

*Map IV Showing Hotel Locations*

Aix is an intriguing city to explore.  The beckoning cobbled streets of the old quarter in particular are fun to wander at night and the illuminated tree-lined Boulevard Mirabeau is enchanting - a bit reminiscent of Paris with its many pavement cafes.  I have returned to Aix a number of times in search of a special hotel in the heart of the old section, but without any success.  However, it is just a fifteen-minute walk in the opposite direction to the very professionally run and attractive Hotel le Pigonnet.  A tree-lined road leads you to this hotel away from the noise and traffic of the center.  Set in its own two and a half acre garden the Hotel le Pigonnet is surrounded by an abundance of flowers and towered over by ancient chestnut trees.  Most inviting on a hot summer day in Provence, the hotel also has a lovely large pool.  Inside, cozy sitting rooms and a large airy restaurant that looks out onto the expanse of back gardens tempt guests to linger.  The hotel's forty-eight bedrooms are pleasantly decorated, commodious and all are with private bathroom.  Le Pigonnet is not a "country inn" but a lovely hotel with first class accommodation and service that maintains a country ambiance and setting within the city of Aix en Provence.

*HOTEL LE PIGONNET*
*Hotelier: M C. Pelaud*
*5, Avenue Pigonnet*
*13090 Aix en Provence*
*Tel: 42.59.02.90 Telex: 410629*
*48 Rooms - Sgl from 391F Dbl to 647F*
*Open: All year*
  *Restaurant closed Sundays*
*Credit cards: All major*
*Restaurant, pool, garden*
*Located 31 km N of Marseille*
*Region: Provence*

With its magnificent blue-grey turrets, the Chateau de Pray dominates the hillside on the outskirts of Amboise.   To locate the hotel, travel northeast out of town, two and a half kilometers on D751.   Set regally in its own beautiful gardens, the Chateau de Pray dates from the thirteenth century and is an appropriate choice of hotel while exploring the castles of the Loire Valley.   Monsieur and Madame Farard are friendly hosts who gladly offer suggestions for regional sightseeing. The public rooms are regal in their decor.   Tapestry-covered chairs, heavy curtains, magnificent tapestries and paintings are staged handsomely against dark wood panelling.   Painted in a rich blue, the dining room is dramatically appointed and guest tables enjoy views out through handsome drapes and thick castle walls to the terrace and gardens.   The bedrooms are traditional in their furnishing, all with private bath or shower and look out over the back garden or down towards the river.   Accommodation may be reserved on a demi-pension basis only.   One of the most attractive features of this chateau-hotel is that on a warm summer night one can enjoy dinner served on the garden terrace, under the castle turrets, overlooking the Loire.   The Chateau de Pray offers travellers a chateau ambiance at a moderate price and the location is ideally suited for exploring the region.

*CHATEAU DE PRAY*
*Hotelier: M A. Farard*
*37400 Amboise Cedex*
*Tel: 47.57.23.67*
*16 Rooms - Sgl from 287F Dbl to 449F*
*Open: 11 February to 2 January*
*Credit cards: All major*
*Restaurant*
*Located 25 km NE of Tours*
*Region: Loire Valley*

Located on the outskirts of Les Andelys, the Hotel la Chaine d'Or looks up to the castle ruins and backs onto the Seine.   Just an hour or so to the north of Paris, Les Andelys is convenient to Charles de Gaulle Airport, Roissy and just a few kilometers from Giverny, Monet's home: a visit to Monet's home and the gardens that inspired his genius will prove a highlight of your trip.   Although the exterior needs a new coat of paint, the hotel benefits from unusually delightful management in the Foucault family, who strive to excel in service and attention to detail.   They take great pride in welcoming guests and overseeing the restaurant.   Each year Monique redecorates a few bedrooms - soon all the accommodation will achieve her desired standard and atmosphere.   The bedrooms, six with private bath, all enjoy views of the Seine and the constant, entertaining parade of barges.   Jean Claude was a baker in Paris before purchasing La Chaine d'Or and reason alone to overnight here would be to sample his breakfast croissants.   The hotel has two lovely restaurants whose windows overlook the Seine and across to a small island with an abandoned manor.   One is intimate and a delightful place for lunch: the service is relaxed and comfortable and the menu offers a limited but appealing selection of items.   A larger room is more formal in atmosphere: the dinner menu more extensive, the tables elegantly set and the service more polished.

*HOTEL LA CHAINE D'OR*
*Hotelier: Jean Claude & Monique Foucault*
*27, Rue Grande, 27700 Les Andelys*
*Tel: 32.54.00.31*
*12 Rooms - Sgl from 285F Dbl to 600F*
*Closed: January*
*Credit cards: AX*
*Restaurant, overlooking Seine*
*Located 92 km NW of Paris*
*Region: Normandy*

Transected by the sweeping Rhone, Arles is a beautiful city, rich with Roman and medieval monuments. Just fifty kilometers to the sea when following the path of the Rhone, Arles has long guarded a strategic location. It is also convenient to all of Provence and an ideal base for exploring the region. The Hotel d'Arlatan is tucked off one of the small streets in the center of Arles near the Place du Forum within easy walking distance of all the city's major sights. In the twelfth, fifteenth and seventeenth centuries the Hotel d'Arlatan belonged to the Counts of Arlatan de Beaumont and served as their private home. It is now the pride of Monsieur and Madame Roger Desjardin who offer you an ideal retreat with charming accommodation and service. This is a quaint hotel, ornamented with antiques and pretty fabrics. Many of the hotel bedrooms overlook a quiet, inner courtyard or garden. Although the hotel does not have a restaurant, a delightful breakfast can be enjoyed in the inviting salon or on the patio. For those travelling by car it is also wonderful to note that the hotel can offer secure parking in their private garage.

*HOTEL D'ARLATAN*
*Hotelier: M & Mme Roger Desjardin*
*26, Rue du Sauvage*
*13200 Arles*
*Tel: 90.93.56.66 Telex: 441203*
*46 Rooms - Sgl from 305F Dbl to 566F*
*Open: All year*
*Credit cards: All major*
*No restaurant*
*Patio, garden*
*Located 30 km SE of Nimes*
*Region: Provence*

In the middle of the seventeenth century a Carmelite convent was erected in Arles by Mother Madeleine St Joseph. It was a residence for nuns until 1770 when the order was expelled in the midst of the French Revolution. The convent then became State property until it was purchased and transformed into a hotel in 1929. In this beautiful old convent, the Hotel Jules Cesar (a member of Relais et Chateaux) has earned a rating of four stars under the directorship of Monsieur Michel Albagnac. The hotel is situated next to and shares a courtyard with the Chapelle de la Charite, also dating from the seventeenth century. The restaurant, "Lou Marques", is lovely and known for its classic and Provencal cooking. In warm weather the restaurant expands into the garden where tables are set on a lush carpet of grass in front of the chapel. Monsieur Albagnac has supervised over the years the renovation and refurbishing of the hotel's sixty-two bedrooms. The majority of rooms are large and spacious: room seventy-two, with windows opening onto the garden, is the choice room - an elegant large room with two double beds. The management has just informed us that a swimming pool is now available for guest use - a welcome addition for those hot summer days in Provence.

*HOTEL JULES CESAR*
*Hotelier: Michel Albagnac*
*Blvd des Lices*
*13200 Arles*
*Tel: 90.93.43.20 Telex: 400239*
*62 Rooms - Sgl from 455F Dbl to 910F*
*Open: 23 December to November*
*Credit cards: All major*
*Restaurant, interior garden, pool*
*Located 30 km SE of Nimes*
*Region: Provence*

We happened upon this lovely eleventh-century chateau a month before it was due to open its doors as a hotel.   The Chateau d'Artannes is the former residence of the archbishops of the city of Tours and is still attatched to an old, neighboring church.   Although now sealed, a private passageway once linked the two buildings. Set in its own garden and park, the home is entered through beautiful old wooden doors at the base of the central turret.   Well worn stone stairs curve up to the seven bedrooms, some of which are furnished in museum quality furniture and tapestries.   No two rooms are alike and yet all have private bath or shower and direct dial phones.   The living room, dining room and library are all panelled in polished dark wood and display an abundance of hunting trophies, paintings, comfortable furniture and other authentic artifacts from previous centuries. French doors in the main salon open out to the peaceful back garden, inviting one to slow one's pace and drink in the historical surroundings.   A stay can be booked on a bed and breakfast or full pension (all meals) basis.   To locate the small, picturesque village of Artannes, travel south from Tours ten kilometers on N10 and then approximately the same distance west from Montbazon along the D17.   As we visited the chateau while it was being readied to accommodate guests, we will look forward to receiving readers' comments on this "new" chateau hotel.

*CHATEAU D'ARTANNES*
*Hotelier: M & Mme Hoffmann*
*Artannes, 37260 Monts*
*Tel: 47.65.70.60 Telex: 752435*
*7 Apartments - Dbl from 950F to 1650F*
*Open: All year*
*Credit cards: All major*
*Restaurant (by reservation only), sauna, jacuzzi*
*Located 21 km SW of Tours*
*Region: Loire Valley*

The Chateau d'Audrieu affords the countryside traveller luxurious accommodation within the walls of a beautiful eighteenth-century chateau. This large, somewhat austere, grey stone manor dominates its own expanse of manicured gardens. On the grounds a lovely pool proves a welcome treat on warm summer days. Always a family home, the furnishings throughout the Chateau d'Audrieu are original to the house and dramatic in that they are authentic of the period. All twenty-eight bedrooms, seven of which are commodious suites, are furnished in elegant antiques and have private bathrooms. Although a chateau demands constant upkeep, the accommodations are beautifully maintained and the family takes pride in refurbishing one or two rooms each year. Bridging the two wings of the chateau are richly appointed drawing rooms, which offer a lovely retreat for house guests to spend a quiet afternoon. There are two intimate dining rooms where service is elegant and formal. Directions: turn off N13, the road that travels between Caen and Bayeux, onto D82, a small country road, in the direction of Tilly sur Seulles. The chateau is set off the road just before the village of Audrieu.

*CHATEAU D'AUDRIEU*
*Hotelier: M & Mme Livry-Level*
*Audrieu, 14250 Tilly sur Seulles*
*Tel: 31.80.21.52 Telex: 171777*
*21 Rooms - Sgl from 570F Dbl to 990F*
*  7 Apts - 1200F to 1600F*
*Open: March to January*
*   Restaurant closed Wednesdays*
*Credit cards: VS*
*Restaurant, pool, park*
*Located 20 km W of Caen*
*Region: Normandy*

An ancient posting station, the Hostellerie de la Poste in Avallon is now a stopover for gourmets.   Detouring from the traditional, heavy Burgundian specialities, the emphasis of the cuisine is now more towards lighter fare and sauces - nouvelle cuisine.   The kitchen is under the careful supervision of Madame P. Gachon-Millot and her chef and they present a delectable array of fish dishes.   Perhaps a bit overpriced, the restaurant's menu is very expensive.   The wine list highlights selections from the neighboring wine regions of Chablis, Cote d'Or and Burgundy. At the Hostellerie de la Poste the dining is superb and bedrooms are reserved to accommodate restaurant guests.   Although the hotel is on a main street of Avallon, the bedrooms are alluringly restful, the majority overlooking a pretty, paved central courtyard.   Avallon is an interesting town, once fortified, that guards its medieval atmosphere.   One can tour the ramparts, enjoy a panoramic view of the town and valley from the "promenade des Petits-Terreaux" and wander the streets, flanked by some lovely old homes of the fifteenth century.   The Hostellerie de la Poste is centrally located in town and Avallon is an easy day trip from Paris and a convenient base for exploring the Cousin river valley and the hilltop village of Vezelay.

*HOSTELLERIE DE LA POSTE*
*Hotelier: Mme P. Gachon-Millot*
*13, Place Vauban*
*89200 Avallon*
*Tel: 86.34.06.12 Telex: 351806*
*23 Rooms - Sgl from 400F Dbl to 550F, Apt 1000F*
*Open: March to November*
*Credit cards: VS, DC*
*Restaurant*
*Located 107 km NW of Beaune*
*Region: Burgundy*

Le Moulin des Ruats is a charming, wood-shingled cottage set on the river's edge, in the shade of the surrounding lush greenery.   Located on a scenic stretch of road as it winds along the banks of the Cousin, between the town of Avallon and the hilltop, medieval village of Vezelay, the setting of this renovated mill is quite peaceful.   Monsieur and Madame Bertier are a lovely couple and very involved with the management of their inn.   In the afternoons they are present in the lobby to welcome their guests and at mealtimes either in the restaurant or on the terrace to offer menu suggestions.   When the weather cooperates, breakfast is quite memorable when enjoyed under a canopy of trees on the edge of the rushing Cousin river.   The setting is quite peaceful and affords a good night's rest.   The accommodations are not luxurious: they are decorated in simple prints, and are almost motel-like in their furnishings, but are moderate in price.   Not all of the hotel's twenty bedrooms have private baths, but the rooms are quiet and clean. The Moulin des Ruats is an inviting hotel and Avallon, a reasonable drive from Paris, would serve as an ideal overnight destination en route to the Burgundy wine region.   Be sure not to venture too far, however, without first visiting the neighboring village of Vezelay and with its acclaimed Romanesque basilica.

*LE MOULIN DES RUATS*
*Hotelier: M & Mme Bertier*
*Vallee du Cousin*
*89200 Avallon*
*Tel: 86.34.07.14*
*20 Rooms - Sgl from 155F Dbl to 360F*
*Open: 3 March to 30 October*
  *Restaurant closed Mondays*
*Credit cards: AX, VS, DC*
*Located 4.5 km from Avallon*
*Region: Burgundy*

Nestled along the river's edge with a terrace banked by flowers in the lovely valley of the Cousin, Le Moulin des Templiers offers a peaceful night's rest at an inexpensive price. The rooms are all very simple in their decor, very few with private bath, small and sparse in furnishings, but fresh, clean and carefully tended to by a charming Madame Hilmoine. Sound the horn in the snug reception area and she will appear to offer a smile and a welcome. The setting here is idyllic. The bedrooms, although not overlooking the rushing Cousin, open up to the sounds of the cascading river, and a small farmyard of roosters, chickens, goats and one lone, lazy boar. If you are blessed with warm sunshine, enjoy either afternoon drinks or breakfast of fresh bread, jam and hot coffee at white wrought-iron tables set along the water's edge. With a number of outstanding restaurants as neighbors (Marc Menau's L'Esperance at St Pere Sous Vezelay is located just a few miles away in the direction of Vezelay) it is a welcome fact that Le Moulin des Templiers does not have a restaurant where one feels obligated to dine. This is a dear little hotel, quite inexpensive in price and convenient to exploring Vezelay and a perfect overnight en route to Burgundy.

*LE MOULIN DES TEMPLIERS*
*Hotelier: Mme Robert Hilmoine*
*Vallee du Cousin*
*Pontaubert, 89200 Avallon*
*Tel: 86.34.10.80*
*14 Rooms - Sgl from 196F Dbl to 282F*
*Open: 15 March to 2 November*
*Credit cards: None*
*No restaurant*
*Located between Avallon and Vezelay on*
*the Route de la Vallee du Cousin*
*Region: Burgundy*

Hotel d'Europe is a classically beautiful sixteenth-century mansion, formerly the home of the Marquis of Gravezon. Just inside the Porte de l'Oulle, on the Place Crillon, the mansion was converted into a hotel in 1799 as it was within walking distance of the River Rhone, a prime location to attract travellers who in that period voyaged predominately by boat. The present owner, Monsieur Daire, purchased the hotel in the early eighties and has completely modernized the hotel with the comfort of his guests as his primary concern, while using handsome furnishings that suit the mood and complement the origins of this grand home. The walls of the marble entry hall, once an open courtyard, and the walls of the upper levels are now hung with magnificent tapestries. The bedrooms of the hotel are all different in character, size and yet are all luxuriously furnished in traditional pieces and antiques. Many of the rooms are quite spacious and extremely comfortable for extended stays. Although within the city walls of Avignon, at least forty percent of the rooms overlook one of the hotel's three courtyards and afford a quiet night's rest. At the front of the building a peaceful, shaded terrace set with tables and chairs buffers the hotel from the activity of the Place Crillon. The hotel has a fine restaurant, the Vieille Fontaine. One can dine in its elegant formality or under the trees in the courtyard on balmy Provencal nights.

*HOTEL D'EUROPE*
*Hotelier: Rene Daire*
*12, Place Crillon, 84000 Avignon*
*Tel: 90.82.66.92 Telex: 431965*
*48 Rooms - Sgl from 435F Dbl to 890F*
*Open: All year*
*Credit cards: All major*
*Restaurant (closed off season)*
*Located 43 km NE of Nimes*
*Region: Provence*

The Hotel Bois Joli is a roadside inn, set on the hill, surrounded by trees just as the road winds away from the river into the resort town of Bagnoles de l'Orne. Very pretty, almost gingerbread in appearance with its red timbered beams and windowboxes, the Bois Joli is a favorite of many who frequent this charming town. I am certain there are other hotels in town whose accommodations equal those of the Bois Joli, and yet no other can boast the same warm and genuine welcome. An extraordinarily lovely hostess, Madame Gabriot, a young, exuberant and handsome woman, is responsible for the hotel's friendly atmosphere as well its fresh new decor. All of the hotel's twenty bedrooms have been refurbished in a traditional French country style. Pretty, colorful wallpapers and prints have been selected and decorate each of the rooms. Accommodations are spotlessly clean and I noticed many thoughtful, feminine touches, such as a spray of fresh heather on a bedside table. The dining room is very inviting and the food which is served in ample portions is quite good. Many guests use the Bois Joli as a base for exploring the region and take advantage of the offered pension plan (room with meals).

*HOTEL BOIS JOLI*
*Hotelier: Mme Chantal Gabriot*
*Avenue Philippe du Rozier*
*61140 Bagnoles de l'Orne*
*Tel: 33.37.92.77 Telex: 171782*
*20 Rooms - Dbl from 300F to 400F*
*Open: 1 April to 1 November*
*Credit cards: All major*
*Restaurant, parking*
*Located 50 km NE of Laval*
*Region: Normandy*

The Hotel La Cardinale is an impressive estate that dominates a position on the banks of the Rhone River. This is an elegant, country residence, ivy-clad and ornamented with heavy shutters. The hotel, dating back to the seventeenth century, is handsomely appointed with traditional pieces and luxurious furnishings. Seven bedrooms are found in the main house, La Cardinale, while two kilometers away additional accommodation is available in a second building, Sa Residence. Surrounded by its own beautiful park, Sa Residence, under the same outstanding management, has five guestrooms and five apartments, all exceptionally furnished and inviting. The home is set in a captivating garden and has a lovely swimming pool, definitely a welcome treat on a hot summer afternoon. Guests staying at Sa Residence return to La Cardinale to experience the gourmet delights of its romantic restaurant, where fine French cuisine is served with great reliabilty, creativity and style. La Cardinale et Sa Residence is a splendid hotel, located in the Rhone Valley, halfway between Burgundy to the north and Provence to the south.

*LA CARDINALE ET SA RESIDENCE*
*Hotelier: Mme M Motte*
*Baix, 07210 Chomerac*
*Tel: 75.85.80.40 Telex: 346143*
*La Cardinale, 5 Rooms -*
  *Sgl from 748F Dbl to 1311F*
*Sa Residence, 10 Rooms -*
  *Sgl from 725F Dbl to 960F*
*Closed: 3 Jan to 16 Feb, & Wed/Thu in Nov*
*Credit cards: AX*
*Restaurant, pool*
*Located 32 km S of Valence*
*Region: Rhone Valley*

The cobblestoned town of Barbizon has attracted artists for many years and the nineteenth-century, timbered Hostellerie du Bas-Breau has also had its share of famous guests.   Robert Louis Stevenson wrote in "Forest Notes" about this hotel and because of this, it is often called "Stevenson's House".   Famous painters who treasured this corner of the Forest of Fontainebleau include Millet, Corot, Sisley and Monet.   Some accommodation is in the main timbered house but most is in a two-story building in the back garden.   Each room is different in decor and has a bath.   The restaurant is superb, drawing dinner guests from as far away as Paris. With unusually attractive flower arrangements on each table, the atmosphere of the dining room is elegant and romantic.   Political leaders from Italy, West Germany, Great Britain, Ireland, Greece, Luxembourg, Denmark and the Netherlands recently selected the hotel as a conference location - you will understand their choice when you dine at Hostellerie du Bas-Breau where the menu features homegrown vegetables and herbs and specialities such as wild boar.   The house wine list is incredible.

*HOSTELLERIE DU BAS-BREAU*
*Hotelier: M Fava*
*77630 Barbizon*
*Tel: (1) 60.66.40.05 Telex: 690953*
*19 Rooms - Sgl from 910F Dbl to 1290F*
*    Apt to 2410F*
*Closed: January to mid-February*
*Credit cards: AX, VS*
*Park, tennis, excellent restaurant*
*On edge of Fontainebleau Forest*
*Located 59 km S of Paris*
*Region: Ile de Paris*

L'Auberge de la Benvengudo is tucked farther along the road from La Cabro d'Or as it winds through the valley travelling away from Les Baux de Provence.   When I first visited the Auberge de la Benvengudo, the Beaupied family offered rooms in their home to overnight guests.   In response to the number of returning guests as well as those who were guided here by their praise, the Beaupieds have expanded their private home into a proper hotel complex.   Sheltered behind a mass of garden, buildings extend out from, and beautifully copy the design of, the original home.   It will take time for the ivy to cover the stucco walls as it does on the main home, but the Provencal sun has already warmed and mellowed the red tile roofs. Green shuttered windows open onto the surrounding rocky hillsides, low green shrubbery and the large swimming pool, tennis court and gardens of the property. Heavy, dark colors (very Mediterranean in flavor) are used to decorate the bedrooms.   Accommodations are comfortable, some quite spacious, all with modern bathrooms.   For those on a longer stay, one might want to reserve a room equipped with a kitchenette.   Although the Beaupieds have changed their policy and no longer request that guests dine at the auberge, the restaurant is lovely, convenient and the menu is tempting in its selection.

*AUBERGE DE LA BENVENGUDO*
*Hotelier: M & Mme Daniel Beaupied*
*Dans le Vallon*
*13520 Les Baux de Provence*
*Tel: 90.54.32.54*
*18 Rooms - Dbl from 380F to 460F, Apt 730F*
*Closed: November, December, January*
*Restaurant (dinner only): Closed Sundays*
*Tennis, pool*
*Located 19 km NE of Arles*
*Region: Provence*

Set in the shadow of the enchanting village of Les Baux de Provence, La Cabro d'Or is under the same ownership as L'Oustau Baumaniere. Compared to its sister hotel, however, La Cabro d'Or does not boast the same grandeur of clientele - a fact which might actually serve as an attraction to others. Its restaurant is lovely and praised highly for its cuisine but it does not receive the same status of gourmet excellence nor does it demand the same prices. Spaciously set in an expanse of beautiful grounds, bathed in the warm air of Provence, the accommodation is very attractive and comfortable and half the price of that offered at L'Oustau Baumaniere. The hotel's twenty-two bedrooms are located in two-story buildings whose green shuttered windows open onto a central courtyard and garden. Also found on the large expanse of grounds are a lovely large swimming pool and tennis courts. La Cabro d'Or is a delightful hotel and children will enjoy feeding the swans and ducks with crumbs from the morning croissants.

*LA CABRO D'OR*
*Hotelier: M Charial*
*Dans le Vallon,*
*13520 Les Baux de Provence*
*Tel: 90.54.33.21 Telex: 401810*
*22 Rooms - Sgl from 448F Dbl to 726F*
*Closed: mid-November to 21 December*
*   Restaurant closed Mondays in low season*
*Credit cards: AX, VS*
*Restaurant*
*Pool, tennis courts*
*Located 19 km NE of Arles*
*Region: Provence*

L'Oustau Baumaniere is a fine hotel with an atmosphere and furnishings rich in antiques and tradition.    Guests enjoy magnificent bedrooms, a beautiful pool and lovely hotel grounds.    Raymond Thuillier, now in his eighties, achieved a level of gourmet excellence in the fifties and sixties by which other restauranteurs set their standards.    He is still ever-present at the hotel, but it is his grandson, Jean Andre Charial, who, with the help of chef Alain Burnel, supervises the kitchen.    The restaurant serves exceptional cuisine accented with the flavors of Provence. Offering such specialities as "Lobster with Ratotouille" or "Herb-stuffed Rabbit", it is often referred to as the finest restaurant in the region.    On a warm afternoon or balmy evening dine on the terrace overlooking the pool - less formal and a refreshing setting.    Products regional to Provence are beautifully packaged and can be purchased in a gift shop opposite the parking area.    The hotel is located not in the hilltop village of Les Baux de Provence but on a country road that winds through the valley beneath it.

*L'OUSTAU BAUMANIERE*
*Hotelier: M Thuillier*
*Dans le Vallon*
*13520 Les Baux de Provence*
*Tel: 90.54.33.07 Telex: 420203*
*25 Rooms - Sgl from 795F Dbl to 910F*
*Closed: mid-January to March*
  *Restaurant closed Wednesday off season*
*Credit cards: AX, VS*
*Restaurant, pool, tennis*
*Located 19 km NE of Arles*
*Region: Provence*

Monsieur and Madame Auregan are your charming and helpful hosts at this lovingly restored eighteenth-century townhome in Bayeux, a picturesque city known for its outstanding tapestry museum.  A large courtyard and stone, semi-circular staircase lead up to the front entry of their hotel, the Hotel d'Argouges, and to a warm welcome.  Off the entry hall, French doors in the beautiful and gracious salon-library lead out to the quiet back garden and terrace.  Sheltered behind its main gate, the Hotel d'Argouges manages to retain the feeling of a quiet country home while its address is, in actuality, downtown Bayeux.  Looking out over the beautiful garden or front courtyard, the bedrooms all have exposed beams and comfortable furniture as well as private shower or bath and phones.  There are also two charming suites which have a small extra room for children.  Next door the Auregans have begun renovating another very old home and some of the bedrooms are found there.  Breakfast can be enjoyed in the privacy of one's room, in the intimate, elegant breakfast salon, or on the back garden terrace overlooking Madame Auregan's vivid flowers.  A veritable haven for travellers visiting Bayeux, the Hotel d'Argouges offers good value in lovely surroundings plus gracious hosts who have great pride in their metier.

*HOTEL D'ARGOUGES*
*Hotelier: Marie-Claire & Daniel Auregan*
*21, Rue St Patrice*
*14400 Bayeux*
*Tel: 31.92.88.86 Telex: 170234*
*25 Rooms - Sgl from 225F Dbl to 350F*
*Open: All year*
*Credit cards: All major*
*No restaurant, garden*
*Located 28 km NW of Caen*
*Region: Normandy*

Monsieur Henri Maria, one of the most gracious and hospitable hotel directors I've met in my travels through France, described La Reserve as a "restaurant avec chambres". Certainly the most luxurious "restaurant with rooms" in France, because La Reserve is one of France's most accredited restaurants. You will be expertly catered to both in the dining room and in the hotel. One may dine in a very elegant restaurant with floor to ceiling windows overlooking the salt-water pool and ocean. This elegant room is bordered by an outside terrace which is used for lunch and dinner in the balmy summer months. There are also two small dining rooms in each wing that can be reserved for private functions: one opens onto the terrace and would make an ideal setting for any special occasion. The swimming pool (heated during the winter months) is filled with sea water and surrounded by a private dock where guests moor for lunch in summer. To accompany your meal, the wine cellar features an excellent selection of local wines and those of Bordeaux and Burgundy. Guests not only return year after year to La Reserve, but request the same room. There are fifty traditionally furnished bedrooms plus three apartments, each with a sitting room and private balcony.

*HOTEL LA RESERVE*
*Hotelier: Henri Maria*
*5, Blvd General-Leclerc*
*06310 Beaulieu sur Mer*
*Tel: 93.01.00.01, Telex: 470301*
*53 Rooms - Sgl from 950F to 1340F*
*  Dbl from 1310F to 2160F*
*Closed: 1 December to 9 January*
*Credit cards: None*
*Restaurant, pool, waterfront setting*
*Located 10 km E of Nice*
*Region: Riviera*

Dating from the fifteenth century, the Chateau de Danzay is very regal with large, high-ceilinged stone rooms, massive walls hung with muted tapestries and enormous, open hearth fireplaces. Stone steps leading up to the six guest bedrooms and one suite are well worn by generations of passage and customarily lit by candles in the evening. All of the comfortable bedchambers have modern private baths and are furnished with large antique pieces, fitting to the grand scale of this castle. The bedrooms are all luxurious, but the public areas are more austere: they do not invite one to sit for a cozy chat, but rather to marvel at what life in the fifteenth century must have been like. Almost historical in tone, the entry hall and grand salon are furnished with sparse heavy antiques, with candelabras casting light on the high stone walls and a few carpets warming the expanse of tile floors. Monsieur and Madame Sarfati purchased the chateau over a decade ago and after extensive renovation, opened it to guests in 1981. Soon to be classified as a hotel rather than a private chateau, the Chateau de Danzay offers modern comforts contained within the stone walls of an elegant fifteenth-century residence. It is located just north from Chinon. Take D749 north of Chinon and then watch for signs at the town of Bourgeuil that will direct you, west, to the chateau.

*CHATEAU DE DANZAY*
*Hotelier: M & Mme J. Sarfati*
*Route de Savigny, 37420 Avoine*
*Tel: 47.58.46.86*
*7 Rooms - Dbl from 550F to 800F, Apt 1050F*
*Closed: 15 November to 1 April*
*Credit cards: VS*
*No restaurant*
*Located 5 km N of Chinon*
*Region: Loire Valley*

Perfect for those on a budget who prefer a countryside setting to the city of Chinon, La Giraudiere is a modest hotel offering excellent value, a rural setting and a pleasant welcome.   Travel the D749 north from Chinon in the direction of Bourgeuil.   At Bourgeuil watch for signs that direct you to "Hotel" and follow them along the V6 in the direction of Savigny en Veron.   Set back off a country road, La Giraudiere is a seventeenth-century farmstead consisting of a cluster of buildings set around a central courtyard.   The reception area and restaurant (breakfast only) are located in a separate building from the hotel's twenty-four bedrooms which are located in neighboring buildings of the complex and back on to open farmland.   These are furnished with reproduction as well as a few effectively placed antiques and a number of them are very picturesque with old beams and stone fireplaces.   All the bedrooms have private bath or shower and we were told that twelve are equipped with kitchenettes.   Breakfast can be enjoyed either in the room, in the restaurant or on the terrace in the shade of the tranquil courtyard.   Much frequented by British tourists, this inn is recommended for its calm, rural setting and bargain rates.

*LA GIRAUDIERE*
*Route de Savigny*
*Beaumont en Veron*
*37420 Avoine*
*Tel: 47.58.40.36*
*24 Rooms - Dbl from 200F to 285F*
*Open: All year*
*Credit cards: All major*
*No restaurant*
*Rural countryside setting*
*Located 5 km N of Chinon*
*Region: Loire Valley*

In the heart of the colorful, medieval town of Beaune, Le Cep offers a gracious welcome, charming and comfortable bedrooms decorated with elegance and taste, and very attentive service. The forty-six bedrooms, individual in decor, vary in size but are all handsome: highly polished wooden antique furnishings are accented by the beautiful, softly colored fabrics used for the curtains, bedspreads and upholstery. In the bar and public areas heavy beamed ceilings, old gilt-framed portraits and fresh flower arrangements add character to the comfort and elegance. The former wine cellar, a cozy room with a low, arched stone ceiling, is used as a breakfast room when the weather does not permit service in the pretty stone outdoor courtyard. Dinner in Le Cep's dining room, with fresh flowers, peach toned curtains, soft hued tapestry chairs, fine silver, china and glassware, is a treat not to be missed. I was sorry to learn the the Falces have sold their hotel, as the excellence of Le Cep has always been a direct reflection of their caring and professional management. However, I have spoken with the new owners, the Bernards, and with guests who have stayed since their acquisition and am assured that the tradition of excellence has been maintained. An ideal base for touring the gourmet wine region of the Cote d'Or, Le Cep combines elegance and warmth in perfect proportions.

*HOTEL LE CEP*
*Hotelier: M & Mme Bernard*
*27, Rue Maufaux, 21200 Beaune*
*Tel: 80.22.35.48 Telex: 351256*
*46 Rooms - Sgl from 350F Dbl to 800F*
*Open: 15 March to 30 November*
*Credit cards: All major*
*New restaurant*
*Located 45 km S of Dijon*
*Region: Burgundy*

Although it is sometimes a bit noisy, there are advantages to staying in a town which is both the capital and at the heart of the Cote d'Or wine region. With Beaune as a base, one can easily venture out to explore and sample some of the world's finest wines. Beaune has an architecturally unique town hall and an interesting wine museum. The famous Hospices de Beaune, founded in 1443, is known the world over because every third Sunday in November, the region's premium wines are auctioned at a public sale. Built in 1660, the Hotel de la Poste came under the management of the Chevillot family when it was purchased by Victor Chevillot in 1904. Today his grandson, Marc Chevillot, continues the family tradition and supervises the excellence of the restaurant. As a wine merchant himself, Marc is also responsible for the selection of the cellar. Some of France's finest Burgundies are a perfect accompaniment to the Terrine of Truffled Duck, Crayfish a la Creme Victor Chevillot, Chicken au Bourgogne and other specialities of the house menu. The restaurant serves both lunch and dinner. This elegant hotel has twenty-five rooms, four of which are luxury suites, all available on a demi-pension basis. To stay at the Hotel de la Poste is to enjoy the ambiance of a French residence in the attentive care of its owners.

*HOTEL DE LA POSTE*
*Hotelier: M Chevillot*
*1, Blvd Clemenceau, 21200 Beaune*
*Tel: 80.22.08.11*
*25 Rooms - Sgl from 695F Dbl to 845F*
*    Apt to 1270F*
*Open: 1 April to 19 November*
*Credit cards: All major*
*Restaurant*
*Located 45 km S of Dijon*
*Region: Burgundy*

L'Auberge de l'Abbaye is a very pretty, Norman, half-timbered inn in an equally charming village. Le Bec Hellouin is a cluster of half-timbered and thatched buildings set around a medieval abbey, nestled along a trickling stream, a peaceful setting removed from the main road (D39). When we entered the cozy, low ceilinged restaurant of the eighteenth-century L'Auberge de l'Abbaye we were greeted by the sight and aroma of a large, freshly baked apple tart. We were told by the welcoming owner, Madame Sergent, that her restaurant is renowned all over the world for apple tarts. Grand Marnier, a specialty of the region, is also featured here, with large bottles present on each table. Madame Sergent has owned the inn for a quarter of a century and her taste and feminine touches are apparent throughout. Lace curtains at the windows, polished copper and faience ornamenting the walls, and pretty fabrics enhance the decor of the inn. The stairway leading to the inn's ten bedrooms is flanked by former exterior walls whose heavy old half timbering add character to this charming auberge. The bedrooms are simple, yet pretty in their furnishings and all have private bath or shower. The rooms either overlook the inn's interior courtyard or look out over a shaded town square. Inside and out this inn is truly what one imagines a simple, country French inn should be.

*L'AUBERGE DE L'ABBAYE*
*Hotelier: Sergent family*
*2780 Le Bec Hellouin*
*Tel: 32.44.86.02*
*10 Rooms - Sgl from 280F Dbl to 360F*
*Open: 28 February to 10 January*
*Credit cards: VS, MC*
*Restaurant*
*Located 42 km SW of Rouen*
*Region: Normandy*

Soon after the publication of the first edition of this guide, I was directed to the Hotel Bonnet and have since returned for repeated visits. Serenely located on a bend of the Dordogne, in the shadow of the impressive Chateau de Beynac, the Bonnet is indeed a "gem". The bedrooms are simple in decor, but the restaurant setting, either indoors with large windows looking onto a river panorama or on the vine-covered terrace, encourages one to linger for hours. The Dordogne meanders through the Perigord, a region whose products have attracted the recognition of true gourmets. Turkeys, ducks, geese, foie gras, crepes, a variety of truffles, plentiful vegetables and fruits (particularly strawberries and raspberries) are all found in abundance. Chef Monzie was trained in Perigord and his excellent cuisine reflects the regional specialities. With the vineyard regions of Bordeaux, Bergerac and Cahors nearby, the Restaurant Bonnet is able to offer you a fine selection of wines to accompany your meal. Generations of the Bonnet family have managed this inn for almost a century and today Mademoiselle R. Bonnet is in residence to act as gracious host. Stay here for a minimum of three nights and take advantage of the fantastic pension rates. This is a reasonably priced, simple, but delightful, inn with an incomparable riverside setting.

*HOTEL BONNET*
*Hotelier: Bonnet family*
*Beynac et Cazenac*
*24220 St Cyprien*
*Tel: 53.29.50.01*
*22 Rooms - Sgl from 152F Dbl to 244F*
*Open: 1 April to 15 October*
*Credit cards: VS*
*Terrace restaurant, riverfront setting*
*Located 64 km SE of Perigueux*
*Region: Dordogne*

L'Auberge les Templiers was built in recent years on the site of an ancient posting house and yet the decor lends an atmosphere of days gone by. Wood timbered furnishings, heavy old beams, warm and colorful fabrics and bountiful flower arrangements decorate this lovely inn. Bedrooms and suites are found in cottages tucked away on the property amidst the trees. Each room is individually styled, each with the flavor of an elegant country inn that has welcomed guests for centuries. The modern bathrooms and luxurious comforts are the only indications as to the true age of L'Auberge les Templiers. Bedroom windows open onto the greenery of the garden and the setting guarantees a peaceful night's sleep. Tennis courts and a lovely large swimming pool provide a means to exercise away the extra calories consumed in the hotel's restaurant. One can review the menu and enjoy an aperitif, fireside, in the lounge bar. Dining is memorable either in one of the elegant dining rooms or on the outdoor terrace. Adjourn after dinner to relax in the smoking room. Before being a posting station, L'Auberge les Templiers proudly traces its beginnings back to when it was a commandery of the Knights of Templiers. Engraved on a central beam in the smoking room is the emblem of the hotel, three knights in arms with a flying banner.

*L'AUBERGE LES TEMPLIERS*
*Les Bezards*
*45290 Nogent sur Vernisson*
*Tel: 38.31.80.01 Telex: 780998*
*30 Rooms - Sgl from 480F Dbl to 980F*
*Closed: 14 January to 15 February*
*Credit cards: AX, VS*
*Excellent restaurant, pool, tennis*
*Located 138 km S of Paris, 1 hr from Orly*
*Region: Ile de Paris*

In 1982 Patrick Gasnier "et sa brigade" (and his staff) took charge of the Domaine de Rochevilaine and under their care the hotel standards have been greatly improved. Domaine de Rochevilaine is dramatically located on Brittany's jagged and rocky coastline and its setting typifies the most spectacular quality of Brittany. The views from the hotel are stupendous, especially when the sun shines on the glistening sea or when the wind howls as the waves crash against the rocks. The vast windows of the dining room overlook a rocky promontory and there is a distinct sensation of being shipboard - all you see from your dining table is the open sea. Beautiful Oriental carpets adorn hardwood floors and on sunny days breakfast is enjoyed in the well kept gardens that are protected from the open sea breezes by whitewashed walls. Bedrooms are handsomely furnished and beautifully appointed. The hotel also has a dramatic salt-water pool built into the rocky promontory below the hotel. The Domaine de Rochevilaine is just a few kilometers from Muzillac - an ideal and dramatic setting for "experiencing" Brittany.

*DOMAINE DE ROCHEVILAINE*
*Hotelier: Patrick Gasnier*
*Pointe de Penlan*
*Billiers, 56190 Muzillac*
*Tel: 97.41.69.27 Telex: 950570*
*28 Rooms - Sgl from 445F Dbl to 990F*
*Open: 20 February to 5 January*
*Credit cards: All major*
*Restaurant with ocean views*
*Salt-water pool*
*Located 25 km SE of Vannes*
*Region: Brittany*

The village streets of the picturesque town of Biot are narrow, a bit difficult to negotiate, and parking is limited, but the effort will be rewarded once you reach the Place des Arcades and the inviting Hotel Galerie des Arcades. Cafe tables monopolize the sidewalk in front of the arched doorways of this little inn. The indoor cafe-bar is always a bustle with local chatter and usually a member of the Brothier family is found here tending the bar. A very friendly and outgoing family, the Brothiers welcome numerous artists, photographers and models as their guests. The inn focuses around the three rooms that Monsieur Brothier opened as a gallery and provincial restaurant more than thirty years ago. Rooms on the upper floors were renovated and offered to overnight guests a decade later. Steep, old tile stairways climb to a maze of rooms that are like an extension of the gallery as they are hung with an array of abstract, original art. The bedrooms are moderate in price and those with private terraces that look out over the rooftops of Biot are a real bargain. Many of the rooms are equipped with private bath, shower, washbasin and toilet. Full of character, the decor is a bit bohemian in flavor and arrangement, with heavy armoirs and often four-poster beds. Facing onto a quiet, picturesque square, the Hotel Galerie des Arcades is a friendly gathering spot and it is easy to transcend time and envision the likes of Van Gogh and Gaugin frequenting the Cafe des Arcades.

*HOTEL GALERIE DES ARCADES*
*Hotelier: Brothier Family*
*16, Place des Arcades, 06410 Biot*
*Tel: 93.65.01.04*
*12 Rooms - Dbl from 150F to 280F*
*Open: January to 20 November*
*Cafe-Restaurant*
*Located 15 km NW of Nice*
*Region: Riviera*

We truly felt that we'd discovered a special little inn when we happened upon the Hotel le Cheval Blanc. Facing the Place de l'Eglise, Le Cheval Blanc is easy to spot with its lovely timbered facade and wrought iron sign of a white horse. Dating from the seventeenth century, this was once an annex for the neighboring church. Now filled in, an old stone archway that once opened onto a passageway to the stables stands as evidence of its earlier history. After the revolution, the building was converted to a cafe-bar and remained a popular, local spot for almost two centuries. It was just a few years ago that Michel and Micheline Bleriot converted the cafe into one of the most charming, most reasonably priced inns in the Loire Valley. The restaurant's decor is charming in its simplicity; a pretty wallpaper covers the walls and wooden chairs and tables dressed with crisp white linen are set beneath dark beams. An inner courtyard latticed with vines and set with white outdoor tables is a delightful spot for breakfast. The bedrooms are unbelievably attractive, particularly when one considers the bargain rates. Each room has its own private bath or shower and overlooks either the central courtyard or a quiet back street. Located just west of Chenonceaux and south of Amboise, Blere is a convenient base from which to explore the castles of the Loire Valley and Le Cheval Blanc is a reasonably priced, delightful inn.

*LE CHEVAL BLANC*
*Hotelier: Michel and Micheline Bleriot*
*Place de l'Eglise, 37150 Blere*
*Tel: 47.30.30.14*
*13 Rooms - Dbl from 210F to 230F*
*Open: All year, closed Sun & Mon (except Jul & Aug)*
*Credit cards: VS*
*Restaurant*
*Located 27 km SE of Tours*
*Region: Loire Valley*

When we stopped to explore Bonnieux, I was happy and very surprised to discover a hotel of such superior quality tucked away in this small hillside village - until I learned that Monsieur Chapotin is a member of a family long responsible for some of France's finest and most prestigious hotels. (His brother owns and operates the lovely Le Clos St Vincent in Ribeauville.) From a finance career in Paris, Monsieur Chapotin has moved to this small eighteenth-century abbey set at the foot of the medieval ramparts of Bonnieux in the beautiful Luberon valley. Le Prieure has a superb restaurant whose menu offers specialities irresistible to even the most disciplined. The restaurant is gorgeous, with pale pink tablecloths, fresh flowers and soft lighting. On warm evenings meals are served in the shade of the garden. A charming bar-saloon has recently been added, with a theme of little Parisian theaters. The traditional bedrooms are beautiful. Lovely antiques and cherished family heirlooms are beautifully displayed in this lovely setting. Take special notice of the magnificent sculptures and paintings throughout the inn: Monsieur Chapotin plans to turn the adjoining chapel into a gallery. Under the care and direction of Remy Chapotin and Charlotte Keller, Le Prieure is in all aspects an outstanding hotel.

*HOSTELLERIE DU PRIEURE*
*Hotelier: Remy Chapotin, Charlotte Keller*
*84480 Bonnieux*
*Tel: 90.75.80.78*
*10 Rooms - Sgl from 330F Dbl to 460F*
*Open: 15 February to 5 November*
  *Restaurant closed Thursday nights*
*Credit cards: None*
*Indoor and terrace restaurants*
*Located 47 km SE of Avignon*
*Region: Provence*

When searching for a luncheon spot for my first tour group to France I was thrilled to discover the enchanting village of Bourdeilles.  Tucked ten kilometers farther up a quiet valley from the larger town of Brantome, the setting of Bourdeilles is idyllic.  In this old village, crowned by a castle, the Hotel des Griffons clings to a narrow bridge.  The hotel met and surpassed my every wish and expectation. Madame Denise Deborde manages the hotel, supervises the restaurant and personally pampers her guests.  Her command of the English language is limited, but she and her husband always sports a welcoming smile.  Bedrooms dressed in pretty fabrics and tucked under old beams are charming and many overlook the quietly flowing river.  The restaurant is intimate and inviting with windows opening up the soothing sound of cascading water.  Tables are set on the terrace on warm summer nights - the outdoor setting is romantic and perfect for enjoying wonderful Perigord specialties.  The food is excellent: beautifully presented and very reasonably priced.  Monsieur Deborde heads off each week to the market and purchases only the freshest ingredients.  The Hotel des Griffons is a delightful inn and an excellent value on the northern boundaries of the Dordogne.

*HOTEL DES GRIFFONS*
*Hotelier: Mme Denise Deborde*
*Bourdeilles, 24310 Brantome*
*Tel: 53.03.75.61*
*10 Rooms - Sgl from 280F Dbl to 350F*
*Open: April to 10 October*
  *Closed Tuesdays 10 April to 1 July*
*Credit cards: VS, DC, MC*
*Restaurant, charming town*
*Located 24 km NW of Perigueux*
*Region: Dordogne*

This storybook chateau is actually located in the small town of Port Boulet on the road between Chinon and Bourgueil. Travelling south from Bourgueil on D749, turn right immediately after the bridge over the railroad tracks where a sign is posted for the chateau. Built by the same family who went on to build the well known chateaux Azay-le-Rideaux and Chenonceaux, the Chateau des Reaux could be out of a fairytale with its twin, red-checked towers and pretty setting. Inside, Madame Goupil de Bouille establishes a friendly atmosphere and is present to genuinely welcome all her guests. Climb the well-worn turret stairs to the salon where aperitifs are served round a table amidst elegance and comfort. Madame's feminine touch is evident throughout and she has managed to make every room an inviting haven of antiques, paintings, polished silver and authentic memorabilia. Many friendships are made and congenial hours spent in the comfy salons and at the large oval dining table table where all the guests may share a meal. The nine bedrooms in the chateau and six in a neighboring annex all have private baths and are charmingly decorated with antiques set off by delicate floral print bedspreads, curtains and wallpapers. We look forward to returning to the Chateau de Reaux, a historical monument that radiates warmth, hospitality and beauty.

*CHATEAU DE REAUX*
*Hotelier: Jean-Luc & Florence Goupil de Bouille*
*Le Port Boulet, 37140 Bourgueil*
*Tel: 47.95.14.40*
*15 Rooms - Dbl from 250F to 450F*
*Open: All year*
*Credit cards: Unknown*
*Family style dining, reservations required*
*Located: 17 km N of Chinon*
*Region: Loire Valley*

Ten years ago the Laxtons took an early retirement and began their search for a country home in the Dordogne River Valley.  They wanted a home where they could host their many friends, met through their travels, from all over the world. Le Chatenet, whose history dates to the seventeenth century, has cream stone walls and a sienna tiled roof and sits on a hillside outside the village of Brantome.  The Laxtons fell in love with this Perigordian manor home, although in a state of disrepair, and dedicated their time and money to restoring it.  Designers by profession, their combined efforts have resulted in a magnificent home.  Local conversation focused on Le Chatenet when it was learned that they had renovated ten rooms and, more impressively, had installed a full bathroom for each one.   It was then that Regis Bulot of Le Moulin de l'Abbaye suggested that the Laxtons rent out rooms to accommodate his overflow of dinner guests since he had too few rooms.   Once one experiences the comforts and luxury of Le Chatenet and the warm, open hospitality and kindness of Philippe and Magdeleine, one returns and shares the glorious discovery with friends.   As a result, the Laxtons' home is now a full time inn, although they describe Le Chatenet as "private but opened to friends and friends of friends".

*LE CHATENET*
*Hotelier: Philippe & Magdeleine Laxton*
*Rte D78 - Direction Bourdeilles*
*24310 Brantome*
*Tel: 53.05.81.08*
*10 Rooms - Dbl to 480F, Suite 650F*
*Open: All year*
*Credit cards: MC, VS*
*No restaurant, pool, tennis court*
*Located 27 km NW of Perigueux*
*Region: Dordogne*

With its beautiful Benedictine abbey, lovely grey-stone homes, peaceful expanses of green, narrow streets crossed by or following the course of the River Dronne, and a unique elbow bridge, Brantome receives many tourists.    Enhancing the charms of this village is the Hostellerie Le Moulin de l'Abbaye.    From its quiet setting straddling the Dronne the inn looks across the span of water to the town.    The twelve romantic bedrooms are beautifully appointed.    The majority of bedrooms are located in the mill and open onto river views, while an additional few are tucked away in an annex across the street.    Word is also out that Monsieur Bulot is looking for another property to accommodate even more guests - possibly in the neighboring village of Bourdeilles.    Currently many of his guests enjoy the hospitality and luxurious accommodation of the Laxtons and their inn, Le Chatenet.    Regis Bulot takes great pride in supervising his renowned kitchen and, whether served on the outdoor terrace or in the elegant dining room, the cuisine is superb (and expensive), having received only accolades and a coveted three stars from Michelin.    Both dining locations profit from this idyllic riverside setting. This is a charming inn, an enchanting village and a wonderful base for exploring the beautiful region of Perigord.

*HOSTELLERIE LE MOULIN DE L'ABBAYE*
*Hotelier: Regis Bulot*
*24310 Brantome*
*Tel: 53.05.80.22 Telex: 560570*
*12 Rooms - Sgl from 470F Dbl to 850F*
*Open: 5 May to 13 Nov*
  *Restaurant closed Mondays*
*Credit cards: AX, VS*
*Restaurant, lovely riverside setting*
*Located 27 km NW of Perigueux*
*Region: Dordogne*

Paul and Jenny Dyer came to the Dordogne Valley from England in search of a country setting in which to raise their two daughters. They discovered this wonderful, eighteenth-century farmhouse, abandoned and in a state of ruin, and spent their time and savings to literally rebuild and restore it. In its fourth season, the Auberge du Noyer, named for the large walnut tree that fronts it, is a warm and inviting inn. Guests have only glowing reports and praise for the accommodation, the food and the hospitality of the hosts. The auberge's intimate dining room has a large, open fireplace and orange and brown tablecloths which blend warmly with the stone walls and sienna tile floors. The Dyers have plans for a veranda to front the home and extend the seating area for morning breakfasts, or dinner on a balmy night. A lovely swimming pool sits on a hill behind the farmhouse. The inn has ten bedrooms all decorated beautifully in Laura Ashley prints and all with private bath or shower. The inn is open later in the season than most of the hotels of the region. Guests return when the weather turns a bit cooler to sit before the large fire, read or don wellingtons and walk the countryside lanes. The atmosphere at the Auberge du Noyer is very relaxed and comfortable and the presence of the Dyers' darling, blond daughters, who leave school bags about, add to the feeling of being "at home".

*AUBERGE DU NOYER*
*Hotelier: Paul & Jenny Dyer*
*Le Reclaud de Bonny Bas, 24260 Le Bugue*
*Tel: 53.07.11.73*
*10 Rooms - Sgl from 250F Dbl to 380F*
*Open: Palm Sunday to December*
*Credit cards: MC, VS*
*Restaurant, pool*
*Located: on D703, 41 km S of Perigueux*
*Region: Dordogne*

Le Lot is overwhelming in its beauty and the splendor of its towns. I was a bit fearful of not being able to find an inn to equal its glory, but I found an outstanding hotel, La Pescalerie, which does justice to the region. Located just two and a half kilometers northeast of the village of Cabrerets (famous for the Grotto du Perche Merle), La Pescalerie is a magnificent weathered-stone manor house in a lovely riverside setting with the tranquil Lot Valley as its backdrop. Ten handsomely appointed bedrooms are divided between two levels and open onto the garden through thick sixteenth- and seventeenth-century walls. The rooms are pleasingly different, yet each an attractive melange of modern furniture and cherished antiques. The top-floor rooms are set under the beams of the house with delightful dormer windows and a few have a loft, perfect for children with a sense of adventure. Opened less than a decade ago, La Pescalerie ideally accommodates those who have the time to linger in the magnificent Lot Valley. It addition to an idyllic riverside setting and spectacular accommodation La Pescalerie has a very attractive restaurant and a lovely bar that opens onto the back terrace.

*LA PESCALERIE*
*Hotelier: Helene Combette*
*A la Fontaine de la Pescalerie*
*46330 Cabrerets*
*Tel: 65.31.22.55*
*10 Rooms - Sgl from 435F Dbl to 650F*
*Open: April to November*
*Credit cards: AX, VS, DC*
*Restaurant, peaceful setting*
*Located 33 km NE of Cahors*
*Region: Lot*

The atmosphere of the Middle Ages prevails in the narrow, winding, cobblestoned streets leading to the Chateau Grimaldi, built by Raynier Grimaldi, the ruler of Monaco, in 1309.   As the streets become narrower, you pass under buildings which form an archway and then arrive at Le Cagnard, which has been in operation for forty years.   Monsieur and Madame Barel make guests feel welcome and at home. Dinner on the terrace, set under a full moon, or indoors with the atmosphere of a medieval castle and candlelight flickering against age-old walls, is a romantic experience and the presentation of the cuisine is exceptional.   Chef Johnay creates a feast of rich delicacies and ensures that specialities such as "foie gras frais de canard" and "carre d'agneau" are professionally and artfully served to tempt the palate.   The lift is charming, biblical paintings changing with each floor, and I found some marvellous rooms and views. Rooms two to twelve have a medieval flavor to their decor.

*LE CAGNARD*
*Hotelier: M & Mme Barel*
*Rue Pontis Long*
*au Haut de Cagnes*
*06800 Cagnes sur Mer*
*Tel: 93.20.73.21*
*19 Rooms - Sgl from 355F Dbl to 1090F*
*Closed: November to 18 December*
   *Restaurant closed: 20 November to 18 December,*
   *and 5 to 20 January*
*Credit cards: All major*
*Terrace restaurant*
*Located 13 km W of Nice*
*Region: Riviera*

Not far from Dieppe, thus a convenient location if one is travelling to or from Britain via the English Channel, the Manoir de Caniel is a lovingly restored and authentically furnished manor home.   Dating from the seventeenth century, the manor has a small, stone entry hall and a staircase that winds and slants as it climbs to the upper floors.   We found Madme Monnier in the high-ceilinged dining room amidst her impressive collection of antique furnishings and old paintings.   The home has four bedrooms and one suite that are enhanced by beautifully painted, original panelling.   The accommodations are very comfortable, decorated with heavy fabrics complemented by period furniture, and have contemporary bathrooms.   The suite, which can comfortably accommodate a family of four, occupies the entire top floor and was still being renovated at the time of our visit. Madame also showed us the "secret garden" at the rear of the house.   Completely walled, with only a hidden pathway leading to its gate, the garden is a private haven for guests of the manor.   The Monniers also have an antique shop with lovely antiques, faience and reproductions, housed in the old stable and Monsieur Monnier has a studio where he studies, repairs and reproduces lovely old tapestries.

*MANOIR DE CANIEL*
*Hotelier: M & Mme Francois Monnier*
*50, Route de Veulettes*
*76450 Cany-Barville*
*Tel: 35.97.88.43*
*4 Rooms - Sgl from 250F Dbl to 410F, Suite 560F*
*Open: All year, but closed Tuesdays off season*
*Credit cards: None*
*No restaurant, breakfasts only*
*Located: 50 km SW of Dieppe*
*Region: Normandy*

Domaine d'Auriac is a lovely ivy-clad manor on the outskirts of Carcassonne.   To locate the hotel, travel two and a half kilometers southeast from the walled city on the D118 and D104.   The twenty-three bedrooms of the Domaine d'Auriac are elegant and quiet and provide a relaxing environment.   The rooms are  nicely furnished and all have bathrooms, direct dial phones, mini-bars and television. The restaurant, overlooking the pool and garden, is most attractive.   Local residents gather here for dinner to enjoy the excellent food and peaceful setting. The bar, in the old wine cellar, is cozy and inviting.   The management provides personal touches and professional service.   Enjoy the swimming pool, tennis courts and surrounding parklands.   The hotel does also provide conference facilities and sometimes caters to business groups either during the day or on an extended stay. Domaine d'Auriac's location affords a proximity to Carcassonne without being in the center of the bustling tourist attraction.   Carcassonne is also a convenient stopover point when travelling between Provence and the Tarn, Basque or Perigord.

*DOMAINE D'AURIAC*
*Hotelier: M & Mme B. Rigaudis*
*Route St Hilaire*
*11000 Carcassonne*
*Tel: 68.25.72.22 Telex: 500385*
*23 Rooms - Sgl from 480F Dbl to 660F*
*Closed: 10 to 31 January*
  *Restaurant closed Sunday evenings low season*
*Credit cards: All major*
*Restaurant, pool, tennis*
*Located 92 km SE of Toulouse*
*Region: Pyrennees Roussillon*

Explore the medieval fortress of Carcassonne and then settle for an evening behind its massive walls in the intimate Hotel de la Cite.   Recessed into the walls near the Basilica St Nazaire, the hotel is on the site of the ancient episcopal palace and offers you the refined comfort of its rooms in a medieval atmosphere.   The bar is a welcome spot to settle for a drink, its walls panelled in ornately carved wood and topped by beautiful and colorful murals that portray the life of days gone by. Tables of the restuarant are regally set on a carpet of Fleur de Lys under a beamed ceiling and surrounded by walls painted with shields and crests.   The hotel's bedrooms, many of which open up onto the ramparts and a large enclosed garden, vary in price according to size, decor and view.   Carcassonne is a magnificent fortress, completely restored to look as it did when first constructed centuries ago. It is impressive when viewed at a distance, rising above the vineyards at the foot of the Cevennes and Pyrenees, but even more spectacular when it can be explored on foot.   Note: although in principle the city is closed to all but pedestrian traffic, guests can enter the city by car (via Porte Narbonnaise), travel the Rue Mayrevieille, the rue Porte d'Aude and the rue St Louis and park at the hotel.

*HOTEL DE LA CITE*
*Hotelier: Dominique Lasserre*
*Place Eglise, 11000 Carcassonne*
*Tel: 68.25.03.34 Telex: 500829*
*51 Rooms - Sgl from 670F Dbl to 850F*
*Open: 20 April to 20 October*
*  Restaurant closed Tuesdays*
*Credit cards: AX, DC*
*Restaurant*
*Hotel within city ramparts*
*Located 92 km SE of Toulouse*
*Region: Pyrennees Roussillon*

The village of Castillon du Gard sits on a knoll surrounded by grey-green olive trees and stretches of vineyards. Housed within medieval walls, the hotel, Le Vieux Castillon, runs the length of one small street in this village of sienna-tiled, sun-washed houses, so typical of Provence. The first floor is a maze of tile floors, light sandstone archways, hallways and intimate sitting rooms. The renowned restaurant, Le Fumoir, overlooks the pool through arched windows. Lunch is sometimes served at tables set in a tiled courtyard. The staging of the pool is magnificent, set against a backdrop of the town ruins with vistas that sweep out over the countryside and neighboring villages. The bedrooms, found in the main building and in a neighboring annex, are furnished with floral wallpapers, complementing curtains and bedspreads and a tasteful mix of antiques and reproduction furniture. The style is one of Mediterranean elegance and leisure. Le Vieux Castillon is a remarkable accomplishment: eight years were spent to renovate a complex of village homes into this luxurious hotel. Care was taken to retain the character of the original buildings and, amazingly, stones were preserved, cleaned and reset within the walls. Directions: take D19 from Remoulins in the direction of Uzes and then travel two kilometers on D228.

*LE VIEUX CASTILLON*
*Hotelier: Roger Traversac*
*Castillon du Gard, 30210 Remoulins*
*Tel: 66.37.00.77 Telex: 490946*
*35 Rooms - Sgl from 560F Dbl to 1190F*
*Open: 10 March to 31 December*
*Credit cards: VS, DC*
*Restaurant, tennis, pool*
*Located 23 km NE of Nimes*
*Region: Provence*

Madame Gautier and her daughter, Delphine, were our gracious hosts at their restored chateau that dates from the twelfth and eighteenth centuries.   Set in a six-acre park, the main chateau houses the majority of guest bedrooms as well as a lovely restaurant with an abundance of fresh flowers, polished dark woods and antique furnishings.   The bedrooms are all furnished with Madame Gautier's refined taste: soft colors, antique or quality reproduction furniture sagely mixed with contemporary pieces and spotless, well-equipped bathrooms - all combining to provide a welcoming haven for the traveller.   Several bedrooms and beautiful apartments are located in a separate stone building that was commissioned to lodge the Knights of Malta, an elite corps of the French military in the twelfth century. Their many different coats of arms are displayed on the shields in the small salon on the way to the luxurious rooms and suites which offer elegant and tranquil accommodations.   These bedrooms are a bit more expensive than those in the chateau, but are worth the extra cost if you would like a room which is larger, very quiet and has a view of the pool and/or garden.   Located just south of the picturesque wine capital of Beaune and just outside Chagny on N6, this twin towered chateau is atmospheric and peaceful, and displays an artistic woman's touch throughout.

*HOSTELLERIE DU CHATEAU DE BELLECROIX*
*Hotelier: Mme Gautier*
*Route Nationale 6, 71150 Chagny*
*Tel: 85.87.13.86*
*19 Rooms - Sgl from 335F Dbl to 785F*
*Open: February to 20 December*
*Credit cards: All major*
*Restaurant, park, swimming pool*
*Located 15 km SW of Beaune*
*Region: Burgundy*

The Hotel Lameloise is named after the remarkable family who owns and manages it.  Set in the middle of the town of Chagny, the Lameloise is principally a restaurant with rooms to accommodate dinner guests.  The Hotel Lameloise is a lovely fifteenth-century house that is handsome with beamed ceilings, heavy dark furnishings against whitewashed walls and contrasting splashes of colorful flower arrangements.  The restaurant, famous for its regional cuisine, is set in old vaults and is delightfully intimate in its pale pink decor.  Jacques Lameloise is now in charge of the kitchen, having learned and perfected his father's, Jean's, flair and talent in the preparation of Burgundian specialties.  The wine list is interesting to review and boasts a number of outstanding regional selections that complement the menu.  The Lameloise family's personal service and attention to detail reconfirm the difference it makes to have the owners personally involved in the managment of a hotel.  The bedrooms of the Lameloise are reserved on a demi-pension basis and are decorated with a touch of elegance and sophistication.  This is a lovely, roadside inn located in the town of Chagny and at the heart of the Burgundy wine district.

*HOTEL LAMELOISE*
*Hotelier: Lameloise family*
*Place d'Armes, 71150 Chagny*
*Tel: 85.87.08.85, Telex: 801086*
*20 Rooms - Sgl from 325F Dbl to 840F*
*Closed: part of July and December*
  *Restaurant closed Wednesdays*
*Credit cards: VS*
*Excellent restaurant*
*Located 15 km SW of Beaune*
*Region: Burgundy*

Chambord is the largest of the castles of the Loire Valley and very impressive in size and appearance.   The castle stands dramatically on a large open expanse of lawn, bounded by forest.   Although almost bare of furniture, it retains its grandeur and enchantment, especially at sunset or shrouded in the morning mist.   Staying at the Hostellerie Saint Michel provides an opportunity to explore the expanse of grounds surrounding Chambord either before you begin your day's adventures or at its end.   It is one of the very few hotels in the Loire Valley that enjoys such a marvellous, close proximity to one of its castles.   The Hostellerie Saint Michel has an inviting terrace restaurant where many, hotel and chateau guests alike, enjoy a refreshing drink and snack.   Indoors is an attractive restaurant and comfortable entry salon.   Accommodation is surprisingly inexpensive.   The rooms are simple in their country prints, basic in furnishings, but comfortable.   Of the forty rooms a choice few look out through the surrounding lacy trees to the Chateau de Chambord.   Of these, the corner rooms are the largest and should definitely be requested as they are no more expensive than the other rooms with a view.

*HOSTELLERIE SAINT MICHEL*
*Le Meur*
*Chambord*
*41250 Bracieux*
*Tel: 54.20.31.31*
*40 Rooms - Sgl from 240F Dbl to 360F*
*Closed: 12 November to 22 December*
*Credit cards: VS, MC*
*Restaurant*
*Faces the Chateau de Chambord*
*Located 18 km E of Blois*
*Region: Loire Valley*

Le Moulin du Roc is a small seventeenth- and eighteenth-century stone mill. With gardens sprawled along the river's edge, secluded even from the small village of Champagnac de Belair, the setting of this small inn is picture-perfect. The twelve rooms, although not large, are each stunning and the bathrooms all modern. One apartment is particularly enchanting: bridging the river below, it has a large room with a marvellous wood canopy double bed and an adjoining small room with a single bed. The bedroom windows overlook the lazy River Drome, the gardens and the beautiful birch-lined pastures. The small, captivating dining room utilizes the weathered old beams and wooden parts and mechanisms of the original mill in its decor. The atmosphere is intimate and the service is very attentive. Madame Gardillou is responsible for the kitchen and the exquisite cuisine. Preserving the traditions of fine gastronomy and employing established Perigord recipes and specialities, she has earned a coveted two-fork rating from Michelin. Menu prices are reasonable considering the excellence of the cuisine. Monsieur Gardillou is a most gracious and charming host. To reach Le Moulin du Roc, travel northeast from the village of Champagnac, six kilometers on D78 and D83.

*LE MOULIN DU ROC*
*Hotelier: M & Mme Gardillou*
*24530 Champagnac de Belair*
*Tel: 53.54.80.36 Telex: 571555*
*12 Rooms - Sgl from 450F Dbl to 700F*
*Closed: mid-November to mid-December,*
*  and mid-January to mid-March*
*  Restaurant closed Tuesdays*
*Crédit cards: All major*
*Marvellous restaurant, ancient mill*
*Located 33 km NW of Perigueux*
*Region: Dordogne*

Helwig was outside with the children and Francois came running from his dried flower workshop to greet us as we drove up to their home, Les Briottieres. The Valbrays are a charming, enthusiastic and artistic young couple who truly make their visitors feel like invited guests. Their grand home dates from 1773 and has been in Francois' family since 1820 when his great, great, great grandfather, the Comte de Valbray, resided here. Old family photos and portraits abound in the gracious salons and we were impressed by Francois' casual friendliness in spite of his noble heritage. It is hard to pick a favorite bedroom, as all are furnished in keeping with the style and mood of the chateau, however, one bedchamber, the Rose Room, is very special: feminine in decor, it was once inhabited by Francois' grandmother. Downstairs the parquet floors, grand chandeliers, and marble fireplaces in the public rooms attest to a very rich and elegant heritage. The elegance of a bygone era continues as guests are privileged to dine with Francois and Helwig at the one long candlelit table which is dressed with family silver and china. Dinner is is priced at 250F per person and includes an aperitif, a multi-course dinner and complementing wines, coffee and afterdinner drinks. A stay of at least two days is recommended to fully appreciate the Valbrays' hospitality and the ambiance of this aristocratic setting.

*LES BRIOTTIERES*
*Hotelier: Francois & Helwig de Valbray*
*Les Briottieres, 49330 Champigne*
*Tel: 41.42.00.02*
*8 Rooms - Sgl from 300F Dbl to 700F*
*Closed: 15 November to 15 February*
*Credit cards: All major*
*Restaurant - on a reservation only basis*
*Located 25 km N of Angers*
*Region: Loire Valley*

The Champagne region of France produces a grape unique in the world. True champagne comes only from this beautiful region located just a few hours east of Paris. In the heart of France's premier wine country, you may enjoy an excellent meal and taste some classic vintages at the Royal Champagne. Renowned for its cuisine, the restaurant of the Royal Champagne is very elegant, with tables set with white linen, crystal, silver and candlelight under a vaulted, beamed ceiling. A large fireplace warms the room and windows look out to spectacular views of the valley and surrounding vineyards. The bedrooms of the Royal Champagne are not traditional in decor, but modern and attractive. They are not exceptionally large and vary only in the color of the wallpaper, but they all have baths and small private terraces overlooking the vineyards. The village of Champillon Bellevue is set high on the hill amongst acres of terraced vineyards and located just a few kilometers north of Epernay, an important town in the Champagne region, making this a good base for champagne enthusiasts. The Royal Champagne is a white stucco building, set just off the road that travels between Reims and Epernay. If you are travelling from Epernay, leave the city to the north and follow the N51 for six kilometers.

*ROYAL CHAMPAGNE*
*Hotelier: M Dellinger*
*Champillon Bellevue*
*51160 Ay*
*Tel: 26.51.11.51 Telex: 830111*
*25 Rooms - Sgl from 430F Dbl to 790F*
*Closed: 3 to 26 January*
*Credit cards: All major*
*Restaurant*
*Located 20 km S of Reims*
*Region: Champagne*

Haute Provence is a region of France whose beauty is bounded by the snow-covered Alps, the fields of lavender and olive trees of Provence and the blue waters of the Riviera.   Villages of soft stone and sienna tiled roofs cluster on hilltops and dot this picturesque landscape.   Haute Provence is a beautiful region and serves as an ideal resting spot when travelling between the regions that bound it.   La Bonne Etape is an old coaching inn, a grey-stone manor house with a tiled roof - blending beautifully and suited to the landscape.   From its hilltop location, it enjoys panoramic views over the surrounding hills.   Dating from the seventeenth century, the hotel has eleven bedrooms and seven apartments, all attractively decorated. The restaurant is recognized for the quality of its cuisine.   Pierre Gleize and his son, Jany, employ local ingredients such as honey, lavender, herbs, lemon, pork, and rabbit to create masterpieces in the kitchen.   Dine in front of a large stone fireplace and sample some of their specialities.   But exceeding the praise for the cuisine are the superlatives guests use to describe the hospitality extended by your charming hosts, the Gleize family.

*LA BONNE ETAPE*
*Hotelier: Pierre & Jany Gleize*
*Chemin du Lac*
*04160 Chateau Arnoux*
*Tel: 92.64.00.09 Telex: 430605*
*18 Rooms - Dbl 500F, Apt 900F*
*Open: 15 February to 3 January*
*Credit cards: All major*
*Restaurant, pool*
*Located 25 km W of Digne*
*Region: Haute Provence*

It seems only appropriate that a region of France's fine wines is also the location of a superior chateau-hotel and restaurant. Set admidst the vineyards, the Hostellerie Fines Roches is a large imposing castle, very feudal in appearance with powerful square turrets binding its corners, surrounded by the golden vineyards of Chateauneuf du Pape. It is surprising, that such an impressive fortress has surprisingly few rooms to offer as accommodation. However, the seven suites are exceptionally spacious and handsomely furnished. Monsieur Estevenin plays host to some very famous guests and acknowledges their preference for privacy and quiet. There has never been a need or desire to advertise: guests faithfully return each year and recommend the Hostellerie Fines Roches to their friends. A junior Monsieur Estevenin is the hotel's chef. Some specialities include "filets de rougets" and a magnificent assortment of desserts. Monsieur Estevenin, rightly very proud of his son's capabilities, has relinquished kitchen duties and his time is now spent looking after his pampered guests. To locate the hotel, travel south from Chateauneuf du Pape for three kilometers on D17.

*HOSTELLERIE FINES ROCHES*
*Hotelier: Henri Estevenin*
*84230 Chateauneuf du Pape*
*Tel: 90.83.70.23*
*7 Rooms - Sgl from 440F Dbl to 690F*
*Closed: Christmas to March*
*  Restaurant closed Mondays*
*Credit cards: VS*
*Excellent restaurant*
*Located 15 km N of Avignon*
*Region: Provence*

Chateau de Chaumontel is a enchanting hotel that once belonged to the family of the Prince de Conde.    The castle gates and surrounding trees frame a breathtaking view of the castle.    Staged with a moat and a glorious expanse of green, lush grass and mounds of colorful flowers it is easy to understand why many French brides select the Chateau de Chaumontel as a setting for their wedding reception.    As a guest of the hotel one can also enjoy the romance of the castle's numerous bedchambers.    A labyrinth of narrow stairways winds up to rooms which are tucked under the beams or perhaps in one of the castle turrets.    All individual in their decor, the twenty rooms of the hotel are furnished with handsome antiques and pretty decorative prints.    A few of the bedrooms are a bit more private as they are located in a pavilion situated near the entrance.    The chateau has facilities to cater large parties and weddings but the guest dining room located in the castle proper is intimate and charming.    Tables are set before a large fireplace or on a warm day one can take advantage of the lovely white tables set in the garden. Directions: follow A1 from Le Bourget or Charles de Gaulle - Roissy airports to D9 then turn on N16 towards Luzarches.    Chaumontel is just north of Luzarches, and the chateau is half a kilometer northeast of Chaumontel.

*CHATEAU DE CHAUMONTEL*
*Hotelier: M et Mme Rigard*
*21, Rue Andre Vassord*
*Chaumontel, 95270 Luzarches*
*Tel: (1) 34.71.00.30 telex: 609730*
*20 Rooms - Sgl from 332F Dbl to 685F*
*Open: All year*
*Credit cards: AX, VS*
*Restaurant, park*
*Located 25 km N of CDG Paris airport*
*Region: Ile de Paris*

On the main road, opposite the gates that open to the road winding to the Chateau de Chaumont, you will discover the lovely Hostellerie du Chateau.  An attractive, timbered building, the location of the hotel is its largest drawback, as it is hard to shut out the traffic noices from the rooms that overlook the road.  But for the Loire Valley the prices are moderate and from the moment you enter the hotel you will be charmed by the wood beamed interior, the glowing fire, the beautiful dining room, quaint salons and Madame Desmadryl's hospitality.  On a warm summer day tables are spread out under the trees in the front garden and provide an inviting spot to rest and enjoy a refreshing drink.  The hallways leading to the upstairs bedrooms are in need of some fresh paint, but the rooms are still quite attractive. The least expensive rooms fall into the moderate price range and are smaller in size and overlook the road.   The more expensive rooms are worth a splurge as they are more commodious and overlook the hotel's back garden and pool and enjoy views of the passing Loire River.  All the rooms are decorated in warm and attractive colors and the bathrooms are modern.  The Hostellerie du Chateau is a well-located hotel for exploring the castles of the Loire   Accommodations are not luxurious, but comfortable and well priced.

*HOSTELLERIE DU CHATEAU*
*Owner: M Bonnigal*
*Hotelier: Mme Desmadryl*
*Chaumont sur Loire, 41150 Onzain*
*Tel: 54.20.98.04*
*15 Rooms - Sgl from 242F Dbl to 544F*
*Open: 1 March to end November*
*Credit cards: MC, VS*
*Restaurant, pool*
*Located 41 km NE of Tours*
*Region: Loire Valley*

Hostellerie le Prieure is a lovely chateau on the banks above the Loire. In season Le Prieure caters to tours and buses do tend to invade the sense of days gone by. However, if you travel off season and can obtain a room in the castle proper you will be rewarded with a sense of regality. Stone steps wind up the castle turret to spacious rooms which are beautifully appointed with large windows set in thick stone walls opening up to fantastic vistas of the flowing Loire River. There are a few rooms built at the base of the chateau, called the terrace rooms, that open onto private patios. They are also handsome in their decor but not as luxurious in size. When heavily booked, Le Prieure also offers more "motel-like" accommodations in bungalows found near the pool. The hotel claims that they advise guests when only bungalow rooms are available as they do not afford the castle experience that one would anticipate. The restaurant, an elegant room surrounded by windows, has earned a reputation for excellent cuisine. Situated in a large estate high above the Loire, this lovely hotel commands panoramic views of the river and makes a convenient base for exploring the enchanting Chateau de Saumur and western stretches of the Loire Valley. Directions: from Saumur, travel northwest eight kilometers on D751 in the direction of Gennes.

*LE PRIEURE*
*Hotelier: M P.H. Doumerc*
*Chenehutte les Tuffeaux*
*49350 Gennes*
*Tel: 41.67.90.14 Telex: 720379*
*36 Rooms - Sgl from 505F Dbl to 1610F*
*Closed: 5 January to 5 March*
*Credit cards: VS*
*Restaurant, pool, tennis, park*
*Located 8 km NW of Saumur*
*Region: Loire Valley*

*Hotel Descriptions*

This hotel is in the town of Chenonceaux and within walking distance of its spectacular castle.   The location of the Bon Laboureur et du Chateau affords one the opportunity to linger close to one of the most elegant of the Loire Valley's Renaissance chateaux.   The hotel's accommodations are simple and moderately priced.   Bedrooms are found in the building above the restaurant as well as in neighboring ivy-covered annexes.   The bedrooms, all with either private bath or shower, vary in price depending on size and whether or not they overlook the road, garden or courtyard.   The hallways that lead to the bedrooms are attractively appointed with antiques and copper pieces.   The hotel's restaurant is intimate and charming in its decor and offers an enticing menu.   Managed for generations by the Jeudi family, a friendly welcome is said to be a tradition at the Bon Laboureur et du Chateau; however, we have recently received a few complaints from our readers concerning a cool reception.   I feel the criticism important to mention, although I recently revisited the hotel and found the management very accommodating.   I would appreciate further feedback from fellow travellers.

*BON LABOUREUR ET DU CHATEAU*
*Hotelier: Jeudi family*
*37150 Chenonceaux*
*Tel: 47.23.90.02*
*29 Rooms - Sgl from 300F Dbl to 490F*
*Open: 1 March  to 1 December*
  *Closed: Tuesdays, November to April*
*Credit cards: AX, VS, DC*
*Restaurant*
*Located 35 km SE of Tours*
*Region: Loire Valley*

Standing proud with its castle turret is the Hotel du Manoir. Newly constructed, the hotel is set on the main road of Chenonceaux, opposite the Hotel Bon Laboureur et du Chateau and just a short distance from the town's beautiful castle. Opened as a hotel just a few years ago, the Hotel du Manoir definitely radiates a pride of ownership. A lovely couple, the Mazzellas offer a warm welcome and the character of the inn reflects the heritage of its Italian owners. Vivid colors, heavy patterns and garish paintings abound and there is lots of detail in the furnishings. The entry salon is comfy, with inviting large overstuffed chairs. A handsome, wide stairway leads up from the lobby to the hotel's seven bedrooms. The restaurant is intimate and charming in its decor: in the evening, candlelight from the individual tables reflects off the room's stone walls and vaulted ceiling. The menu boasts a number of Italian specialties, such as "Lasagne a la Maison". Afternoon tea is served at tables set round an old well at the center of the flagstone terrace. One can also relax in the shade of a garden that extends out at the back of the hotel. The Hotel du Manoir is a delightful inn because of its endearing owners.

*HOTEL DU MANOIR*
*Hotelier: M & Mme Carlo Mazzella*
*1, Rue La Roche*
*37150 Chenonceaux*
*Tel: 47.23.90.31*
*7 Rooms - Dbl from 280F to 560F*
*Open: March to November*
*Credit cards: Unknown*
*Restaurant, park*
*Located 35 km SE of Tours*
*Region: Loire Valley*

Chinon is a pretty riverside town with narrow cobblestoned streets which climb to the ruins of its crowning castle. This is where Jeanne d'Arc met Le Dauphin and is an interesting stop for any Loire Valley itinerary. The Hotel Diderot is well located just off the Place Jeanne d'Arc in a residential district of town. The Hotel Diderot is owned and managed with care by Theo Kazamias and his family who came to France from Cypress ten years ago in search of a new life. He purchased and completely renovated the home, installing bathrooms and decorating with a homey touch. Off the entryway, a breakfast room set with country tables and chairs before a large fifteenth-century fireplace, is where one enjoys breakfast complete with homemade jams and the chatter and good spirits of the many British travellers who frequent this hotel. An old wooden stairway and hallways with exposed walls and beams lead to eighteen of the bedrooms. Another room is found in the pavilion, and three additional rooms, converted from the stables, are located at street level and are equipped for handicap access. All of the bedrooms are furnished with a mixture of antique and contemporary pieces with bathrooms that are adequate and spotless. The Hotel Diderot offers simple comforts and moderate prices. Your host is a kind and very interesting man who genuinely cares about his guests.

*HOTEL DIDEROT*
*Hotelier: Theo Kazamias*
*4, Rue Buffon, 37500 Chinon*
*Tel: 47.93.18.87*
*22 Rooms - Sgl from 160F Dbl to 350F*
*Closed: Christmas holidays*
*Credit cards: MC, VS*
*No restaurant*
*Located 48 km SW of Tours*
*Region: Loire Valley*

Travelling east from Tours on N76, look for signs before you reach Montrichard for the Chateau de Chissay in the small town of Chissay en Touraine. At the top of a small hill, the arched stone entryway between twin towers is actually a side entrance to this "petite" chateau. Walk through the vaulted stone walls over old cobblestones to reach the inner courtyard with its fountain and open cloister side which lets in cool breezes and looks out over a vista of the Loire Valley. Tapestry covers the chairs in the intimate restaurant, and heavy antique furnishings dress the grand salons. At the time of our visit the bedrooms were all occupied but a helpful management described them as all having private baths and beautifully traditional furnishings. From the lovely decor and refined taste evident throughout the public areas of the chateau, we are sure the twenty bedrooms and seven apartments are very comfortable and pleasant. Located in a twenty-acre estate, this romantic castle is a former royal residence containing a dungeon that dates from the eleventh century. Despite its white stone walls and floors, and heavy, forbidding old wooden doors, the Chateau de Chissay provides a warm and luxurious ambiance from which to explore the many other chateaux of the Loire Valley.

*CHATEAU DE CHISSAY*
*Hotelier: M. Philippe Savry*
*Chissay en Touraine, 41400 Montrichard*
*tel: 54.32.32.01 telex: 750 393*
*27 rooms - Sgl from 445F Dbl to 790F*
*　Apt to 1390F*
*Closed: January to 15 March*
*Credit Cards: VS*
*Restaurant, pool, park*
*Located 43 km SE of Tours*
*Region: Loire Valley*

A converted mill, this ivy-covered complex of buildings is situated along the River Orne just downstream from the old stone bridge. It is an idyllic setting ablaze with masses of flowers and the sound of the river tumbling past the former mill is quite soothing. The Moulin du Vey has a lovely terrace set with tables and shaded by a lacy willow tree. If you choose to dine indoors, the restaurant is in an adjacent building. Twelve bedrooms tucked away in the former mill could use a little sprucing up but they are comfortable and equipped with either private bath or shower. Three kilometers from the mill is the Relais de Surone, an annex, where seven additional bedrooms are offered. The Relais is an old home built in the style of a church or a priory. Although away from the river and without a restaurant, the rooms of the Relais are more attractive and spacious than those of the Moulin. Breakfast can be taken in the salon, in the bedroom, or, on a nice day, in the front garden. Clecy le Vey is the capital of the beautiful district referred to as Swiss Normandy. The Moulin du Vey is located two kilometers east of Clecy in the village of Le Vey. The Relais is located on the other side of Clecy le Vey, just off the road that travels between Caen and Domfort (route D962).

*LE MOULIN DU VEY*
*Hotelier: Mme Leduc*
*14570 Clecy le Vey*
*Tel: 31.69.71.08*
*12 Rooms (Mill) - 7 Rooms (Relais)*
*  Sgl from 310F Dbl to 460F*
*Open: Moulin du Vey - February to December*
*     Le Relais - Easter to October*
*Credit cards: AX, DC, VS*
*Restaurant, park on river's edge*
*Located 37 km S of Caen*
*Region: Normandy*

Colroy la Roche is a town typical of the Alsatian region. The Hostellerie la Cheneaudiere, set on a hillside overlooking the town and surrounding valleys, was built to resemble a country tavern. The bedrooms are very luxurious in their decor and appointments. Beautiful wallpapers, handsome paintings, a tasteful blend of antique and contemporary furnishings and wall-to-wall carpets enhanced by Oriental rugs have all been selected and achieve an elegant environment in the bedrooms. Each room is equipped with a telephone, television, mini-bar and remarkably spacious bathroom. Many of the hotel's twenty-eight rooms also enjoy the privacy of a covered terrace. Breakfast served on your own patio with views out over the village of Colroy is a treat. The hotel has two dining rooms whose formal atmosphere is warmed by a large fire. The cuisine is prepared under the supervision of Chef Jean Paul Bossee and includes specialities such as "millefeuille de foie gras & truffes" and "tartare de saumon sauvage". The hotel has a large spacious lounge and a few elegant boutiques. La Cheneaudiere also organizes private hunting parties in the summer, autumn and winter months.

*HOSTELLERIE LA CHENEAUDIERE*
*Hotelier: M & Mme Francois*
*Colroy la Roche*
*67420 Saales*
*Tel: 88.97.61.64 Telex: 870438*
*28 Rooms - Dbl from 606F Dbl to 836F*
*    Apt from 1000F to 1436F*
*Open: March to December*
*Credit cards: All major*
*Restaurant, tennis, garden setting*
*Located 62 km SW of Strasbourg*
*Region: Alsace*

Turn south off N89 (halfway between Perigueux and Brive) at Le Lardin and continue in the direction of Montignac for one kilometer to Conde where you turn east towards Coly. A sign before Coly directs down a private drive enclosed by cornfields to this old mill in its idyllic setting where tables are set in a garden bounded by stone walls, colorful flowers and a rushing stream. The flock of geese inhabiting a nearby lawn complete the postcard scene. The original core of this ivy-covered manor house was a forge and dates from the thirteenth century. Belonging to the Hamelin family for over three hundred years, the forge later became a mill and other sections were added with distinctive arched windows and doors. Family antiques decorate the salons, halls and bedrooms, including a magnificently tall grandfather clock on the stair landing. On the second floor the six bedrooms are attractive in their simplicity and all have well appointed bathrooms. The floors are wooden and can be a bit noisy, but most guests retire early after one of Madame's gourmet meals. Guests are expected to dine here and Madame will tailor her cuisine to the wishes of any on an extended stay. The Manoir d'Hautegente proves to be a picturesque, tranquil and convenient base from which to explore northern Perigord.

*MANOIR D'HAUTEGENTE*
*Hotelier: Mme Edith Hamelin*
*Coly, 24120 Terrasson*
*Tel: 53.51.68.03*
*6 Rooms - Dbl from 390F to 550F*
  *Menu: 180F per person, drinks extra*
*Open: 15 November to 1 April*
*Credit cards: AX*
*Restaurant, riverside setting*
*Located 25 km SW of Brive*
*Region: Dordogne*

Hotel la Belle Etoile is an expensive, elegant hotel situated on the southern coast of Brittany looking out to the sheltered bay of Le Cabellou.   Although the address is Concarneau, Cabellou beach is approximately three miles from the walled city and looks out over a quiet harbor and moored boats.   Should you decide to arrive by yacht, La Belle Etoile has its own private mooring.   The gardens stretch down to the sandy shore and extend the lines of the hotel to form the image of a ship.   An anchor off to the side and a flagpole serving as a mast complete this picture. Tennis courts are there for those who wish to play.   Inside heavy rope is looped through the balustrades of the bannister, again playing on the theme of a ship. The bedrooms, however, are more commodious than any seaboard accommodation. Firm beds, well appointed bathrooms, excellent lighting, large closets in addition to handsome furnishings guarantee a good night's rest. Also expensive, the restaurant is elegant and looks out onto the bay and the entrance to the harbor of Concarneau.   To reach the hotel by car, from Concarneau travel east on D783 and C22, five and a half kilometers to Cabellou Beach.

*HOTEL LA BELLE ETOILE*
*Hotelier: Marie & Paul Raout-Guillou*
*La Plage du Cabellou*
*29110 Concarneau*
*Tel: 98.97.05.73*
*30 Rooms - Sgl from 640F Dbl to 890F*
*Closed: February*
  *Restaurant closed: December to March*
*Credit cards: AX, DC, VS*
*Restaurant, bay views*
*Located 24 km SE of Quimper*
*Region: Brittany*

The medieval village of Conques overlooks the Dourdou Gorge.  Tucked off the beaten track, the village is glorious in the gentle light of evening or in the mist of early day.  Conques' pride is an eleventh-century abbey, directly across from which is a simple hotel, the Ste Foy.  The shuttered windows of our room opened up to the church steeples and we woke to the melodious sound of bells.  The decor is neat and attractive and one can't fault the location.  The restaurant is reserved exclusively for guests of the hotel and is open for breakfast and dinner.  The interior restaurant is lovely and rustic in its decor, the walls hung with an exhibition of French, English and American paintings and on warm summer nights dinner is served family-style on a sheltered courtyard terrace.  One can order a la carte or select from a well-chosen three- or four-course fixed menu at a very reasonable price.  The restaurant offers a number of regional dishes.  The Roquefort cheese produced in the area is exceptional and the house "salade verte aux noix et roquefort et huile de noix" is a perfect first course to any meal.  A wide selection of fine French wines from the various provinces comprise the wine list.  The hotel's finest feature is Madame Cannes, whose charm, welcoming smile and eagerness to please create the wonderful atmosphere of the Ste Foy.

*HOTEL STE FOY*
*Hotelier: M & Mme Jean Cannes*
*    and Mme Garcenot*
*Conques, 12320 St Cyprien*
*Tel: 65.69.84.03*
*20 Rooms - Sgl from 162F Dbl to 424F*
*Open: 10 April to 6 October*
*Restaurant*
*Located 37 km NW of Rodez*
*Region: Lot*

Vieux Cordes is an enchanting, medieval hilltop village.   It is a treasure and found at the center of this medieval city is the Hotel du Grand Ecuyer.   Once the home and hunting lodge of Raymond VII, Comte de Toulouse, this is a grand hotel that seems to improve with age.   Found along the upstairs hallway whose floors creak and slant, the fifteen bedrooms are very impressive in their decor.   Decorated with period furnishings, a few of the rooms boast magnificent four poster beds and some even enjoy large fireplaces.   The bedroom windows, set in thick stone walls, open on to glorious vistas of the surrounding countryside.   The reputation of the hotel's restaurant reflects the expertise of Monsieur Yves Thuries, under whose direction and guidance selections from the menu are further enhanced by artful and creative presentation.   His specialty is desserts and they are divine in taste as well as presentation.   If you want to try your own talent in the kitchen, purchase a copy of his book, "La Nouvelle Patisserie".   Vieux Cordes is a gem.   It is a medieval village that proves to be a highlight of many a trip and the Hotel du Grand Ecuyer is the final polish that makes Cordes an ideal stopover for any itinerary.

*HOTEL DU GRAND ECUYER*
*Hotelier: M Yves Thuries*
*Rue Voltaire*
*81170 Cordes*
*Tel: 63.56.01.03*
*15 Rooms - Sgl from 340F Dbl to 630F*
*Open: 1 April to 20 October*
  *Restaurant closed Mondays*
*Credit cards: AX, DC, VS*
*Restaurant*
*Medieval city*
*Located 25 km NW of Albi*
*Region: Tarn*

An alternative for travellers who would like to avoid the crowds on the island of Le Mont Saint Michel, the ivy-clad, grey-stone Manoir de la Roche Torin is a lovely hotel. This stately manor was a private residence for twenty-five years before it was converted to a hotel. A short tree-lined drive past an ancient chapel on the front lawn leads to the front steps. The highlights of this hotel are the mix of antique furnishings in the public rooms and the magnificent view from the dining room where one looks out over sheep grazing on the tidal grasslands to Le Mont Saint Michel. The regional specialty known as "pre-salted lamb", sheep who have grazed on the salty grass, is roasted over a large open hearth in the restaurant. Two stately grandfather clocks watch over the dinner guests. It is important to note that hotel guests are expected to dine in the Manoir's restaurant. The twelve bedrooms of the Manoir de la Roche Torin are furnished with modern pieces and sometimes overly bright colors have been chosen for their decor. The rooms, however, are clean, cheerful and reasonably priced. All but one room is equipped with private bath. Considering its location, priceless views and the warm welcome extended by the Barraux family, this hotel is a bargain and a tranquil haven near an otherwise congested tourist destination.

*MANOIR DE LA ROCHE TORIN*
*Hotelier: M & Mme Barraux*
*50220 Courtils*
*Tel: 33.70.96.55*
*12 Rooms - Sgl from 190F Dbl to 400F*
*Open: March to December*
*Credit cards: All major*
*Restaurant*
*Located 9 km E of Le Mont St Michel*
*Region: Normandy*

The Dordogne River makes a panoramic journey through a rich valley studded with castles. The ancient village of Domme has for centuries stood guard fifteen hundred feet above the river, and commands a magnificent panorama. The town itself is enchanting, with ramparts that date from the thirteenth century, and narrow streets that wind through its old quartier and past a lovely fourteenth century Hotel de Ville. At the center of town under the old market place one finds access to some interesting stalactite and stalagmite grottos. But most visitors come to Domme for its spectacular valley views and the best vantage point is from the Terrasse de la Barre. Very near to la Barre, facing the church, is a hotel which enables you to savor the village long after the tour buses have departed: Monsieur et Madame Gillard extend a warm and friendly greeting at the Hotel de l'Esplanade. Rene Gillard is both your host and chef. In the dining room he'll propose some excellent regional specialties that feature the delicious cepes, truffles, foie gras and local fish. There are two restaurants to choose from, both attractive and very country in decor. The hotel's twenty rooms, all with either bath or shower, are located in the main building or in a neighboring annex that was once a building of the church and dates from the seventeenth century. The bedrooms are simply decorated, reasonably priced and commodious.

*HOTEL DE L'ESPLANADE*
*Hotelier: M Rene Gillard*
*24250 Domme*
*Tel: 53.28.31.41*
*20 Rooms - Dbl from 240F to 420F*
*Open: Dec to end Jan & Mar to end Oct*
*Credit cards: AX, VS, MC*
*Restaurant*
*Located 75 km SE of Perigueux*
*Region: Dordogne*

At first glance this hotel appears a typically French roadside restaurant, pretty with natural wood shutters and flowerboxes overflowing with a profusion of red, pink and white geraniums at every window. The wonderful surprise one discovers is that this restaurant also offers forty rooms in a quiet rear wing, all far removed from any traffic noises. Beautifully appointed, all but two of the bedrooms (both singles) have private bath or shower and all rooms are equipped with direct-dial telephones and mini-bars. With all these modern conveniences one still has the impression of staying in a country home. Antiques, well chosen paintings and Oriental rugs warm the length of the hallways. The bedrooms are delightfully fresh in their decor, hung with pretty flowered wallpapers and furnished in antique reproductions. With a good night's rest in mind, the layout of the hotel was constructed so that all the bedrooms overlook the garden. Fourteen of the accommodations are suites with private patios in the very tranquil annex. The public areas, including the well known and respected restaurant, are all very charming with many warm decorative touches and tasteful antiques. Monsieur Houard, the chef, is renowned in the region. The Jean-Paul Perardel family manage the Aux Armes de Champagne with care and taste. This is an ideal haven for overnight accommodations while touring the Champagne district.

*AUX ARMES DE CHAMPAGNE*
*Hotelier: Denise & Jean-Paul Perardel*
*51460 L'Epine*
*Tel: 26.66.96.79 Telex: 830998 Fax: 26.66.92.31*
*40 Rooms - Dbl from 375F to 490F*
*Closed: 9 January to 13 February*
*Credit cards: AX, VS, MC*
*Restaurant, garden, mini-golf*
*Located 40 km SE of Reims*
*Region: Champagne*

Monsieur and Madame Treillou have opened up their home to guests. This ivy-covered former rectory is just across the cobblestone courtyard from the church. The reception area is a cozy sitting room with an oft used fireplace, warm tile floors and a gallery of treasured paintings. Madame Treillou is an antique dealer and has a shop housed in a wing of the building. The entire hotel is lovingly furnished with her selections of antiques which add a richness and warmth to the decor. Every bedroom is tasteful and unique and all have a lovely armoire. What were once the children's rooms have all been tastefully supplied with television, mini-bar, direct dial phones and all have a modern private bath or shower. Madame tends the lovely "English" garden, still in full bloom at the time of our fall visit. The tables in the garden courtyard invite a leisurely breakfast or an afternoon read. If the weather does not cooperate, a cozy fire is lit every morning in the open hearth fireplace of the breakfast room. Although Le Prieure is near the main road that travels through Ermenonville, the mellow chimes of the adjacent church will temper any traffic noises. The Treillous are extremely gracious hosts and we are fortunate that they now offer their home to guests. We hope to return very soon.

*HOTEL LE PRIEURE*
*Hotelier: Jean Pierre & Marie Josie Treillou*
*Chevet de l'Eglise*
*60950 Ermenonville*
*Tel: 44.54.00.44 Telex: 145 110*
*10 Rooms - Dbl from 410F to 460F*
*Open: All year*
*Credit cards: EC, VS*
*No restaurant, garden*
*Located: 47 km NE of Paris*
*Region: Ile de Paris*

The vine-covered Hotel Cro Magnon was built on the site where the skull of prehistoric Cro Magnon man was unearthed and a beautiful collection of prehistoric flints can be seen in the hotel. Managed by the third generation of the Leyssales family, this is a tranquil country-style hotel with beautiful furnishings from the Perigord region. The hotel has a large swimming pool, perfect for warm summer days, and a park of four acres. There are twenty-three rooms, some of which are in the annex added in 1962. Rooms are priced according to their location and size. Back bedrooms in the annex look out through shuttered windows onto the expanse of colorful garden and pool. The restaurant is truly delightful in its country French decor and the menu features Perigordian specialties that, alone, are a prime attraction of the region. The hotel's front terrace is set under the shade of draping vines and is an ideal place to linger over lunch or enjoy an aperitif. Les Eyzies is a popular tourist destination and the town is rich in accommodation. The Cro Magnon hotel proves to be a choice and favorite of many which is a direct reflection on the standards of service and welcome set by the Leyssales family.

*HOTEL CRO MAGNON*
*Hotelier: M & Mme J. Leyssales*
*24620 Les Eyzies de Tayac*
*Tel: 53.06.97.06 Telex: 470382*
*23 Rooms - Sgl from 265F Dbl to 510F*
*Open: 16 April to 11 October*
*Credit cards: All major*
*Restaurant, pool, flower garden*
*Located 45 km SE of Perigueux*
*Region: Dordogne*

For more than a thousand years this majestic chateau has soaked up the sun and looked across the beautiful blue water of the Mediterranean. Rising twelve hundred feet above sea level, the medieval village of Eze looks down upon Cap Ferrat and Nice. You can happily spend an entire afternoon on the secluded hotel terrace overlooking the pool and the stunning coastline vistas. In the sparkle of evening lights, the coastal cities seem to dance along the waterfront. The bedchambers open onto views of the Riviera or surrounding hillsides. Often on two levels, the rooms are tastefully appointed with the most modern conveniences. Room nine has a private terrace with unsurpassed views. Enjoy a drink in the bar just off the pool while studying the day's menu selections. For lunch or dinner, a meal at the Chateau de la Chevre d'Or is a wonderful experience because of Chef Mazot's cuisine and the incredible views. The restaurant is popular with the local community and the many celebrities who have homes on the Riviera, so reservations are as difficult to get as room reservations. Attentive service, superb cuisine, beautiful views and a peaceful, serene medieval atmosphere make the Chateau de la Chevre d'Or a hotel to which you will eagerly return.

*CHATEAU DE LA CHEVRE D'OR*
*Hotelier: Pierre de Daeniken*
*Rue de Barri, 06360 Eze Village*
*Tel: 93.41.12.12 Telex: 970839*
  *Fax: 93.41.06.72*
*11 Rooms - Dbl from 1310F to 2200F*
*Open: March to December*
  *Restaurant closed Tuesdays*
*Credit cards: AX, VS, DC*
*Restaurant, lovely coastal views, pool*
*Located 13 km E of Nice*
*Region: Riviera*

Monsieur Andre Rochat in the fabled tradition of Swiss excellence has renovated the former chateau of Prince William of Sweden and converted the magnificent residence into a hotel of superb luxury. The Chateau Eza is located in the medieval village of Eze, perched thirteen hundred feet above the coastline of the Riviera. The hotel's bedrooms are found in a cluster of buildings that front onto Eze's narrow, winding, cobbled stoned streets. Most of the nine rooms have a private entry and blend beautifully as part of the village scene. Accommodation can only be described as extremely luxurious apartments or suites. The decor is stunning, with priceless antiques and Oriental rugs and a number enjoy fireplaces that are well-stocked with wood. Each room enjoys spectacular views and some have private terraces that extend out over the rooftops of the village. The Chateau Eza has a renowned restaurant with views and service to equal the excellent cuisine. A multi-level tea room with its hanging garden terraces is a delightful and informal spot for afternoon tea or a light meal. This is a hotel for the wealthy or a wonderful splurge before departing France: the international airport at Nice is just fifteen minutes from Eze Village by the Autoroute. Note: as Eze is closed to all but pedestrian traffic look for the reception at the base of the village - it is easy to spot as two donkeys, "the bagagistes", are stabled out front.

*CHATEAU EZA*
*Hotelier: Andre Rochat*
*06360 Eze Village*
*Tel: 33.93.41.12.24 Telex: 470 382*
*9 Rooms - Dbl from 920F Suite to 3620F*
*Open: April to November*
*Credit cards: All major*
*Restaurant*
*Located 15 km NW of Nice*
*Region: Riviera*

The Hostellerie du Chateau is a lovely and luxurious chateau hotel. Set in a magnificent park, fifty-five miles from the Charles de Gaulle - Roissy airport, the Hostellerie du Chateau guarantees a peaceful night's rest whether it is your first or last night in France. The chateau has twenty individually decorated bedrooms to offer as accommodation. The decor is elegant. The walls are covered with beautiful materials that complement the bedspreads and drapes; the beds are large and comfortable; the bathrooms spacious; the location is peaceful and the views are splendid. Room twenty-nine, in the old tower, is decorated in feminine pinks and whites and offers views of the valley through its windows set deep in the old stone walls. Rooms twenty and twelve are both large, lovely apartments. Outdoor facilities include tennis courts and a new nine-hole golf course. Looking out onto the expanse of garden through lovely floor-to-ceiling windows, the restaurant is dressed in elegance with a display of beautiful linens, silver and crystal and offers a magnificent menu, with pastries too tempting to resist. The vaulted wine cellar maintains an excellent selection of fine French wines. Travel north from Fere en Tardenois, three kilometers on D967 to the outskirts of town.

*HOSTELLERIE DU CHATEAU*
*Hotelier: Blot family*
*02130 Fere en Tardenois*
*Tel: 23.82.21.13 Telex: 145526*
*20 Rooms - Sgl from 598F Dbl to 896F*
*  Suite to 1300F*
*Closed: January and February*
*Credit cards: AX, VS, DC*
*Restaurant, tennis, pool, golf*
*Located 90 km NE of CDG Airport*
*Region: Champagne*

The Chateau de Fleurville is a less expensive alternative for travellers with a longing to stay in a castle. Conveniently located for touring the Burgundy and Rhone wine regions, this sixteenth- and eighteenth-century farmstead chateau is found on D17 between Beaune and Macon. Although set in a pleasant garden, the chateau still suffers from some traffic noise as it is separated from the main road only by a stone wall. Ask for a room nearer the pool to be assured of a quieter stay. The fourteen bedooms (two with handicapped access) and one small apartment are comfortable but not luxurious; the color schemes and wallpapers do not always make up an entirely pleasing ensemble. However, all are clean and equipped with private bath or shower. The dining room is decorated in a simple country French style: stone walls surrounding the wooden chairs and tables set with pretty pottery before a large open fireplace. Simple fare is offered at a reasonable price, so wine, dine and enjoy the hospitality of the Naudin family. An after dinner brandy can be enjoyed in the tile-floored salon with its tapestry chairs and couches and old marble fireplace. A good choice for a family, complete with three sweet-tempered collie dogs to romp with on the front lawn, this modest chateau is for those seeking homey rather than elegant accommodation

*CHATEAU DE FLEURVILLE*
*Hotelier: Naudin family*
*71260 Fleurville*
*Tel: 85.33.12.17*
*15 Rooms - Dbl from 330F to Apt 620F*
*Closed: 15 November to 26 December*
*Credit cards: All major*
*Restaurant, park, pool*
*Located 17 km N of Macon*
*Region: Rhone Valley*

La Regalido, converted from an ancient oil mill, is a lovely Provencal hotel, with its cream stone facade and sienna tile roof, whose shuttered windows peek out through an ivy-covered exterior. Running the length of this hotel is a beautiful garden bordered by a multitude of brilliantly colored roses. I was pleased to find the interior equally attractive and inviting. In the entry lovely paintings and copper pieces adorn the walls and plump sofas and chairs cluster before a large open fireplace. An arched doorway frames the dining room whose tapestry-covered chairs are placed round elegantly set tables and whose windows look out to the rose garden and terrace. The inviting restaurant is renowned for the excellence of its regional cuisine and for its wine cellar. Monsieur Michel spends much of his day tending to the kitchen and is often seen bustling about the hotel, dressed in his chef's attire, but never too busy to pause for a greeting. His wife's domain is the garden - the French say that she has a "green hand" instead of just a "green thumb", and it shows. The bedrooms of La Regalido are very pretty in their decor and luxurious in size and comfort. Approximately half of the rooms enjoy the privacy of their own terrace and look out over the tile rooftops of Fontvieille.

*LA REGALIDO*
*Hotelier: Michel family*
*Rue Frederic Mistral*
*13990 Fontvieille en Provence*
*Tel: 90.97.60.22 Telex: 441150*
*13 Rooms - Sgl from 560F Dbl to 1120F*
*Closed: December & January,*
   *Restaurant closed Mondays*
*Credit cards: All major*
*Restaurant, converted oil mill*
*Located 10 km NE of Arles*
*Region: Provence*

The owner, Madame Hubert, describes Le Manoir du Stang as "not really a small hotel or inn, but a comfortable family home where we receive guests".  Set behind its own moat and arched gateway and tower, it is, however, a dramatic home and affords some regal accommodation.  A sixteenth-century manor house, the Manoir du Stang is surrounded by well-tended flower gardens, a small lake, woods and acres of farmland.  The interior furnishings manage to retain the original atmosphere of a private chateau.  The hallway leading to the bedrooms is a bit motelish, but the rooms themselves are decorated in period pieces in keeping with the mood of the building.  The hotel offers twenty-six rooms, all equipped with modern conveniences and comforts.  The Louis XV dining room is handsomely appointed, with tables set before a large fireplace.  Waitresses adorned in costumes of the southern coast of Brittany provide service and lend an air of festivity to the meal.  Accommodation is offered on a demi-pension basis.  To locate take D783 between Concarneau and Benodet, then follow D44 to the center of La Foret Fouesnant and then V7 in the direction of Quimper.  Less than a mile out of town watch for signs that will direct you down a long tree-lined drive to the manor.

*LE MANOIR DU STANG*
*Hotelier: M & Mme Guy Hubert*
*29133 La Foret Fouesnant (Finistere)*
*Tel: 98.56.97.37*
*26 Rooms - Sgl from 600F Dbl to 1100F*
  *Note: price includes breakfast and dinner*
*Open: 1 May to 30 September*
*Credit cards: None*
*Restaurant, tennis, park*
*Located 16 km S of Quimper*
*Region: Brittany*

Located just around the corner from the Chateau de Gace, a small chateau dating from the 1200s and 1400s on a green town square, Le Morphee is set behind tall iron gates and a driveway that circles a fountain from an ancient spring. This stately brick manor has two stories and our spacious room was tucked cozily under the eaves. It was extremely attractive with exposed dark wooden beams and was papered in a pink floral print with matching rose bedspreads and curtains. The bathroom was spotless and contained all the modern conveniences as well as thoughtful touches such as a small traveller's sewing kit. Downstairs we found an intimate dining room with a beautifully restored panelled ceiling. Request a window seat if eating breakfast downstairs, as the garden view is pretty. The sitting room across the main hall from the billiard room is jewel-like, with another beautifully restored ceiling, a chandelier, decorative plaster relief work on the walls, a lovely parquet floor and a small piano. The fortunate traveller will be treated to selections played by Madame Lecanu. Lavish praise for Le Morphee in the guest book attests to the main attraction of this hotel, the hospitality of its owners, the Lecanus.

*LE MORPHEE*
*Hotelier: M & Mme Lecanu*
*2, Rue de Lisieux*
*61230 Gace*
*Tel: 33.35.51.01*
*10 Rooms - Sgl from 250F Dbl to 310F*
*Open: 1st March to 1st January*
*Credit cards: All major*
*No restaurant*
*Located 46 km NE of Alencon*
*Region: Normandy*

On the outskirts of the medieval town of Gordes is a small secluded hotel, Les Bories. Recognized principally for its restaurant, very few guests even realize that Les Bories also offers accommodation. However, with only four luxurious bedrooms, this should truly be titled, not a hotel, but rather a "restaurant with rooms", and if you are fortunate enough to secure a reservation you will feel like a privileged guest in a private home. The restaurant occupies a number of rooms where heavy wooden tables, copper pieces, flowers and a fire all add warmth, while the owner, Madame Rousselet, supplies the charm and hospitality. The dining room has a panoramic view of the Luberon Valley. Guests are often amazed to learn that this small hotel, with Monsieur Rousselet as your accomplished chef, has been awarded two red forks by Michelin and is highly praised by Gault-Millau. Nestled on a hillside, Les Bories' quiet location ensures an exceptional rest and its marvellous restaurant affords a sampling of gourmet cuisine. To find this small inn travel northwest of Gordes two kilometers along the Route Abbaye de Senanque.

*LES BORIES*
*Hotelier: M & Mme Gabriel Rousselet*
*Route de Senanque*
*84220 Gordes*
*Tel: 90.72.00.51*
*4 Rooms - Sgl from 395F Dbl to 535F*
*Closed: December and Wednesdays*
  *Restaurant closed Sunday to Thursday*
*Credit cards: Unknown*
*Restaurant - excellent food*
*Located 38 km E of Avignon*
*Region: Provence*

Just outside the medieval village of Cordes, in the direction of Senanque, is a engaging complex of cream stone houses converted to an exclusive hotel. Set on the hillside the buildings sit amongst gardens and stretches of green lawn. The main building dates back to when it was a private home, regionally referred to as a "mas", and houses a beautiful restaurant and six bedrooms. The restaurant occupies most of the first floor. Tables are spaciously set before floor to ceiling windows that look out over the valley, in front of a magnificent stone fireplace or in a secluded corner. A quiet sitting room and bar are also available for guests' use - a perfect spot to enjoy a game, read a book or write some cards. The Bergerie and Fermettes are neighboring, newly constructed buildings that offer luxurious suites and apartments as accommodation. With cream stone walls and tile roofs, the exteriors are attractively modeled after the original home and in kepping with the flavor of the region and all but two rooms in this section of the complex have a private terrace, patio or garden. The accommodations at the Domaine de l'Enclos are superlative, decorated with Provencal prints and treasured antiques, the bathrooms are spacious and equipped with every modern convenience. The Domaine's buildings are set to maximize views of the countryside and the setting is rural and tranquil.

*DOMAINE DE L'ENCLOS*
*Hotelier: Serge Lafitte*
*Route de Senanque, 84220 Gordes*
*Tel: 90.72.08.22 Telex: 432119*
*14 Rooms - Dbl from 780F Apt to 2900F*
*Open: 12 Apr to 31 Oct, Rest closed Mon*
*Credit cards: AX, VS*
*Restaurant, pool, tennis, park*
*Located 38 km E of Avignon*
*Region: Provence*

Gordes is a very picturesque village whose terraced buildings cling to a rocky hillside that is dominated by its church and chateau.   Located less than twenty miles east of Avignon and in the heart of Provence, this medieval village is worth a detour for a visit regardless of one's base of exploration.   Since 1970 the Vasarely Museum (closed Tuesdays), which focuses on the evolution of painting and cinema art, has been installed inside the walls of the old chateau.   The narrow streets stumble through town and shelter a number of interesting art and craft shops. Should you decide to stay in Gordes, La Mayanelle is a moderately priced hotel and enjoys a central location at the heart of this medieval village.   Monsieur Mayard extends a warm welcome: he is your host as well as chef for the hotel's lovely restaurant.   La Mayanelle's ten bedrooms are small (room number four being the largest), but comfortable and pleasing in their decor.   Since the hotel is perched on the side of the village, the bedrooms whose windows open out to the Luberon Valley enjoy some magnificent views.   I was here at the time of a festive wedding reception and had the only room not occupied by a wedding guest.

*LA MAYANELLE*
*Hotelier: M Mayard*
*84220 Gordes*
*Tel: 90.72.00.28*
*10 Rooms - Sgl from 186F Dbl to 350F*
*Closed: January and February*
*  Restaurant closed Tuesdays*
*Credit cards: All major*
*Restaurant*
*Located 38 km E of Avignon*
*Region: Provence*

A small sign directed me along a dirt road and through a small town as I searched for the Chateau de Roumegouse. I was not certain I had followed the sign correctly. Suddenly, a large majestic tower, peering above the treetops, revealed the location of the chateau. A very cordial Monsieur Lauwaert, who speaks perfect English, was the only person at the chateau when I arrived. I wrongly assumed that due to the isolated location of the hotel, no one knew about it: as it turned out, the reason for the lack of guests was that Monsieur Lauwaert had closed for the season a week earlier. When open, the hotel and restaurant are very popular - even Pompidou and de Gaulle have dined here. Monsieur and Madame Lauwaert retired five years ago and the management of the chateau is now in the capable hands of their daughter and her husband, Monsieur and Madame Laine. Elegant furnishings are found throughout. In keeping with the mood of the castle, the bedroom suites are extremely handsome while the dining rooms are in Louis XV decor. In summer dinner is served on the terrace overlooking the Lot Valley The Laines request that overnight guests lunch or dine at the hotel. To locate the hotel, travel northwest from the town of Gramat, four and a half kilometers on N140.

*CHATEAU DE ROUMEGOUSE*
*Hotelier: M & Mme Laine*
*46500 Gramat*
*Tel: 65.33.63.81 Telex: 532592*
*14 Rooms - Sgl from 360F Dbl to 770F*
*Open: April to mid-November*
 *Restaurant closed Tuesdays*
*Credit cards: All major*
*Restaurant*
*Located 57 km SE of Brive*
*Region: Dordogne*

The Chateau de Locguenole, surrounded by acres of woodland, is dramatic and isolated. Standing proud, the property of this stately manor extends down to the edge of the Blavet. This chateau has been the family home of the de la Sabliere family since 1600 and today Madame de la Sabliere runs it as an exclusive hotel. The hotel glories in the tradition and heritage of the family's pride and possessions. Antiques abound. Many of the bedrooms have majestic fireplaces and all have lovely views. The service and attention to detail is very professional and refined, befitting the high standards outlined by the prestigious Relais et Chateaux chain of hotels. The restaurant of the hotel is set in the formal dining room. Michel Gaudin presents a wonderful menu complemented by an excellent wine list (both expensive). Two minutes by car from the Chateau, isolated on the silent moors of Brittany, the Residence Kerniaven, a genuine Morbihan cottage, shelters twelve additional luxurious rooms. Set on the southern coast of Brittany, Hennebont is a convenient base from which to explore the region and the Chateau de Locguenole makes your base a luxurious and extremely comfortable one as well. Directions to the hotel are to travel south from Hennebont, four kilometers on D781.

*CHATEAU DE LOCGUENOLE*
*Hotelier: Mme de la Sabliere*
*Route de Port-Louis*
*56700 Hennebont*
*Tel: 97.76.29.04 Telex: 950636*
*36 Rooms - Sgl from 573F Dbl to 1080F*
*Open: 1 March to 15 November*
*Credit cards: All major*
*Restaurant, pool, tennis*
*Located 10 km NE of Lorient*
*Region: Brittany*

Honfleur is one of the world's most picturesque port towns and I am certain that you will want to spend time here. On the outskirts of town, in a residential district, I have recommended the moderately priced Hotel l'Ecrin and just outside of town, the very expensive and excellent La Ferme St Simeon. Should these hotels be full, or if your budget needs some monitoring, there is an alternate, budget selection, the Hotel du Dauphin. Off St Catherine's Square just near the port, the hotel has a central location, but the port is teeming with activity so a quiet night's sleep is not guaranteed. The rooms of the hotel are very simple and spartan in their decor, but clean and inexpensive. A maze of stairways and confusing double doors ramble through the building and lead to the various rooms. Flowerboxes adorn the timbered facade. The Hotel du Dauphin has an informal bar and cafe, but no restaurant: however, there are numerous cafe-restaurants that specialize in fish bordering the scenic harbor. The Hotel du Dauphin offers basic, clean and inexpensive accommodation at the heart of picturesque Honfleur.

*HOTEL DU DAUPHIN*
*Hotelier: Philippe Alfandari*
*10 Place Pierre Berthelot*
*14600 Honfleur*
*Tel: 31.89.15.53*
*30 Rooms - Sgl from 262F Dbl to 287F*
*Closed: January*
*Credit cards: VS*
*No restaurant*
*Budget hotel*
*Located 63 km E of Caen*
*Region: Normandy*

An alternative to the very expensive Relais et Chateaux Hotel, La Ferme St Simeon, located outside the town of Honfleur, is the moderately priced Hotel l'Ecrin. This hotel is conveniently located within walking distance of the picturesque harbor, yet benefits from the quiet of a residential district. We've chosen this hotel, converted from a private home, because of its location and price. However, the decor would be considered by many to be overly ornate. We felt it would be difficult to improve upon the following description provided by one of our readers, Bill Simpson:

*"Our room was very large, convenient, with all the amenities. The bathroom was completely modern and well-equipped. The staff was friendly and helpful. The decor, to say the least, was flamboyant. Red velvet and gilt, lavishly applied, the fanciest French furniture, a multitude of paintings of all descriptions and a wide-ranging assortment of decorations including stuffed birds, a larger-than-lifesize painted statue of a Nubian slave and a smiling portrait of Maurice Chevalier."*

Honfleur is truly one of France's most picturesque port towns and the Hotel l'Ecrin offers a quiet, convenient, moderately priced, if colorful, base.

*HOTEL L'ECRIN*
*Hotelier: M & Mme Blais*
*19, Rue Eugene Boudin*
*14600 Honfleur*
*Tel: 31.89.32.39*
*16 Rooms - Sgl from 275F Dbl to 500F*
*Open: All year*
*Credit cards: AX, VS, DC*
*No restaurant*
*Located 63 km E of Caen*
*Region: Normandy*

Set on the coastal hills just outside the picturesque port town of Honfleur, La Ferme St Simeon is a typical Normandy home with flowerboxes adorning every window.   Under the management of the Boelen family, La Ferme St Simeon is an excellent hotel.   Recently seventeen new rooms have been added, set in the same gardens where painters such as Monet, Boudin and Jongkind set up their easels. Of these, three are suites and, like the other rooms, all are individually styled and handsomely decorated with fine antiques.   The intimate decor of the restaurant is beautifully accented by a beamed ceiling and colorful flower arrangements decorate each table.   The restaurant's new chef, Jean Pierre de Boissiere, has earned recognition in some of France's most prestigious restaurants and utilizes the high quality fresh produce for which the region is famous to make the most of his talents in creating exquisite dishes.   Offered on an a la carte basis, the cuisine is delicious but also very expensive.   Reservations for the hotel as well as for the restaurant are a must and should be made well in advance.

*LA FERME ST SIMEON*
*Hotelier: M & Mme Roland Boelen*
*Route A.-Marais*
*14600 Honfleur*
*Tel: 31.89.23.61 Telex: 171031*
*35 Rooms - Sgl from 900F Dbl to 1780F*
*Open: All year*
*  Restaurant closed Tuesdays*
*Credit cards: VS*
*Tennis, countryside estate*
*Located 63 km E of Caen*
*Region: Normandy*

This thirteenth-century fortress, located in a small village nestled amongst vineyards, offered a safe haven to its owners of yore and now, having withstood centuries of strife, it welcomes guests into its ancient walls. A medieval ambiance reigns in the entry hall, salon, and especially in the dining room where diners are seated before a crackling fire in an enormous, open-hearth stone fireplace. Tapestry chairs and prettily set tables are the perfect stage for the delicious cuisine served here. An after dinner drink can be savored in the adjoining salon. Bedchambers are reached by climbing the well-worn turret stairs and passing through heavy old wooden doors. The six bedrooms and six apartments are furnished for the most part with antique reproductions enhanced by some period pieces and details. All have private bath and are personalized with a vase of fresh flowers on your arrival. A well priced and friendly member of the Relais et Chateau group of hotels, the Chateau d'Ige is a wonderful, atmospheric base from which to explore the Romanesque churches of Cluny and Vezelay and the wine region of the Cote d'Or.

*CHATEAU D'IGE*
*Hotelier: M Henri Jadot*
*Ige, 71960 Pierreclos*
*Tel: 85.33.33.99 Telex: 351915*
*12 Rooms - Dbl from 490F Apt to 910F*
*Open: 5 February to 5 November*
*Credit cards: All major*
*Thirteenth-century castle*
*Restaurant*
*Located 14 km NW of Macon*
*Region: Rhone Valley*

Winding through the foothills of the Vosges Mountains, the wine route of Alsace is extremely picturesque.  It meanders through delightful towns and is exposed to enchanting vistas of a countryside carpeted with vineyards and dotted by neighboring towns clustered around their church spires.  The village of Itterswiller, nestled on the hillside amongst the vineyards, is a wonderful base from which to explore the region and the Hotel Arnold is a charming country hotel.  The accommodation and restaurant are in three separate buildings.  Although the color wash of the individual buildings varies from white to soft yellow to burnt red, each is handsomely timbered and the windowboxes hang heavy with a profusion of red geraniums.  Most of the twenty-eight bedrooms are located in the main building of the Hotel Arnold set just off the road on the edge of the village.  The bedrooms are at the back of the hotel and look out over the surrounding vineyards. On the town's principal street, standing next to the hotel's restaurant, the Winestub Arnold, is a selection of lovely rooms in La Reserve.  Set under lovely old beams with provincial cloths and decorative flower arrangements adorning the tables, the Winestub Arnold is an appealing place to dine on regional specialities and the estate's wines.

*HOTEL ARNOLD*
*Hotelier: Gerard Arnold*
*Route du Vin, Itterswiller*
*67140 Barr*
*Tel: 88.85.50.58 Telex: 870550*
*28 Rooms - Sgl from 310F Dbl to 465F*
*Open: All year*
   *Restaurant closed Sundays & Mondays*
*Credit cards: VS*
*Located 41 km SW of Strasbourg*
*Region: Alsace*

The Chateau du Plessis is a lovely, aristocratic country home.   Madame Benoist's family have lived here since well before the revolution, but the antiques throughout the home are later acquisitions of her great, great, great grandfather, as the furnishings original to the house were burned on the front lawn by the revolutionaries in 1793.   Furnishings throughout the home are elegant, yet the Benoists also establish an atmosphere of homey comfort.   Artistic fresh flower arrangements abound and one can see Madame's cutting garden from the French doors in the salon that open onto the lush grounds.   The well-worn turret steps lead to the beautifully furnished accommodations.   In the evening the large oval table in the dining room provides an opportunity to enjoy the company of other guests and the country-fresh cuisine of Madame Benoist.   She prepares a four course meal and Monsieur Benoist selects a different regional wine to complement each course.   The Benoists are a handsome couple who take great pride in their home and the welcome they extend to their guests.   To reach La Jaille-Yvon travel north of Angers on N162 and at the town of Le Lion d'Angers clock the odometer eleven kilometers further north to an intersection, Carrefour Fleur de Lys.   Turn east and travel two and a half kilometers to La Jaille-Yvon and the Chateau du Plessis on its southern edge.

*CHATEAU DU PLESSIS*
*Hotelier: M & Mme P. Benoist*
*La Jaille-Yvon, 49990 Chambellay*
*Tel: 41.95.12.75*
*6 Rooms - Sgl from 480F Dbl to 630F*
*Open: 1st April to 1st November*
*Credit cards: All major*
*Restaurant by reservation only*
*Located   30 km N of Angers*
*Region: Loire Valley*

Nestled in the coutryside just a few kilometers outside Tours, the Hotel du Chateau de Beaulieu is well located for visiting the castles of the Loire Valley.   The formal garden setting is highlighted by vividly colored flowers and nearby swimming pool and tennis courts.   A somewhat Oriental theme pervades in the grand entry hall and on the staircase where collections of Oriental war spears, tapestries and carpets are displayed.   The nine bedrooms in the chateau and ten in a nearby pavilion annex are attractively appointed and are priced according to size, view and whether they have a bath or a shower (less expensive).   The management requests guests stay here on a demi-pension basis.   There are two menus offered daily priced at 150F and 180F.   Dinners are enjoyed in the gracious dining room surrounded by fresh flowers and attentive waiters.   Reduced rates are offered for guests who stay three or more days.   Comfortable and atmospheric, this hotel offers a chateau ambiance without the higher prices of its more luxurious neighbors.   Directions: Just south of Tours travel east on D86 and then D207 following signs to Villandry.

*HOTEL DU CHATEAU DE BEAULIEU*
*Hotelier: Jean-Pierre Lozay*
*Route de l'Epend*
*37300 Joue les Tours*
*Tel: 47.53.20.26*
*19 Rooms - Sgl from 335F Dbl to 585F*
*Open: All year*
*Credit cards: All major*
*Restaurant*
*Private pool, public tennis courts adjacent*
*Located 5 km SW of Tours*
*Region: Loire Valley*

Kayersberg is one of Alsace's greatest splendors. The village sprawls up the hillside and the Hotel l'Arbre Vert is tucked away along a street in Haut Kayersberg. This delightful country inn whose facade is colored by boxes of overflowing geraniums has been a family business for three generations. The Hotel l'Arbre Vert is a simple, comfortable inn, rustic in its decor and reasonably priced. The atmosphere is friendly and the Kieny and Wittmer families extend a personal welcome. Monsieur Kieny who supervises the kitchen offers a number of interesting Alsatian specialities that are complemented by the regional wines. Even if the cuisine weren't such a gastronomic delight it would be a memorable treat to dine in the charming, country restaurant. The hotel also has a cozy wine cellar where one can sample some of the famous as well as local Alsatian wines. Should the Hotel l'Arbre Vert be full, the Hotel la Belle Promenade (tel: 89.47.11.51), directly across the square, is also attractive, a bit more modern in decor, but benefiting from the same gracious and hospitable management.

*HOTEL L'ARBRE VERT*
*Hoteliers: Kieny & Wittmer families*
*Rue Haute du Rempart*
*68240 Kayersberg*
*Tel: 89.47.11.51*
*23 Rooms - Sgl from 180F Dbl to 290F*
*14 Rooms (Annex - Belle Promenade)*
*Closed: 5 January to 5 March*
*Credit cards: None*
*Restaurant*
*Located 11 km NW of Colmar*
*Region: Alsace*

Just inside the walls of the charming village of Kayersberg is a wonderful, recently opened hotel, the Residence Chambard. Each of the rooms is decorated differently, the majority with an emphasis on regal luxury. (A few annex rooms are a bit modern but comfortable, and one should specify a preference when making reservations.) Of the twenty bedrooms, two (rooms 206 and 207) are lovely apartments, well worth the additional nominal surcharge. Room 206 is particularly enchanting with a turret sitting area. Just off the entrance hall is a lovely lounge, and downstairs in the basement is a charming bar. The Restaurant Chambard is in a separate building, just in front of the hotel. This is Pierre Irrmann's pride and joy. The decor is handsome: high-back, tapestry-covered chairs set round intimate tables before a large, open stone fireplace. It has earned three forks and one toque from Michelin. Specialities of the house include "foie gras frais en boudin", "fricassee de la mer" and "mousse chambard" and the wine list highlights some delicious Rieslings and Pinot gris.

*HOTEL RESIDENCE CHAMBARD*
*Hotelier: Pierre Irrmann*
*13, Rue General de Gaulle*
*68240 Kayersberg*
*Tel: 89.47.10.17 Telex: 880272*
*20 Rooms - Sgl from 385F Dbl to 520F*
*Closed: 1-15 December and 1-21 March*
   *Restaurant closed Sundays Evenings*
     *and Mondays*
*Credit cards: All major*
*Located 11 km NW of Colmar*
*Region: Alsace*

Perched regally above the flowing River Dordogne, the Chateau de la Treyne has been renovated and returned to its earlier state of grandeur. A fairy-tale fortress, the chateau will enchant you with its presence, its grace, its regal accommodation and excellent restaurant. Michele Gombert-Devals has opened her home to a privileged few, not as a hotel, but, more intimately, as a "chateau-prive". Set on three hundred acres of parkland formal French gardens stage the entry of the Chateau de la Treyne. Inside, heavy wood doors, wood panelling and beams contrast handsomely with white stone walls and the rich, muted colors of age-worn tapestries. Public rooms are furnished dramatically with antiques and warmed by log burning fires. In summer, tables are set on a terrace with magnificent views that plunge down to the Dordogne. On brisk nights, the dining room is romantically lit with candlesticks and tables are elegantly set with silver, china and flowers. In season (June, July, August) guests are asked to dine at the chateau. Off-season meals are prepared when requested in advance. The chateau's bedrooms are all luxuriously appointed and furnished. Individual in their decor, size and location, the windows of the rooms open either on to dramatic river views or onto the lovely grounds. From N20 take D43 three kilometers west towards Lacave - Rocamadour: just over the bridge are the gates to the chateau.

*CHATEAU DE LA TREYNE*
*Hotelier: Mme Michele Gombert-Devals*
*Lacave, 46200 Souillac*
*Tel: 65.32.66.66*
*12 Rooms - Dbl from 550F to 1000F*
*Closed: January to Easter*
*Credit cards: All major*
*Restaurant, pool, tennis*
*Located 49 km S of Brive*
*Region: Dordogne*

Chateau de Brindos is a superb Spanish-style castle in the Basque region.  It is an attractive white building with an orange tile roof that sits sheltered in its own expanse of green park.  The medieval hall, grand salon and dining rooms are impressive.  Of the fifteen luxurious bedrooms it is hard to choose a favorite but rooms seventeen (a corner room facing the lake with an antique four-poster canopy) and eleven (a large room, with twin beds, decorated in gold, with a round salon) are exceptional.  The facilities (pool, tennis courts, practice golf course) and refined service make the Chateau de Brindos more of a resort than hotel.  An afternoon can easily be spent lounging poolside and ordering exotic drinks.  The Chateau de Brindos is situated on the Lac de Brindos with its own dock at the lake where ducks and swans set a graceful scene.  The Chateau de Brindos stages a very romantic setting.  Directions to the hotel are from Biarritz.  From the city, follow the N10 in the direction of the airport, and turn off to Lac de Brindos just after the airport or "aerogare".

*CHATEAU DE BRINDOS*
*Hotelier: M & Mme Vivensang*
*Lac de Brindos*
*64600 Anglet*
*Tel: 59.23.17.68 Telex: 541428*
*15 Rooms - Dbl from 840F to 1140F*
*Open: All year*
*Credit cards: AX, VS*
*Restaurant*
*Pool, tennis, practice golf*
*Located 5 km SE of Biarritz*
*Region: Basque*

Why would anyone tackle a winding mountain road and travel for an hour off the main road to reach the small town of Lamastre? - A question I posed myself as the sun was setting on what had already been a full day on the road.   The answer is the lovely Chateau d'Urbilhac.   Set high above the town, this is a beautiful chateau with extensive grounds and a stunning swimming pool surrounded by statues. Very reasonable in price, the chateau attracts European families on holiday who appear very "at home" here and comfortable in their regal surroundings.   Madame Xompero, the owner, extends a gracious welcome and genuinely cares that her guests enjoy their holiday.   There is no lift and the bedrooms are scattered on three floors.   We stayed in a small room on the third floor which was once the servants' quarters.   There are a number of more spacious, grand rooms: fourteen and fifteen both have beautiful antique double beds, twelve, a corner room, has antique twin beds and twenty-four has twin brass beds.   The dining room is small and friendly and the menu boasts a number of regional specialities - beautifully prepared and thoughtfully served.   Removed from any tourist destination, the Chateau d'Urbilhac offers calm and quiet, a perfect hideaway for those who want to relax.   The chateau is tucked in the wooded hills above Lamastre: travel the D2, Route de Vernoux, for two kilometers.

*CHATEAU D'URBILHAC*
*Hotelier: Mme Xompero*
*Route de Vernoux, 07270 Lamastre*
*Tel: 75.06.42.11*
*14 Rooms - Sgl from 400F Dbl to 600F*
*Open: 1 May to 11 October*
*Credit cards: All major*
*Restaurant, gorgeous pool, tennis*
*Located 40 km NW of Valence*
*Region: Rhone Valley*

Levernois is a country village located a five-minute drive on D970 from Beaune. Here the ivy-clad Hotel le Parc offers a countryside alternative for those travellers seeking to guard their pocketbook as well as avoid city noises. Monsieur and Madame Moreau-Tanron own and manage their hotel with pride and care. Actually, Monsieur Moreau-Tanron informed us that he mainly tends to the flower garden and small park, while his wife scrupulously handles all facets of the hotel. The twenty rooms are almost always full with returning clients, who also enjoy congregating before dinner in the convivial bar near the cheerful entry salon. Prettily papered hallways lead to the simple, but charming bedrooms, all but one of which have their own spotlessly clean bath or shower. Antique pieces are strategically placed throughout the hotel, especially in the breakfast room which boasts an old country hutch filled with colorful plates, a large antique mirror and matching wooden tables and chairs which look out through French doors onto the flower-filled courtyard. Reserve early in order to be able to enjoy the warm hospitality of the Moreau-Tanrons in this tranquil setting. Travel five kilometers southeast of Beaune on Route de Verdun sur le Doubs D970 and D111.

*HOTEL LE PARC*
*Hotelier: M & Mme Moreau-Tanron*
*Levernois, 21200 Beaune*
*Tel: 80.22.22.51*
*20 Rooms - Dbl from 166F to 220F*
*Closed: 28 February to 16 March and*
   *22 November to 11 December*
*Credit cards: None*
*No restaurant*
*Located 5 km SE of Beaune*
*Region: Burgundy*

It was late in the day, but we were spurred by a sense of adventure to follow a small inviting sign for the Manoir de Caudemonne.   One sign led to another, tempting us deeper and deeper into the pastoral, picture-perfect Normandy countryside.   The old timbered farmhouse cluster of the Manoir de Caudemonne suddenly appeared before us, immediately transporting us back to a simpler place in time.   As we approached past tumble-down outbuildings we came upon the two guests of the manor, an English couple engaged in a leisurely game of cards on the front lawn. The only audible sound was the occasional squawk of geese or hens.  Madame Dudouit greeted us at the front door under an ancient turret and amiably ushered us inside her rustic farm inn.   It was easy to imagine a country banquet of long ago in the dining hall furnished with its one long heavy trestle table before a massive stone fireplace with open hearth.   Madame led us up the steep and narrow curved staircase to the very simple and basic guest rooms.   The two rooms share facilities and in fact adjoin, so two parties would almost be sharing a room.   A farm-country breakfast is included in the cost of an overnight stay, so this country homestead is a real bargain - budget.   A family-style restaurant with rooms, Le Manoir de Caudemonne is for the traveller who seeks not modern comfort, but rather an evening in an ancient, peaceful, pastoral setting.

*LE MANOIR DE CAUDEMONNE*
*Hotelier: Edith Dudouit*
*La Chapelle Haute Grue, 14140 Livarot*
*Tel: 31.63.53.74*
*2 Rooms - Dbl 170F*
*Open: All year, Restaurant closed Wednesdays*
*Credit cards: Unknown*
*Restaurant, farm setting*
*Located 10 km N of Gace*
*Region: Normandy*

Domaine de Beauvois is the choice of many who decide to spend some time in the Loire Valley, a fifteenth- and seventeenth-century chateau surrounded by a lovely wooded estate of three hundred and fifty acres. Its forty rooms are furnished with antiques and offer you a holiday equal to that enjoyed by the many lords and ladies who came to the Loire Valley for relaxation long ago. It was once a residence for the knights of the fifteenth century and there are some very historical rooms with exposed old stone walls in the original tower. The ceiling of one bedroom looks up dramatically to the original old oak beams that form a stunning pattern and a chamber once occupied by Louis XIII has its own fireplace and a vaulted ceiling. From the bedrooms one looks down over a pool surrounded by grass, over a courtyard, its reflecting pool and fountain or up to the dense forest. On most nights one large, beautiful room whose floor to ceiling windows overlook the courtyard terrace is elegantly set for dinner. There is also, however, a smaller, more intimate dining room. The service is professional and it is worth asking the "sommelier" for a tour of the remarkable wine cellar. For sports enthusiasts there are also tennis courts, lovely marked trails in the surrounding forest and fishing nearby. To the northwest of Tours, at the heart of the Loire Valley, the Domaine de Beauvois is found outside Luynes, four kilometers northwest on D49.

*DOMAINE DE BEAUVOIS*
*Hotelier: Patrick C. Ponsard*
*37230 Luynes*
*Tel: 47.55.50.11 Telex: 750204*
*40 Rooms - Dbl from 610F to 1310F*
*Closed: mid-January to mid-March*
*Credit cards: VS*
*Restaurant, pool, tennis, park*
*Located 13 km NW of Tours*
*Region: Loire Valley*

The Chateau de la Caze is a fairytale fifteenth-century castle, majestically situated above the Tarn. With its heavy doors, turrets and stone facade, it is a dramatic castle and yet intimate in size. It was not built as a fortress, but rather as a honeymoon home for Sonbeyrane Alamand, a niece of the Prior Francois Alamand. She chose the idyllic and romantic location and commissioned the chateau in 1489. Today this spectacular chateau offers accommodation and now one will be royally attended to by Madame and Mademoiselle Roux. Inside the chateau vaulted ceilings, rough stone walls, tile and wood-planked floors are warmed by tapestries, Oriental rugs, dramatic antiques, paintings, copper, soft lighting and log-burning fires. Each bedroom in the castle is like a king's bedchamber. Just opposite the chateau "la Ferme" offers six additional, attractive apartments. Room six, the honeymoon apartment of Sonbeyrane, is the most spectacular room: it has a large canopied bed and an entire wall of windows overlooking the Tarn and its canyon. On the ceiling there are paintings of the eight sisters who later inherited the chateau, and according to legend, were very beautiful, having secret rendezvous each night in the garden of the castle with their lovers. The restaurant enjoys spectacular views of the canyon and house specialties include a delicious "truite Sonbeyrane" and "caneton Chateau de la Caze". Directions: from La Malene travel northeast five and a half kilometers on D907.

*CHATEAU DE LA CAZE*
*Hotelier: Mme & Mlle Roux*
*La Malene, 48210 Ste Enimie*
*Tel: 66.48.51.01*
*14 Rooms - Sgl from 465F Dbl to 710F*
*Open: May to 15 October, Restaurant closed Tuesdays*
*Credit cards: AX, VS, DC*
*Located 42 km NE of Millau*
*Region: Tarn*

For fifteen hundred years the Manoir de Montesquiou was the residence of the Barons de Montesquiou. With the canyon walls at its back the Manoir de Montesquiou faces onto the street in the small town of La Malene at the center of the Tarn Canyon. This is a moderately priced chateau hotel, not luxurious but very traditional in furnishings. The welcome and service is warm and friendly. The Manoir de Montesquiou serves as a delightful and comfortable base from which to explore the spectacular beauty of the Tarn Canyon, "Gorges du Tarn". Here you can enjoy a wonderful meal and then climb the tower to your room. All the bedrooms are with private bath and those that overlook the garden at back are assured a quiet night's rest. Each bedroom is unique in its decor, some with dramatic four-poster beds, and the carvings on the headboard in room six are magnificent. Although the setting and accommodation of the Manoir de Montesquiou are not as spectacular as the Chateau de la Caze, it is a less expensive alternative and well located at the heart of the Tarn Canyon. With the Manoir de Montesquiou as a base, you can venture out by day to boat, fish, hunt, explore and walk.

*MANOIR DE MONTESQUIOU*
*Hotelier: M Bernard Guillenet*
*La Malene*
*48210 Ste Enimie*
*Tel: 66.48.51.12*
*12 Rooms - Sgl from 245F Dbl to 450F*
*Open: April to 1st October*
*Credit cards: DC*
*Restaurant*
*Located 42 km NE of Millau*
*Region: Tarn*

Chateau de Marcay is a a fifteenth-century fortress that was transformed into a luxurious hotel in 1970. It is a dramatic castle, built of stone, with twin end turrets, situated six kilometers south from Chinon following the D749 on D116 and surrounded by vineyards, enjoying the quiet and calm of the lovely Vienne Valley which creates a restful and welcoming environment. There are twenty-seven bedrooms in the chateau and eleven in a modern "motel" annex. In the chateau the rooms are unique and lovely. Room eleven is spacious with twin beds and a dark red color scheme that blends with the richly dark wooden beams. Room twenty-five is a plain double room, but the bathroom is magnificent, larger than the room itself, located in one of the end turrets with blue and white tiles, beamed walls and ceiling. In the public areas the Chateau de Marcay has a lovely salon with comfortable chairs set before the warmth of a large fireplace, high stools gathered around an inviting bar and a very elegantly staged restaurant. Plan on spending the quiet hours of early evening on the terrace that overlooks the serene Vienne Valley. On the expanse of grounds that surrounds the chateau, guests will find a large swimming pool, tennis courts and a pretty garden. The Chateau de Marcay is a very luxurious, expensive chateau-hotel.

*CHATEAU DE MARCAY*
*Hotelier: M Philippe Mollard*
*Marcay, 37500 Chinon*
*Tel: 47.93.03.47 Telex: 751475*
*38 Rooms - Sgl from 473F Dbl to 1095F*
*Closed: mid-January to mid-March*
*Credit cards: AX, VS*
*Restaurant*
*Pool, tennis, park*
*Located 6 km S of Chinon*
*Region: Loire Valley*

Timbered houses, windowboxes colored with geraniums, and sloping vineyards are typical of the Alsace region of France.   Marlenheim is praised as a typical Alsatian village and the Hostellerie du Cerf represents the typical Alsatian inn.   It is in fact an old coaching inn at the start of the Route du Vin d'Alsace.   Settle in one of its nineteen pleasantly furnished bedrooms or in one of the three more spacious apartments.   Dine indoors in the cozy elegance of the restaurant or in the sheltered courtyard, bordered by a multitude of flowers, under the skies that bless the region's grapes.   This reasonably priced hostelry highlights local specialties. Both father and son, Robert and Michel, supervise the kitchen and their recommended "carte de marche", a menu that changes daily based on the freshest produce, meats and fish available, is always enticing.   Both the hotel and restaurant are closed on Mondays and Tuesdays, but breakfast, lunch and dinner are served the rest of the week.   Family pride and the desire to maintain a tradition of fine Alsatian cuisine inspire Robert and Michel Husser to keep an excellent kitchen.   The Hostellerie du Cerf is a charming roadside inn and a perfect base from which to explore the vineyards of Alsace.

*HOSTELLERIE DU CERF*
*Hotelier: Robert Husser*
*30, Route du General de Gaulle*
*67520 Marlenheim*
*Tel: 88.87.73.73*
*22 Rooms - Sgl from 220F Dbl to 350F*
*Open: All year*
  *but closed on Mondays and Tuesdays*
*Credit cards: AX, VS*
*Located 20 km W of Strasbourg*
*Region: Alsace*

The village of Millac is nestled on the river bank near the prettiest and most dramatic bend in the River Dordogne, "la Cingle de Tremolat".   On the river's edge, set in the shadow of a small bridge, is the engaging Hotel de la Poste.   We were so thrilled to "discover" this true French country inn and are now very proud to recommend it.   It is simple, spotlessly clean, unpretentious and has been family-run for generations.   Madame Mirabel Courtey takes pride carrying on the standards of service and hospitality established by her family and it shows. Glistening polished copper pieces adorn the walls, unrivalled flower arrangements take central focus in the salon or dining room, crisp clean sheets are all indications of her efforts.   Very popular with locals, the large, airy dining room is charmingly decorated with country tables and chairs, and red checkered tablecloths - all set under heavy beams.   Multi-course menus are offered at amazingly low prices (55F, 65F, 90F, 110F) and boast regional specialties such as "pate maison", "melon au Montbazillac" and "ris de veau sur canape".   The bedrooms are very simply decorated, a few have private bath, some have only toilet, but they are clean, comfortable,inexpensively priced and eight enjoy views of the river.

*HOTEL DE LA POSTE*
*Hotelier: Mme Mirabel Courtey*
*Mauzac, 24150 Lalinde*
*Tel: 53.22.50.52*
*18 Rooms - Sgl from 140F Dbl to 280F*
*Open: 1st March to 31 October*
*Credit cards: AX, VS, MC*
*Restaurant, river setting*
*Located 63 km S of Perigueux*
*Region: Dordogne*

There is an enchantment about this beautiful castle high above Mercues and the Lot Valley.   Once you have seen it you will not be able to take your eyes away or to drive through the valley without stopping.   It appears to beckon you.   Here you can live like a king with all the modern conveniences.   The chateau has been restored and decorated in keeping with formal tradition.   The twenty-three guestrooms in the chateau are magnificent - the furnishings are handsome and the windows open to some splendid valley views.   Unique and priced accordingly, room 419 (in a turret) has windows on all sides and a glassed-in ceiling that opens up to the beams.   In recent years an additional twenty-two rooms have been added in the newly constructed annex, the Hotel des Cedres.   Here bedrooms are modern in decor and less expensive.   Enjoy a memorable dinner in the elegantly beautiful restaurant.   The Vigouroux family own vineyards which produce sumptuous wines bottled under the Chateau de Haut Serre label.   They have just built some large cellars under the gardens connecting the chateau to store their produced and acquired wines.   The owner's daughter, Anne-Catherine, markets the estate's wine internationally.

*CHATEAU DE MERCUES*
*Owner: M Georges Vigouroux*
*Hotelier: Yves & Brigitte Buchin*
*Mercues, 46090 Cahors*
*Tel: 65.20.00.01 Telex: 521307*
*23 Rooms (castle) - Sgl from 500F Dbl to 1570F*
*22 Rooms (Cedres) - Sgl from 380F Dbl to 520F*
*Open: 12 April to 2 November*
*Credit cards: All major*
*Restaurant, pool, tennis, park*
*Located 9 km NW of Cahors on N20*
*Region: Lot*

The Chateau de Meyrargues was once the stronghold of the mightiest lords in Provence. Built in the shape of a horseshoe, this large, imposing stone fortress is reached by taking a small winding road from the center of Meyrargues. Large heavy doors open on the outside to the central courtyard and inside to the lofty entry halls and sparsely decorated hallways that lead to various wings of the chateau and its fourteen bedrooms. It is impressive in a chateau of its size and age that thirteen of the fourteen rooms are handsomely decorated with period furnishings. The pride and effort of new ownership are wonderfully apparent in the fresh decor, the newly refurbished bathrooms and the standard of service and comfort. The entire hotel is fit for nobility and the cuisine that originates in the chateau's charming kitchen hung with heavy copper pans is delicious. One can savor traditional French cuisine in one of the two restaurants or on the wonderful terrace that enjoys spectacular valley views. A swimming pool and outdoor grill have just been added and tennis courts are available nearby. The Chateau de Meyrargues is a dramatic castle-hotel located just fifteen kilometers north of the city of Aix en Provence. Take the A51 to the Sisterton exit, N96, and follow signs the short distance farther to Meyrargues. The chateau is easy to spot, crowning the village.

*CHATEAU DE MEYRARGUES*
*Hotelier: Valerie Ferrand*
*13650 Meyrargues*
*Tel: 42.57.50.32*
*14 Rooms - Dbl from 800F to 1070F*
*Open: February to November*
  *Restaurant closed Sundays & Mondays*
*Credit cards: AX, DC*
*Restaurant*
*Located 47 km NE of Marseille*
*Region: Provence*

Overpowered by the walls of the towering Jonte Canyon, the picturesque houses of Meyrueis huddle along the banks of the River Jonte.   From this quaint village you take a farm road to the enchanting Chateau d'Ayres.   Hidden behind a high stone wall, the chateau has managed to preserve and protect its special beauty and peace.   Built in the twelfth century as a Benedictine monastery, it has been burned and ravaged over the years and at one time was owned by an ancestor of the Rockefellers.   It was purchased by recent owners when Monsieur Teyssier du Cros came to the castle to ask for the hand of his wife and recognized the grounds where he had played as a child.   The Teyssier du Cros family operated the Chateau d'Ayres for a number of years until they sold it in the late 1970s to a young and enthusiastic couple, Jean-Francois and Chantal de Montjou, under whose care and devotion the hotel is managed today.   Now there are twenty-three beautiful bedchambers instead of the original two.   Works of art are created in the kitchen daily.   The Chateau d'Ayres, its character formed by so many events and personalities, is a lovely and attractive hotel.   Directions to the Chateau d'Ayres are to travel east from Meyrueis for one and a half kilometers on D57.

*CHATEAU D'AYRES*
*Hotelier: M & Mme de Montjou*
*48150 Meyrueis*
*Tel: 66.45.60.10*
*23 Rooms - Sgl from 250F Dbl to 470F*
*Open: 25 March to 15 October*
*Credit cards: DC, VS, AX*
*Restaurant, tennis*
*Located 42 km E of Millau*
*Region: Tarn*

Relais la Metairie is a charming country hotel nestled into one of the most irresistible regions of France, the Dordogne. La Metairie is an attractive soft yellow stone manor set on a grassy plateau. Views from its tranquil hillside location views are of the surrounding farmland and down over "la cingle de Tremolat", a scenic loop of the River Dordogne. The nine bedrooms and one apartment are tastefully appointed and profit from the serenity of the rural setting. Rooms open onto a private patio or balcony terrace. The bar is airy with a decor of white wicker furniture. The restaurant is intimate and very attractive with tapestry-covered chairs and a handsome fireplace. In summer grills and light meals are served on the terrace by the swimming pool. Relais la Metairie is found on a country road that winds along the hillside up from and between Millac and Tremolat, and, without a very detailed map, a bit of a struggle to find. We found the reception to be somewhat cool, but will hope for a warmer welcome on our next visit as this is a lovely country inn with an idyllic, peaceful setting.

*RELAIS LA METAIRIE*
*Hotelier: Mme Francois-Vigneron*
*at Millac, Mauzac*
*24150 Lalinde*
*Tel: 53.22.50.47*
*10 Rooms - Sgl from 380F Dbl to 740F, Apt 860F*
*Open: 28 April to 2 January*
  *Closed: Tuesdays October to 2 January*
  *Restaurant closed Wednesdays at lunch*
*Credit cards: MC, VS*
*Restaurant, pool, park*
*Located 63 km S of Perigueux*
*Region: Dordogne*

Alongside a small lake with lily pads, ducks and a few colorful rowing boats is the quaint Les Moulins du Duc, dating from the sixteenth century. This charming mill once belonged to the Dukes of Brittany. Under beamed ceilings, looking out to the garden and small stream, the dining is enchanting: both the atmosphere and specialities provide the ingredients for a perfect evening. The owner, Monsieur Quistrebert, is ever present. He bustles about ensuring that the service is professional and attentive. Guestrooms are found in stone cottages that are spaced along a pathway following the course of the babbling stream. On a recent visit we found the grounds and the gardens absolutely beautiful in a multitude of color but were disappointed to find the original bedrooms a bit musty in smell and in need of refurbishing. Additional cottages have been built and house some lovely apartments, attractive and equipped with modern bathrooms, lofts, sitting areas and often a fireplace. The apartments, however, are not spacious and seem a bit overpriced. Les Moulins du Duc for the most part is extremely charming, does enjoy an idyllic setting and boasts an excellent restaurant. I will hope that reviews from readers contradict my findings and that fresh paint and carpets will precede my next visit. To find the mill, travel two kilometers northwest from the village of Moelan sur Mer. Signs for the mill are well posted.

*LES MOULINS DU DUC*
*Hotelier: Quistrebert Family*
*29116 Moelan sur Mer*
*Tel: 98.39.60.73 Telex: 940080*
*27 Rooms - Sgl from 430F Dbl to 720F*
*Closed: mid-January to end February*
*Credit cards: All major*
*Excellent restaurant, indoor pool*
*Located 10 km S of Quimperle*
*Region: Brittany*

Haute Provence is a beautiful region of rugged terrain and villages of warm sandstone buildings and tiled roofs, nestled between the Riviera, the Alps and Provence. Wanting to find an alternate to the Bastide de la Tourtour, we happened upon Le Calalou. Monsieur and Madame Vernet built this hotel in the shadow of Moissac to match the village architecturally and blend beautifully into the landscape. Although Madame does not always extend a warm greeting, she is a perfectionist and the guests benefit as she demands that rooms be spotlessly clean, the public areas fresh, the garden immaculately groomed and the terrace swept. Monsieur Vernet is very approachable and the staff nice and accommodating. The bedrooms are simple and basic in their decor, but have very comfortable beds, a modern bathroom and look out over the swimming pool to spectacular valley views or open on to a private terrace. One can dine either in the glass-enclosed restaurant, a smaller more intimate dining room or on the garden terrace. During season, May through mid-September, the Vernets request that guests stay at Le Calalou on a demi-pension basis. Off season, take advantage of the hotel's proximity to the village of Tourtour, "village dans le ciel", and discover its many charming restaurants tucked along medieval streets.

*HOTEL LE CALALOU*
*Hotelier: M & Mme Armande Vernet*
*83630 Moissac-Bellevue*
*Tel: 94.70.17.91, Telex: 461 885*
*40 Rooms - Dbl from 492F to 641F*
*Closed: 1 December to 8 February*
*Credit cards: AX, DC, MC*
*Restaurant, pool*
*Located 29 km NW of Draguignan*
*Region: Haute Provence*

Chateau d'Artigny is world-famous for its cuisine and accommodation. This is a grand and luxurious chateau hotel whose stature rivals its regal neighbors - Azay le Rideau, Chambord, Amboise. The public rooms are elegant and spacious with their high ceilings, ornate furnishings, crystal chandeliers, gilded fixtures and Oriental carpets. The restaurant is formal in atmosphere, decor and service. There are thirty-eight rooms and seven apartments in the chateau and eight bedrooms in an annex on the river's edge. The Chateau d'Artigny hosts a number of enchanting musical "soirees" from November to March. The evenings have become very popular, begin with a cocktail at 7:30PM and feature the concert a half an hour later. One can also enjoy the concert followed by a romantic candlelit dinner. Contact the chateau for their season schedule of events and for reservation information. The Chateau d'Artigny will please those who seek luxury: for those in search of a country inn the Chateau d'Artigny might prove a bit too formal. The hotel is located just outside Montbazon, to the southwest on D17.

*CHATEAU D'ARTIGNY*
*Owner: Rene Traversac*
*Hotelier: Alain Rabier*
*37250 Montbazon*
*Tel: 47.26.24.24 Telex: 750900*
*53 Rooms - Sgl from 575F Dbl to 1270F*
*    Apt from 840F to 1370F*
*Open: 9 January to 30 November*
*Credit cards: VS*
*Restaurant, pool, tennis*
*Located 12 km S of Tours*
*Region: Loire Valley*

Domaine de la Tortiniere has a relaxed and inviting atmosphere and provides everything needed to make wonderful lasting memories. The chateau, built in 1861, has an intricate exterior, a lovely swimming pool and grounds that invite exploration and contain a path which was once a Roman road. The bedrooms combine the height of elegance with comfort. You might choose one of the castle's dramatic turret rooms or perhaps settle under beams in a cozy apartment in the neighboring pavilion. Located at the entrance to the property is an annex with a few ultra-modern rooms which are not as convenient nor as charming as those in the main castle. The dining room is small, attractive and the cuisine is excellent. Madame Olivereau Capron, your charming hostess, runs the hotel with the help of her three children: Sophie, Xavier and Gregoire. In recent years the chateau has sponsored five-day cooking classes that serve as an introduction to fine regional cuisine. Recipes are selected from those served at the finest tables among the privately owned chateaux and manors of the Touraine. Instruction includes preparation of complete menus and one has the opportunity to dine with the owners in their chateaux. For reservations and information, please contact the hotel direct. The chateau is located just off the N10, two kilometers north of Montbazon and ten kilometers south of Tours.

*DOMAINE DE LA TORTINIERE*
*Hotelier: Mme Capron*
*37250 Montbazon*
*Tel: 47.26.00.19 Telex: 752186*
*21 Rooms - Sgl from 375F Dbl to 850F*
*Open: 15 March to 15 November*
*Credit cards: MC, VS*
*Restaurant, swimming pool, garden paths*
*Located 10 km S of Tours*
*Region: Loire Valley*

*Hotel Descriptions*

Montpellier is the capital of Languedoc-Mediterranean, rich in monuments and buildings of the seventeenth and eighteenth century. The old university quarter still retains its medieval appeal and character. Montpellier's museum, "Le Musee Fabre" (closed Mondays) is the home for one of France's most impressive collections of Italian, Spanish, Flemish, Dutch and seventeenth-, eighteenth- and nineteenth-century French painters. Demeure des Brousses is a lovely country manor on the outskirts of this large city. Surrounded by vineyards, on acreage shaded by trees, this eighteenth-century house was rescued from decay in 1968 when it was renovated as a hotel. The hotel is spacious and grand: the sitting room is inviting and the seventeen bedrooms are beautifully furnished. Room sixteen is the most expensive and the best, with its own balcony and splendid views. The hotel provides a hearty country breakfast and delightful dinners are served in the restaurant, L'Orangerie. To reach the hotel, travel east from Montpellier four kilometers on D24 and D172E.

*DEMEURE DES BROUSSES*
*Hotelier: M & Mme Antoine Marechal*
*Route de Vauguieres*
*34000 Montpellier*
*Tel: 67.65.77.66 & 67.64.03.58*
*17 Rooms - Sgl from 305F Dbl to 500F*
*Closed: January & February*
  *Restaurant closed Sundays and Mondays*
*Credit cards: AX*
*Restaurant*
*Located 52 km SW of Nimes*
*Region: Provence*

The Chateau de la Salle is tucked romantically away in the scenic countryside of Cotentin, Normandy. Once part of a private estate, this thirteenth-century stone mansion has only ten bedchambers all of which are spacious, with either a bath or a shower, and are handsomely decorated with period pieces. There are two rooms furnished with dramatic four-poster beds: one (reserved for honeymoon couples) remains in its authentic condition, historically romantic but a bit small, and the second has been enlarged to fit a double mattress. The small restaurant has a few heavy wooden tables and tapestry-covered chairs positioned before a large open fireplace. The dining room occupies what was once the kitchen, actually very modern for its time. Take notice of the well. If you are lucky perhaps you will secure the table next to the hearth where a small wooden door at table height opens to expose a small round oven where pastries were once baked. Views look out through windows set deep in the thick stone walls. This is a jewel of a chateau tucked away in the quiet of the rural Normandy landscape. Our arrival coincided with a wet, grey day but we were greeted by Madame Lemesle with a warm welcome and found an inviting fire blazing in the grate. From Coutances, take D7 towards Villedieu and then head for Cerisy la Salle on D27. A small road, D73, will turn off before Cerisy and continues on to the chateau just outside Montpinchon.

*CHATEAU DE LA SALLE*
*Hotelier: Mme Cecile Lemesle*
*50210 Montpinchon*
*tel: 33.46.95.19*
*10 Rooms - Sgl from 480F Dbl to 530F*
*Open: 24 March to 10 November*
*Credit cards: AX*
*Restaurant*
*Located 13 km SE of Coutances*
*Region: Normandy*

If you want to stay on the island of Mont St Michel, I recommend the Hotel Mere Poulard. The hotel is found immediately on the left as you enter the town gates. You will be tempted inside by the aroma and cooking display of the famous Mere Poulard omelette. The cheery bright restaurant is famous for this omelette, created here almost a century ago by Mere Poulard. The preparation of the omelette can be seen from the street and is an attraction in its own right. The eggs are whisked at a tempo and beat set by the chef and then cooked in brightly polished copper pans over a large open fire. The restaurant is open for both lunch and dinner and reservations are strongly recommended. Although the restaurant is found inside the walls of the fortress of Mont St Michel and does not enjoy a view of the encircling landscape, its menu far surpasses any other on the island both in quality and price. Dramatic in its presence and setting, Mont St Michel is understandably a popular tourist destination and in the tourist season is mobbed with people, particularly at midday. You can stay overnight at the Hotel Mere Poulard and experience the town in the quiet of the early morning and late evening hours. The small bedrooms are comfortable and simply furnished. The hotel remains one of the nicest on the island. The Heyraud family request that reservations are made on a demi-pension basis.

*HOTEL MERE POULARD*
*Hotelier: M & Mme Heyraud*
*50116 Mont St Michel*
*Tel: 33.60.14.01*
*27 Rooms - Sgl from 283F Dbl to 468F*
  *Demi-pension only*
*Open: 14 February to 12 November*
*Credit Cards: AX, DC, VS*
*Located 66 km N of Rennes*
*Region: Normandy*

Although south of the scenic region of the Dordogne and west of the Lot River Valley, we stayed at the Chateau de Monviel to bridge the driving distance between Bordeaux and the Lot. This is a handsome seventeenth-century stone manor house that guards the site of a previous fourteenth- century castle, elevated above the surrounding farmland. Located on a small country lane, the chateau's most attractive feature is its isolated, countryside setting. A series of steps lead up to the reception and large, tiled entry. A grand stone staircase and second floor balustrade overlook the entry hall and lead to the seven rooms of the chateau. The rooms have poetic names and their color schemes reflect these titles. Our room, "L'Automne", although small, was attractively decorated in warm tones of rust and brown, and had a modern bathroom. Four larger rooms, reserved for guests on a longer stay, are located in a stone annex at the base of the chateau. One can relax on a peaceful garden terrace set with tables or lounge poolside with magnificent views extending out over the cornfields and acres ablaze with sunflowers. The restaurant is a cluster of intimately placed tables, very romantic in its atmosphere. We thoroughly enjoyed our meal of fresh fish complemented with regional wine. This is a lovely hotel and one cannot fault its accommodation or comfort. However, we found the management a bit aloof.

*CHATEAU DE MONVIEL*
*Hotelier: M & Mme Leroy*
*Monviel, 47290 Cancon*
*Tel: 53.01.71.64*
*11 Rooms - Dbl from 445F to 590F, Apt 700F*
*Open: end March to beg January*
*Credit cards: AX, DC*
*Restaurant, pool*
*Located 41 km S of Bergerac*
*Region: Dordogne*

In the heart of the Burgundy wine region, between the prestigious wine towns of Nuits St Georges and Gevrey Chambertin, this family-run hotel is off a quiet street in the village of Morey St Denis and right next door to a small wine making cooperative. Madame Jarlot and her family take great care to preserve a feeling of the past with their many antique furnishings, paintings and other memorabilia. From the cozy, low-ceilinged bar and reception area, to the television salon with its comfy couches, this is an unpretentious inn known locally for its cuisine. The dining room is a pleasant hodge-podge of many tables, tapestry chairs, antiques, plants and other cherished family knick-knacks. The bedrooms are all located either in the main, eighteenth-century manor house or in the older annex, a former church and monastery dating from the twelfth and thirteenth centuries. All rooms have private bath or shower except one. Do not expect luxury, merely comfort and atmosphere in this family-run country inn. To find the Castel de Tres-Girard, take N74 north through the vineyards from Beaune to Morey St Denis and then follow signs and backstreets in town to this endearing hotel.

*AUBERGE LE CASTEL DE TRES-GIRARD*
*Hotelier: Herve Jarlot family*
*Morey St Denis*
*21220 Gevrey Chambertin*
*Tel: 80.34.33.09*
*13 Rooms - Sgl from 215F Dbl to 370F*
*Open: All year*
*Credit cards: All major*
*Restaurant*
*Located 16 km S of Dijon*
*Region: Burgundy*

Whenever I hear the name Le Moulin de Mougins, I recall the charm and splendor of this small inn.  The hotel, a sixteenth-century oil mill, is located in a quiet setting just off the main road from Cannes - only a few miles from the bustling Cote d'Azur.  The accommodation is described by the owner himself as providing "comfort and quiet as in a friend's house".  With the focus on the restaurant, the inn has only five apartments for overnight guests.  The accommodation is extremely pleasant, with a cozy country ambiance.  The cuisine is prepared by the owner, Roger Verge.  Blessed by the sun of the French Riviera, produce is bountiful and meats, fish, herbs, vegetables and fruits are picked up fresh every morning and dictate the selections on the menu.  Here one can experience truly fine French dining, and service is very attentive.  If you would like to return home with souvenirs of your holiday visit the boutique which Denise Verge has opened offering delicacies created by her husband, antiques and gift items.  For those who want to learn how to cook some of the entrees they have sampled, Monsieur Verge has a cooking school above his other restaurant, L'Amandier.  Five- and ten-day courses are offered.

*LE MOULIN DE MOUGINS*
*Hotelier: M Roger Verge*
*Notre Dame de Vie, 06250 Mougins*
*Tel: 93.75.78.24 Telex: 970732*
*5 Rooms - Dbl from 700F to 1200F*
*Open: 20 March to 20 November*
  *Restaurant closed Mondays*
*Credit cards: AX, DC, VS*
*Gourmet restaurant, cooking school*
*Located 32 km W of Nice*
*Region: Riviera*

A long drive (follow the D739 east of Nieuil) leads to the enchanting Chateau de Nieuil which possesses everything a "fairytale" chateau should have: dramatic towering turrets, a deep moat, intricate gardens and a surrounding forest that was once the king's favorite hunting ground. A number of the bedrooms are handsomely decorated with antiques, while a few others are quite small and makeshift in their furnishings. An apartment located in one of the turrets has a magnificent chandelier, old paintings, beautiful mirrors, tapestries, attractive wallpaper and an enormous bathroom. The dining room is beautifully panelled and has heavy wood display cabinets. The owners, Monsieur and Madame Pierre Fougerat, have turned the management of the hotel over to their grandson, J. Michel Bodinaud - his wife is the chef. Monsieur Bodinaud was once an art teacher and because of this interest has housed an art gallery in the outbuildings. The gallery highlights some Aubusson tapestries, paintings and porcelain. The Chateau de Nieuil is a beautiful and dramatic castle, whose setting and ambiance are enchanting even if the accommodations are not always consistent in comfort or decor.

*CHATEAU DE NIEUIL*
*Hotelier: M J. M. Bodinaud*
*16270 Nieuil*
*Tel: 45.71.36.38 Telex: 791230*
*15 Rooms - Sgl from 400F Dbl to 700F*
*Open: 29 April to 12 November*
*Credit cards: AX, VS*
*Restaurant, pool, tennis*
*Located 65 km W of Limoges*
*Region: Dordogne*

Ideally situated on the tourist route that winds through the chalky plains of the "Haute de Cote de Nuits", just northwest of the center of Nuits St Georges as you travel the Route de Meuilley for one and a half kilometers, La Gentilhommiere is a charming and very reasonably priced hotel.  The hotel can be seen set just a short distance off the road, but as it is built in the pale grey stone so typical of the region it blends beautifully with the landscape.  The reception, restaurant and bar are found in the former sixteenth-century hunting lodge.  Staged handsomely, the upstairs restaurant is lovely.  Tapestries cover the dramatic stone walls and high-back tapestry chairs set round heavy wood tables add character to the decor.  The bedrooms are in a newly constructed wing that stretches along a trout stream, behind the former lodge.  All the rooms are identical in style and size and vary only as to whether they have a double or twin beds.  The furnishings are simple, functional, but pleasant.  The rooms, although not spacious, are comfortable and all are equipped with private bath.  The Gentilhommiere is a pleasant inn set on the wine route of Burgundy, offering travellers an excellent location, a scenic setting and attractive rates.

*LA GENTILHOMMIERE*
*Hotelier: Jack Vanroelen*
*Route de Meuilley O*
*21700 Nuits St Georges*
*Tel: 80.61.12.06 Telex: 350401*
*20 Rooms - Sgl from 295F Dbl to 350F*
*Open: All year*
  *Restaurant closed Mondays*
*Credit cards: AX, DC*
*Located 17 km N of Beaune*
*Region: Burgundy*

Once a hunting pavilion of the Count de Rostaing, the Domaine des Hauts de Loire is a beautiful chateau opened this past decade as a hotel. It is managed and owned by Mme Bonnigal, who also oversees the successful, but much more moderately priced, Hostellerie de Chateau in the town of Chaumont sur Loire. The Domaine des Hauts de Loire is a few miles away from the Loire River, bounded by six acres of park and forest. From the town of Onzain take the D152 then turn north on D1 and travel three kilometers in the direction of Herbault. A private, wooded drive leads up to this elegant hotel. With its grey slate roof and ivy-covered facade the regal home is framed by trees and reflected in a small lake that fronts it. The chateau has twenty-two large, elegantly decorated rooms and four exceptionally lovely apartments - all with spacious modern bathrooms - and a lovely dining room. Accommodations are located in the chateau as well as in a lovely, timbered annex. The public salons are quiet, and elegantly furnished with antiques. The restaurant is gorgeous, with soft pastel linens, silver candlesticks, silver and china dressing every table. Everything about this chateau says "luxury".

*DOMAINE DES HAUTS DE LOIRE*
*Hotelier: Mme Bonnigal*
*41150 Onzain*
*Tel: 54.20.72.57 Telex: 751547*
*26 Rooms - Sgl from 560F Dbl to 1120F,*
  *Apt from 1390F to 1590F*
*Open: 15 March to 1 December*
*Credit cards: AX, VS*
*Restaurant, tennis, beautiful chateau*
*Located 44 km NE of Tours*
*Region: Loire Valley*

Vieux Perouges is a charming, medieval village with the atmosphere of a time long gone by.   In one of the quaint old timbered buildings that lean out over the narrow, cobblestoned streets, you will find a captivating restaurant, the Ostellerie du Vieux Perouges.   Traditional and regional cuisine of the Bressane and Lyonnaise districts which are the pride of the chef are served in the thirteenth-century dining room of this charming hotel.   Enhancing the atmosphere are waiters dressed in regional costumes.   Open for breakfast, lunch and dinner, the restaurant also profits from a wine cellar with a wonderful selection of fine Burgundies.   The bedrooms are located in two separate buildings.   The fifteen rooms in the manor, "Au St Georges et Manoir", are fabulously decorated with antiques and a few even have their own garden.   The annex, "a l'Annexe", houses more simply decorated rooms - not as attractive as those in the main building, but quite pleasant and perhaps more appealing since they are less expensive.

*OSTELLERIE DU VIEUX PEROUGES*
*Hotelier: M. Georges Thibaut*
*Place du Tilleul, Vieux Perouges*
*01800 Meximieux*
*Tel: 74.61.00.88*
*15 Rooms (Manor) -*
  *Sgl from 450F Dbl to 1000F*
*10 Rooms (Annex) -*
  *Sgl from 450F Dbl to 500F*
*Open: All year, Restaurant closed Wed*
*Credit cards: VS*
*Restaurant, lovely old timbered building*
*Located 39 km NE of Lyon*
*Region: Rhone Valley*

There are certain characteristics and qualities I will always recall and associate with each of the hotels I have visited. My stay at the Chateau de Violet will forever draw memories of an encouraging, friendly welcome and the amazing woman responsible for it, Madame Faussie. She and her husband purchased the chateau twenty years ago: Madame Faussie is in charge of the hotel and the restaurant and Monsieur Faussie supervises the care of the vineyards. The castle dates from the eleventh century, was renovated in the twelfth and nineteenth centuries and then converted to a hotel in 1966. It stands at the center of the vineyards with a terrace, park and lovely view over the Black Mountains. When I visited the hotel I found only two rooms worthy of mention: "Empire" and "Archeveque". Since my visit, Madame Faussie has written to tell me that many of the additional thirteen bedrooms have been renovated to compare in decor with these lovely rooms and that they have plans to add an art gallery. The Chateau de Violet is not a luxurious hotel, but is reasonably priced and a wonderful place for families. To reach the chateau, travel north one kilometer from the town of Peyriac on the D35.

*CHATEAU DE VIOLET*
*Hotelier: M et Mme Faussie*
*11160 Peyriac Minervois*
*Tel: 68.78.10.42, Telex: 505077*
*15 Rooms - Sgl from 315F Dbl to 645F*
*Open: All year: however,*
   *From 1 October to 1 June by reservation only*
*Credit cards: All major*
*Restaurant, pool*
*Located 24 km NE of Carcassonne*
*Region: Pyrenees Roussillon*

This handsome stone manor is the result of one man's lifelong dream and years of hard work. Monsieur Bernard had a vision of what a chateau should be and has created it here in Pleugueneuc. The Chateau de la Motte Beaumanoir is an oasis in the heart of Brittany's farmland, set in sixty acres of forest and pasture, facing its own private lake and moat. Eric Bernard, the personable son, manages the chateau and is present to  welcome and escort guests to one of the chateau's eight bedchambers. Each room is different in its decor, but all reflect the artistry of Monsieur Bernard and offer luxury, spaciousness and modernly appointed bathrooms. The large bedroom windows frame enchanting scenes of either the lake or forest. In the evening, the Bernards often host a convivial aperitif for all guests in their living room. Seated in comfortable chairs and couches before the massive, stone fireplace one can truly appreciate the advantage of a "chateau prive". If dining, guests are then escorted to a light and airy salon where tables are set before French doors opening on to the lake. Le Chateau de la Motte Beaumanoir is a private home offering rooms to paying guests and does not provide the formality and variety of service associated with a hotel. But to wake in the morning to the sound of swans taking flight and to have received the gracious hospitality of the Bernard family is truly a unique and memorable experience.

*CHATEAU DE LA MOTTE BEAUMANOIR*
*Hotelier: Bernard family*
*35720 Pleugueneuc*
*Tel: 99.69.46.01*
*8 Rooms - Sgl from 435F Dbl to 685F*
*Open: All year*
*Credit cards: VS*
*Restaurant - by reservation only*
*Located 25 km SW of Dinard*
*Region: Brittany·*

*Hotel Descriptions*

It is always a pleasure to visit the endearing Auberge du Vieux Puits. Although set on a main road in the town of Pont Audemer, its lovely timbered facade shelters a melange of charming rooms in which to dine and a back wing of rooms that overlook an oasis of "Shakespearean" garden. L'Auberge du Vieux Puits translates to mean the inn of the old well and is a typical Normandy home dating from the seventeenth century. It was used as a tannery in the nineteenth century, was converted to an inn in 1921 and has been in the Foltz family for three generations. Madame Foltz is an attractive and gracious hostess and Monsieur Foltz has established himself as a highly acclaimed chef. The restaurant is divided into a multitude of alcoves where tables are set under low, heavy beams, before a large open fireplace and surrounded by copper, paintings and antiques. A large portion of the inn was destroyed in World War II and only eight of the original twenty bedrooms were able to be salvaged. These eight rooms are small, modest, yet extremely charming. Five of the bedrooms have showers. In 1985 another timbered wing was renovated to accommodate six bedrooms, slightly more contemporary in decor, all with private bath. It is a treat to be awakened with a tray of fresh coffee, hot rolls, homemade jams and country fresh butter.

*AUBERGE DU VIEUX PUITS*
*Hotelier: M & Mme Foltz*
*6, Rue Notre-Dame du Pre, 27500 Pont Audemer*
*Tel: 32.41.01.48*
*14 Rooms - Sgl from 160F Dbl to 390F*
*Open: 23 Jan to 26 Jun & 7 Jul to 18 Dec*
 *Restaurant closed Mondays and Tuesdays*
*Credit cards: VS*
*Excellent restaurant, lovely garden*
*Located 52 km SW of Rouen*
*Region: Normandy*

Tucked away in the beauty and quiet of the Black Mountains is a fantastic hotel - the Chateau de Montledier.  (To find the hotel, travel five kilometers northeast out of Mazamet on D109 and D54.)  Once you've arrived at the Chateau de Montledier and developed a taste for the splendor and elegance it offers, you will not want to leave and when you do, you will resolve to return.  With just ten guestrooms the Chateau de Montledier is intimate in size and atmosphere.  The accommodations are magnificent in their furnishings, luxuriously appointed, with commodious, modern bathrooms.  "Raymond", with its two stunning canopied beds, is one of the loveliest bedrooms.  The restaurant of the hotel is staged in the cellar: cozy and intimate, it is a romantic setting in which to sample the excellent cuisine and impressive service.  The Chateau de Montledier is a superb hotel, where everything - service, decor, cuisine - is done to perfection and with superb taste.

*CHATEAU DE MONTLEDIER*
*Hotelier: M F. Sidobre*
*Route d'Angles*
*Mazamet*
*81660 Pont de Larn*
*Tel: 63.61.20.54*
*10 Rooms - Sgl from 340F Dbl to 575F*
*Open: All year*
  *Restaurant closed January and Sundays*
*Credit cards: AX, DC, VS*
*Restaurant, park*
*Located 47 km N of Carcassonne*
*Region: Tarn*

Le Clos St Vincent is set in a vineyard on the Alsatian wine route. On the outskirts of the town of Ribeauville a sign directs you up a small road which winds through the vineyards to the hotel. Positioned high on the hill, the hotel looks out over marvellous views of surrounding vineyards to the Alsatian Valley and across to the Black Forest in Germany. The bedrooms are individually identified by a different flower or fruit pattern. Ground-floor bedrooms benefit from a small partitioned patio where one can lounge and enjoy a drink and the panoramic view before dinner. (Each room has its own mini-bar.) The patio is an ideal picnic spot if you decide to pack a light supper of fruit, a crusty baguette and local cheese. (I was disappointed, however, on my most recent visit to see that the bedrooms needed some refurbishing.) The restaurant is very well known for its wine and menu. Depending on the weather, tables are set either indoors in a glass-enclosed room or on the surrounding outdoor terrace. Breakfast, a basket piled high with croissants, brioche and an assortment of breads, is served with fresh-squeezed orange juice, cafe au lait and the morning paper in the privacy of your room or in a cheerful dinette.

*LE CLOS ST VINCENT*
*Hotelier: M Chapotin*
*Route de Bergheim*
*68150 Ribeauville*
*Tel: 89.73.67.65*
*11 Rooms - Sgl from 500F Dbl to 700F*
*Open: mid-March to mid-November*
  *Restaurant closed Tuesdays and Wednesdays*
*Credit cards: VS*
*Restaurant*
*Located 15 km NW of Colmar*
*Region: Alsace*

Chez Melanie, located on a street in the small town of Riec sur Belon, is a simple white, three-story building with three rows of shuttered windows hung with a bounty of colorful flowerboxes. Once an "epicerie" or local grocery store, it was converted to a restaurant in 1920. Over the years a few upstairs rooms were remodeled to accommodate guests and it has remained over the decades a very popular "restaurant with rooms". Considered one of the finest local restaurants of the region, the Chez Melanie offers a beautiful dining room where you can feast on seafood specialities. Waitresses dress in festive, regional costume and their intricate lace hats and aprons add a touch of elegance to the service. The first time I visited the Chez Melanie it was owned and managed by a very gracious Madame Trellu. On a recent visit I felt fortunate to meet a handsome young couple, the Tallecs, who only two weeks earlier had acquired the hotel. I feel confident that this dear inn will only blossom under their care. The restaurant will change little: platters of "les huitres fines Belon" and "le homard Melanie a la creme", to mention just a few of the house specialties, will still appear on the menu. The Tallecs do, however, plan to slowly refurbish the hotel's simple bedrooms. Not all rooms are with private bath, but they are very commodious, clean and offer a comfortable as well as inexpensive night's rest.

*CHEZ MELANIE*
*Hotelier: M & Mme Tellec*
*Place de l'Eglise, 29124 Riec sur Belon*
*Tel: 98.06.91.05*
*7 Rooms - Sgl from 185F, Dbl to 275F*
*Open: March to October, Restaurant closed Tuesdays*
*Credit cards: AX, DC*
*Excellent regional restaurant*
*Located 13 km SW of Quimperle*
*Region: Brittany*

The Moulin de la Gorce is set amongst rolling farmland.  This sixteenth-century mill has been converted to a lovely countryside hotel and a superb restaurant.  In the various buildings clustered along the edge of a quiet pond and brook are luxurious, antique-furnished bedrooms whose walls are hung with tapestries. (The tapestries are hand-painted replicas from a factory in Rambouillet, and are for sale.)  The wallpapers and materials chosen for the decor are sometimes overbearing, but the rooms are all with private bath or shower and very comfortable.  A few open onto a grassy terrace.  The restaurant, intimate in size, is romantically furnished in soft pastel tones: tables are set before a lovely fireplace and the restaurant's atmosphere is surpassed only by the unusually beautiful presentation of each course.  The care and attention to detail that the Bertranet family strive for is evident throughout.  There are currently only six rooms in the mill but the Bertranets have built an additional three in an adjacent building.  A lovely retreat, and, as a result, a bit difficult to find.  From St Yrieix La Perche travel on the D704 northeast out of town in the direction of Limoges and then twelve kilometers on to La Roche l'Abeille.

*MOULIN DE LA GORCE*
*Hotelier: M & Mme Bertranet*
*La Roche l'Abeille*
*87800 Nexon*
*Tel: 55.00.70.66*
*9 Rooms - Sgl from 300F Dbl to 550F*
*Closed: 16 November to 2 December and*
*  25 January to 20 February*
*Credit cards: AX, DC, VS*
*Restaurant*
*Located 40 km S of Limoges*
*Region: Dordogne*

*Hotel Descriptions*

During the Middle Ages the Chateau d'Isenbourg was the cherished home of the prince bishops of Strasbourg and more recently it was owned by wealthy wine growers.  On the hillside above the town of Rouffach, the chateau is still surrounded by its own vineyards.  There are forty bedrooms, nine of which are modern additions that overlook either the vineyards, the wide plain of Alsace or the castle park.  A number of rooms are exceptionally elegant with massive, hand-painted ceilings: room one is an especially beautiful apartment.  Room fourteen is not as expensive but is also impressive in furnishings.  The grounds feature a large swimming pool and tennis courts.  The kitchen is the domain of the chateau's young and remarkable chef, Eric Orban.  You can appropriately savor a delicious meal and fine Alsatian wines (select from the chateau's own reserve) in the vaulted fifteenth-century wine cellar or on the panoramic terrace.  An open-air luncheon is offered in summertime.  Between October and January you might want to plan your stay around one of the musical evenings that the hotel sponsors.  The soirees begin at 7:30 pm over a cocktail and the concerts begin punctually at 8:00 pm, followed by a candlelit dinner.

*CHATEAU D'ISENBOURG*
*Hotelier: M Daniel Dalibert*
*68250 Rouffach*
*Tel: 89.49.63.53 Telex: 880819*
*40 Rooms - Sgl from 575F Dbl to 1095F*
*Closed: beg January to mid-March*
*Credit cards: VS*
*Restaurant, pool, tennis*
*Located 15 km S of Colmar*
*Region: Alsace*

*Hotel Descriptions*

Your vivacious hostess at the seventeenth-century Manoir les Prouillacs, Audrey Summerskill-Bronte, offers a true slice of rustic, yet gracious country life. The atmosphere she encourages is more of a casual houseparty rather than a hotel, thus children are not especially welcome. Audrey, a descendant of the well-known writers Emily and Charlotte Bronte, spends only her summers at the Manoir les Prouillacs. She thoroughly enjoys playing hostess and prepares all the meals herself while treating clients like invited guests. The dining room is furnished with an intricately carved light wood antique dining room set, including one long table where all are invited to sit. After dinner drinks might be taken in the English style living room with its well worn chairs and couches, array of books and a piano and all set before a large stone fireplace. Conversation tends towards literature, the arts and local history as befits this setting and your hostess, who also organizes an annual music festival in the town of St Amand de Vergt. Some of the five bedrooms share a bath, but all are high-ceilinged and spacious and furnished with a mix of antique furniture. To fully enjoy the ambiance here, one must be able to appreciate the rural setting amidst the cornfields and pastures as well as the quiet that prevails. Follow small signs at St Amand de Vergt's only intersection in the direction of Peyrebrane/St Maurice to Les Prouillacs.

*MANOIR LES PROUILLACS*
*Hotelier: Audrey Summerskill-Bronte*
*St Amand de Vergt, 24380 Vergt*
*Tel: 53.54.96.61*
*5 Rooms - Dbl 900F, includes 5-course dinner & wines*
*Open: Easter to October*
*Credit cards: None*
*Restaurant, pool*
*Located 27 km S of Perigueux*
*Region: Dordogne*

Monsieur Kubons has recently retired from Paris and restyled his country home in a tiny half-timbered hamlet into a charming country inn. Across the country lane from the old cemetery and church, the Auberge du Prieure is a former rectory. Its thatched roof, half-timbers, windows hung heavy with geraniums, odd angles and interesting sections dating from the thirteenth century lend much character to this peaceful inn. The low-ceilinged dining hall offers a wide variety of Madame Kubons's gourmet specialties. The centuries-old aroma of a log-burning fire mingles with the mouth-watering scents from the kitchen. One sits in the restaurant, which is very rustic in decor, on pew benches and tapestry chairs at long trestle tables placed in the firelight. In the morning, one is tempted to join the flock of ducks and geese in the lush back garden that faces the rose-covered stone wall of the auberge. Monsieur Kubons proudly showed us all of his seven bedrooms including one commodious duplex. The accommodations all have spotless and modern bathroom facilities (no easy task in a building of its age), large comfortable beds and dark beamed ceilings and are accented by handsome antique furnishings. Colors are muted earth tones and there is a very masculine touch to the decor. We felt very fortunate to have happened on the Auberge du Prieure and only wish our schedule had permitted us to stay longer.

*AUBERGE DU PRIEURE*
*Hotelier: M & Mme Kubons*
*St Andre d'Hebertot, 14130 Pont l'Eveque*
*Tel: 31.64.03.03*
*7 Rooms - Sgl from 325F Dbl to 480F*
*Open: All year*
*Credit cards: None*
*Restaurant*
*Located 11 km SE of Deauville*
*Region: Normandy*

Beyond the ruins of a medieval arched gateway, the Hotel de la Pelissaria, nestled at the foot of St Cirq Lapopie, is an engaging inn whose character is enhanced by its artistic owners, the Matuchets. With only six rooms, it is a fortunate few who can enjoy a stay here. Fresh and simple in its decor, the inn's whitewashed walls contrast handsomely with dark wooden beams and sienna tile floors - strikingly reminiscent of the Mediterranean. Thick stone walls and shuttered windows frame the idyllic scene of St Cirq Lapopie perched high above a wide band of the meandering Lot River. The restaurant is limited in seating, so it is wise to make reservations well in advance in order to savor Marie-Francoise's delicious and fresh regional cuisine - one can select from a reasonably priced menu or order a la carte. It is incredible how efficient and creative Marie-Francoise can be in the confines of her small kitchen. Francois's talents are in the field of music. A piano and string instruments decorate the intimate, candlelit restaurant, and his own recordings stage a romantic mood. St Cirq Lapopie is truly one of France's most picturesque villages. With only forty-four year-round residents, this hamlet of steep, narrow, winding cobbled streets, sun-warmed tile roofs, mixture of timber and stone facades, and garden niches is a postcard-perfect scene. It is wonderful to find an inn which so perfectly complements the beauty of this village.

*HOTEL DE LA PELISSARIA*
*Hotelier: Francois & Marie-Francoise Matuchet*
*St Cirq Lapopie, 46330 Cabrerets*
*Tel: 65.31.25.14*
*6 Rooms - Sgl from 250F Dbl to 360F*
*Open: 1 Apr to 1 Nov, Restaurant closed Mon*
*Credit cards: DC, VS, MC*
*Gourmet restaurant*
*Located 33 km E of Cahors*
*Region: Lot*

The Auberge du Sombral is a small country inn facing onto the main square of the picturesque village of St Cirq Lapopie. In such a small, remote village it was amazing to learn that editors of *Gourmet* and *Le Figaro* had already discovered the auberge and praised it for its restaurant. It is owned by the Hardevelds, with Monique a charming hostess and Giles the acclaimed chef. Cafe tables are set on the front porch and provide an inviting spot to linger and enjoy a cool drink after an afternoon of exploring the narrow and steep cobbled streets of the village. Inside, the restaurant is furnished with a melange of country tables and chairs set on a warm tile floor, watercolors that paint country scenes and a glorious, enormous, central arrangement of flowers. Offered are a number of well priced menus or a tempting a la carte selection. Specialties feature regional gastronomic delights such as "terrine de foie de canard frais" and "omellette aux truffes". The wine list highlights excellent regional wines. The inn's ten bedrooms are found at the top of a wooden stairway. All are with bath or shower and they are clean, basic and many look out over the rooftops of St Cirq Lapopie. During high season (May through September) the Hardevelds offer rooms on a demi-pension basis only. The Auberge du Sombral is a little inn with a stone facade and simple accommodations offering both moderately priced rooms and superb country French cuisine.

*AUBERGE DU SOMBRAL*
*Hotelier: M & Mme Gilles Hardeveld*
*St Cirq Lapopie, 46330 Cabrerets*
*Tel: 65.31.26.08*
*10 Rooms - Sgl from 210F Dbl to 310F*
*Open: 15 March to 11 November*
*Credit cards: VS*
*Restaurant*
*Located 33 km E of Cahors*
*Region: Lot*

The wine town of St Emilion was introduced to us in all its splendor.   It was a day that the town was dressed with banners, filled with music and laughter and visited by all the dignitaries of the region.   It was a warm day in late September, a day to commence the "vendage" - the beginning of the wine harvest.   The day was captivating and we fell in love with the town.   Crowning a hillside with vistas that stretch out to the surrounding vineyards, St Emilion is a medieval village of tradition, long considered the capital of the Bordeaux wine region.   The Hotel Plaisance opens on to the square, in the shade of the church, and its walls have echoed over the centuries the first church bells commemorating the start of the wine harvest.   To stay here one could not be more central to the activity and town's events.   The hotel has only twelve rooms, most of which were understandably occupied at the time of our visit.   All are individual in decor and from their windows views extend out over vineyards and the maze of tile rooftops.   The dining room is lovely and extremely popular, with tables set against windows whose views appear to plunge over the valley.   Service is gracious and accommodating. La Plaisance is the place to stay in town and St Emilion is the most charming town of the Bordeaux wine region.

*HOTEL LA PLAISANCE*
*Hotelier: Louis & Samira Quilain*
*Place du Clocher*
*33330 St Emilion*
*Tel: 57.24.72.32 Telex: 573032*
*12 Rooms - Dbl from 594F to 764F*
*Open: All year*
*Credit cards: AX, VS*
*Restaurant*
*Located 39 km E of Bordeaux*
*Region: Dordogne*

This authentic, eighteenth-century mill has been lovingly converted into a true French country inn. Family-run and far from the closest town, Moulin d'Hauterive is located in a peaceful country setting, soothed by the sound of an adjacent rushing stream and surrounded by miles of unspoilt French countryside. The bedrooms of the mill are not overly large, but all have private bath, television and mini-bar, are furnished individually in soft colors and profit from the feminine touch of Madame Moille. The restaurant consists of two charming stone, low-ceilinged rooms, where intimate tables are dressed with pretty china and silver and silver plate covers are proudly displayed. Dining here, one is as likely to meet out-of-towners and international guests as well as locals, since the kitchen is known for its refined cuisine in this pastoral setting. To find this uncut jewel in the countryside of Burgundy, travel south from Beaune on D970 towards Verdun sur les Doubs until the turnoff to St Gervais en Valliere on D183. Look for signs as you continue deeper into the countryside and you'll see the ivy-covered inn on your left.

*MOULIN D'HAUTERIVE*
*Hotelier: M & Mme Moille*
*71350 St Gervais en Valliere*
*Tel: 85.91.55.56 Telex: 801395*
*19 Rooms - Sgl from 282F Dbl to 360F*
*   3 Apt at 550F*
*Closed: 1 December to 2 January*
*Credit cards: All major*
*Restaurant*
*Pool, tennis, sauna*
*Located 20 km SE of Beaune*
*Region: Burgundy*

Hotel de Chantaco is a lovely Spanish villa in an isolated quiet position on the outskirts of St Jean de Luz, a picturesque port town, on the road that winds up into the Basque hills and some truly charming villages.   To reach the hotel, travel east two kilometers from St Jean de Luz on D918.   Facing a challenging eighteen-hole golf course, the hotel serves as an ideal retreat for golfers.   For those who want to settle in Basque, the Hotel de Chantaco offers a comfortable and well-located retreat.   Architecturally, the hotel blends beautifully with the region.   Just off the road, but against a backdrop of greenery, this cream-stone, tile-roofed villa has shuttered windows and arched entryways draped with vines.   The decor is austere but well suited to this weathered villa.   The grand entry and salons are airy, spacious and classically furnished.   The hotel was full when we visited and so we were able to view only a few additional rooms but found them individual and comfortable in decor.   The restaurant, El Patio, is inviting and the service is friendly.   For its accommodation, restaurant and service, the Hotel de Chantaco adds to the enchantment of the Basque province.

*HOTEL DE CHANTACO*
*Hotelier: M P. Larramendy*
*64500 St Jean de Luz*
*Tel: 59.26.14.76*
*24 Rooms - Sgl from 450F Dbl to 950F*
*Open: April to October*
*Credit cards: AX, DC, VS*
*Restaurant, faces golf course*
*Located 15 km S of Biarritz*
*Region: Basque*

An ancient Relais de Poste, Le Lievre Amoureux is located to the northwest of the Rhone Valley at the base of the Vercors and Isere massifs. It is a pretty, ivy-covered building with shutters and flowerboxes at each of its windows. Le Lievre Amoureux is a charming inn that reflects the ideals of the management - Gisele Carmet wants guests to be as comfortable and relaxed as they are at home, but pampered with gracious service. The restaurant is quite popular locally and the cuisine, under the excellent chef's direction, is delicious. He composes the menu based on the freshest ingredients and products available. Tables are set romantically before a warming fire or on the terrace under old lime trees in summer. A number of rooms have been added since my last visit, of which six are very commodious suites. I am informed that the majority of rooms are now located in an annex adjacent to the main building and restaurant. The bedrooms have all been decorated with pretty fabrics and comfortable furnishings. This is a pretty inn in a lovely and peaceful setting. Le Lievre Amoureux is located between St Marcellin and Romans, formerly the meeting point of hunting parties.

*LE LIEVRE AMOUREUX*
*Hotelier: Claude Breda & Gisele Carmet*
*St Lattier*
*38840 St Hilaire du Rosier*
*Tel: 76.64.50.67 Telex: 308534*
*12 Rooms - Dbl from 300F to 420F*
*Open: mid-January to mid-December*
*Credit cards: AX, DC, VS*
*Restaurant, pool*
*Located 30 km NE of Valence*
*Region: Rhone Valley*

La Chapelle St Martin is a small grey-wash manor that rests on a velvet green lawn. Although there is very little exterior ornamentation (even the shutters are painted to blend with the facade) the interior decor is very ornate and detailed. Colorful patterned papers, complementing carpets, paintings hung in heavy gilt frames, lavish chandeliers, tapestries and miniature statues decorate the rooms of the hotel. Known for its restaurant, La Chapelle St Martin serves meals in three elegant, small dining rooms. The setting and service is formal, with lovely porcelain, crystal, china and silver used to enhance the presentation of Chef Yves Leonard's masterful creations. La Chapelle St Martin is only a few minutes from Limoges, a city famous for its porcelain. Although many guests venture from Limoges for dinner, the manor does have eleven rooms to accommodate overnight guests. The bedrooms are decorated with the same flavor as the restaurant and public rooms. Very commodious, the rooms are all with private bath and look out onto the hotel gardens and greenery. The surrounding farmland and two ponds complete the storybook atmosphere of La Chapelle St Martin.

*LA CHAPELLE ST MARTIN*
*Hotelier: M Jacques Dudognon*
*St Martin du Fault*
*87510 Nieul*
*Tel: 55.75.80.17*
*11 Rooms - Sgl from 490F Dbl to 750F*
*Open: March to January*
*  Restaurant closed Mondays*
*Credit cards: VS*
*Outstanding restaurant, tennis*
*Located 12 km NW of Limoges on N147 & D35*
*Region: Dordogne*

La Colombe d'Or is located opposite the main square at the gates to the fortified town of St Paul de Vence. The hotel is attractive and elegant in its rustic ambiance, the theme of its decor focusing around the colors of the home and region. Antiques worn over the years to a warm patina are placed on terracotta floors, set under rough wooden beams before open fireplaces. Walls are washed white, heavy wooden doors contrast handsomely and throw pillows, wall hangings, and flower arrangements add colors of rusts, oranges, browns and beiges. The hotel also boasts a fantastic collection of art. In the past a number of now famous painters paid for their meals with their talents - and now the walls are hung like a gallery and the reputation of the inn dictates that the value of the art complements the cuisine. The restaurant of La Colombe d'Or is both excellent and attractive. Dine either in the intimacy of a room warmed by a cozy fire or on the patio whose walls are draped with ivy at tables set under the shade of cream umbrellas. In the evening stars and candles illuminate the very romantic setting. The entrance to the fortified town of St Paul de Vence is just up the street from La Colombe d'Or. After a day of sightseeing, return to La Colombe d'Or and enjoy its refreshing pool set against a backdrop of aging stone wall and greenery.

*HOTEL LA COLOMBE D'OR*
*Hotelier: M & Mme Roux*
*Place de Gaulle*
*06570 St Paul de Vence*
*Tel: 93.32.80.02 Telex: 970607*
*24 Rooms - Sgl from 760F Dbl to 1000F*
*Closed: 5 November to 20 December*
*Credit cards: All major*
*Restaurant, pool, art collection*
*Located 20 km NW of Nice*
*Region: Riviera*

Le Hameau is an old farm complex set on the hillside just outside the walled city of St Paul de Vence. The whitewashed buildings, tiled roofs aged by years of sun, shuttered windows, arched entryways, heavy doors and exposed beams all create a rustic and attractive setting. The bedrooms of this inn are found in four buildings clustered together amidst fruit trees and flower gardens. Each building has its own character and name: L'Oranger, L'Olivier, Le Pigeonnier and La Treille. Three of the largest bedrooms have a small room for an infant and the attraction of their own balcony (rooms one and three with twin beds and two with a double bed). Of the rooms, eleven, with antique twin beds and a lovely view onto the garden, was my favorite. I was very impressed with the quality of this provincial inn. Monsieur Xavier Huvelin is a charming host and is graciously attentive to the needs of his guests. Le Hameau does not have a restaurant but a delicious country breakfast can be enjoyed in the garden or in the privacy of your room. I highly recommend Le Hameau as a wonderful inn and a great value.

*LE HAMEAU*
*Hotelier: M & Mme X. Huvelin*
*528, Route de la Colle*
*06570 St Paul de Vence*
*Tel: 93.32.80.24*
*16 Rooms - Sgl from 240F Dbl to 390F*
*  Apt from 440F to 480F*
*Credit cards: AX, VS*
*Open: February to 15 November*
*No restaurant, terraces, gardens*
*Located 20 km NW of Nice*
*Region: Riviera*

Les Orangers welcomes you to St Paul de Vence. Nestled amongst olive and orange trees, the hotel has a view looking back to the village of St Paul de Vence and down towards the French Riviera. The hotel is not located within the walls of St Paul de Vence, but just on its outskirts, on the Route de la Colle. A lovely large living room serves as a welcoming place to settle: a handsome antique hutch, comfortable sofa and chairs and a cozy fireplace tempt one to linger while mapping out the day's itinerary. Madame Biancheri's loving touch is especially apparent in the ten charming bedrooms which are in a building off the reception area. Pretty provincial prints have been chosen to adorn the beds and frame the windows while lovely antiques and Oriental rugs warm the rustic tile floors. Bathrooms are all spotlessly clean and supplied with fresh country soaps and fresh, soft towels. Although the hotel is no longer associated with the restaurant, Les Oliviers, located just below it on the hillside, there are numerous eating places to choose from in the medieval walled village of St Paul. Since each of the bedrooms at Les Orangers has its own terrace, with grape vines entwined in the corner and the fragrance of orange blossoms wafting from below, there is no place more romantic to enjoy a country breakfast.

*LES ORANGERS*
*Hotelier: Mme Biancheri*
*06570 St Paul de Vence*
*Tel: 93.32.80.95*
*10 Rooms - Sgl from 300F Dbl to 580F*
*Open: 15 March to 3 January*
*No restaurant*
*Lovely views, beautiful garden*
*Located 20 km NW of Nice*
*Region: Riviera*

Dining in the care of Marc Meneau is truly an enchanting and memorable experience. Relax and study the daily offerings in the salon, subtle in its soft beiges, greys, well-placed mirrors and abundance of green plants. Casual yet quietly elegant, the restaurant looks out onto outdoor greenery through floor-to-ceiling windows. Tables are set with soft pastel linen, stunning flower arrangements, elegant crystal and silver. Marc Meneau is a tall, handsome man, who sports a tie under his chef's white and is ever-present to welcome guests before attending to his culinary creations. His lovely wife, Francoise, graciously supervises the attentive, professional staff of waiters. She bustles about to extend greetings, pour wine, assist with the service and offer a welcoming smile. Shadowed by his devoted Doberman, Volt, Marc Meneau reappears in the lounge after dinner to relax with guests over coffee. For those fortunate enough also to secure a room reservation, there are thirteen beautifully appointed bedrooms upstairs, traditional in furnishings. There are an additional three suites and five bedrooms, lovely and more rustic in decor, situated in a renovated mill just three hundred meters from the reception. L'Esperance is located three kilometers southeast of Vezelay on D957.

*L'ESPERANCE*
*Hotelier: Marc & Francoise Meneau*
*St Pere sous Vezelay*
*89450 Vezelay*
*Tel: 86.33.20.45 Telex: 800005*
*21 Rooms - Sgl from 330F Dbl to 1205F*
*Closed: January*
*Restaurant closed Tuesdays & Wednesday lunch*
*Credit cards: AX, VS, DC*
*Located 12 km E of Avallon*
*Region: Burgundy*

The Chateau des Alpilles was purchased a few years ago by the Bons and they have renovated this magnificent manor to its former state of grandeur. The Chateau des Alpilles is grand, with high ornate ceilings, decorative wallpapers and tall windows draped with heavy fabrics. The public rooms are attractively decorated with period pieces but, without rugs, are a bit austere. A breakfast room contrasts dramatically with the rest of the house as it is furnished with white plastic chairs and tables. Upstairs tiled hallways hung with tapestries lead to the twelve lovely bedrooms. Soft, subdued colors such as rose and Dutch blue have been selected for fabrics and papers. Large armoirs, beds, desks and chairs arrange easily in the spacious rooms, each with private bath, and make for a very comfortable stay. The corner rooms are especially nice with four large shuttered windows overlooking the shaded gardens that are planted with a multitude of exotic species of trees. On the top floor, the Bons suggest three smaller rooms that share a bath and toilet as ideal accommodation for children. The Bons have also renovated a small chapel into a beautiful apartment and hope soon to convert an adjacent farmhouse. On summer evenings a barbecue of lamb, beef or pork and a buffet of large salads are offered poolside. The rest of the year, as the Chateau les Alpilles does not have a restaurant, meat and cheese platters, omelettes, foie gras and wines are available.

*CHATEAU DES ALPILLES*
*Hotelier: Mme & Mlle Bon*
*Route D31, 13210 St Remy*
*Tel: 90.92.03.33 Telex: 431 987*
*16 Rooms - Sgl from 580F Dbl to 790F*
*Open: Easter to 10 November & Christmas*
*Credit cards: All major*
*Pool, tennis, sauna*
*Located 40 km E of Nimes*
*Region: Provence*

The Chateau de Besset sits on the top of a hill looking down upon fifty acres of park in the heart of the province of Vivarais. Built of beige and brown bricks with a warm sienna tile roof, this imposing fifteenth-century chateau offers luxurious comfort and quiet to its visitors with ten spacious chambers as accommodation. Regal in their decor, the rooms are decorated with dramatic wallpapers and fabrics chosen to complement the beamed ceilings, antique furnishings and Oriental rugs. The rooms, each characteristic of a certain style, are elegant and grand. The bathrooms, ultra modern and remarkably appointed, also deserve mention. In the restaurant one can feast on delicious food and excellent local wines. The dining room is handsomely set with tables on a terra cotta floor before an open fire. You will want to savor this impressive and marvellous hotel and the facilities give you reason and excuse to do so. With the beautiful and serene Ardeche hills as a backdrop, the swimming pool enjoys a tranquil setting. Tennis courts and the equestrian center will tempt the sport enthusiast and the park of fifty acres offers an unlimited number of walks. Directions to the hotel: travel nine kilometers northwest of St Peray to St Romain de Lerps on D287, then continue three kilometers southwest from St Romain.

*CHATEAU DE BESSET*
*Hotelier: Dominique Couture*
*St Romain de Lerps, 07130 St Peray*

*Tel: 75.58.52.22 Telex: 345261*

*6 Rooms - Dbl 1700, 4 Apt 2200*
*Open: 27 March to 27 October*
*Credit cards: AX, VS, DC*
*Restaurant, pool, tennis, riding*
*Located 15 km W of Valence*
*Region: Rhone Valley*

*CLOSED*

The true French meaning behind their saying "chez soi" can be defined and experienced at the Hostellerie du Levezou. This is a simple hotel housed within the walls of a fourteenth-century chateau and lovingly run and managed by the entire Bouviala family: parents, sons, daughters and the dog. The Bouvialas do not boast a hotel of luxurious comfort, but rather a place where one can enjoy good food and comfortable accommodations at a reasonable price. Monsieur Bouviala's pride is his restaurant. Inviting in its decor the dining room is lovely and, when the weather permits, outdoor seating is set on a terrace that extends out in front of it. The focal point of the restaurant is a large fireplace where Monsieur Bouviala grills his delicious specialities. The thirty bedrooms of the Hostellerie du Levezou are basic, cheerful in their decor, a few with private bath or shower and all extremely reasonable in price. At the heart of the ancient fortified village of Salles Curan, with a beautiful view over Pareloup Lake and the countryside, the Hostellerie du Levezou, once the medieval summer residence of the Bishops of Rodez, offers a friendly welcome and good-value lodging.

*HOSTELLERIE DU LEVEZOU*
*Hotelier: M Bouviala*
*12410 Salles Curan*
*Tel: 65.46.34.16*
*30 Rooms - Sgl from 75F Dbl to 300F*
*Open: 1 April to 15 October*
*  Restaurant closed Sunday evenings & Mondays*
*Credit cards: All major*
*Restaurant, fourteenth-century chateau*
*Located 37 km NW of Millau*
*Region: Tarn*

Captivating L'Abbaye de Ste Croix was built in the ninth and twelfth centuries. For seven hundred years it was a residence of Cistercian monks but abandoned and left to ruin in the nineteenth century. In 1969 it was purchased and converted into a hotel by the Bossard Family. Sprawling along the contours of the hillsides of Provence, the abbey commands a peaceful and idyllic location and enjoys a splendid panorama over the surrounding countryside. Vaulted ceilings, antiques, tiled floors and open fires warm the atmosphere of the abbey. A labyrinth of narrow stairways, low, small arched doorways and stone passageways lead to the rooms that are named for saints. Since the bedrooms' history dates back to when they accommodated Cistercian monks who came to savor the peaceful setting and facilities, they tend to be a bit small and dark, with deep-set windows that peek out through thick stone walls. A few enjoy the extension of a private terrace. The restaurant opens up to spectacular vistas out over the Salon Valley and highlights Provencal cuisine. L'Abbaye is located five kilometers to the northeast of Salon de Provence following D16 and a private drive.

*L'ABBAYE DE STE CROIX*
*Hotelier: Bossard family*
*Route du Val de Cuech*
*13300 Salon de Provence*
*Tel: 90.56.24.55 Telex: 401247*
*19 Rooms - Sgl from 540F Dbl to 860F*
*5 Apt to 1400F*
*Open: March to November*
*Credit cards: All major*
*Restaurant, large pool*
*Located 35 km NW of Aix en Provence*
*Region: Provence*

Nestled in the area bordering Spain, the Hotel Arraya has captured the tradition and rustic flavor of this Basque region. Long ago the hotel was founded to provide lodgings for pilgrims on the road to Santiago de Compostela. Today it accommodates guests who have fallen in love with this dear inn and return time and again. The Hotel Arraya is decorated with an abundance of seventeenth-century Basque antiques and is a comfortable and hospitable country manor. The entry, lobby and breakfast nook are charming. Cozy blue and white gingham cushions pad the wooden chairs that are set round a lovely collection of antique tables. The restaurant offers regional Basque specialities and you must stay long enough to sample them all: "foie de canard frais poele aux poires", pigeon with salami sauce, country hams, goat cheese made by the mountain shepherds and "pastiza", a delicious Basque almond cake filled with cream or black cherry preserve. The bedrooms are all individual in decor and size but are attractive with their white-washed walls, exposed beams and pretty fabrics. The hotel is managed by Paul Fagoaga who welcomes his guests as friends in the traditional way, round the "zizailua" or bench near the fire.

*HOTEL ARRAYA*
*Hotelier: M Paul Fagoaga*
*Sare, 64310 Ascain*
*Tel: 59.54.20.46*
*21 Rooms - Sgl from 330F Dbl to 420F*
*Open: 11 May to 2 November*
*Credit cards: AX, VS, MC*
*Restaurant*
*Located 24 km SE of Biarritz*
*Region: Basque*

The Domaine de Bassibe is a hotel you have to stay at to realize its charms. Set in a region popular for its health spas and resorts, the hotel is a beautiful vine covered homestead. The setting, atop a gently rolling hill overlooking the countryside of Geroise, is extremely restful and serene. The use of large floral prints dominates the bedroom decor, quite modern in contrast to the character of the building. After a morning by the pool and an exquisite lunch served at the poolside with luxurious linens, crystal and china I felt quite ready to recommend the hotel to you. The staff are extremely hospitable, making the Bassibe a romantic hideaway as well as an ideal holiday spot for families. The restaurant in the converted stables proves popular with guests and locals alike. The rough wooden beams have been painted in fresh white and contrast attractively with the warm orange color of the walls. Tables are spaciously set on a tile floor around a warming log fire: on warm afternoons they are placed in the courtyard under the shade of low hanging trees. On a Sunday, locals will linger here an entire afternoon over a delicious meal. To reach the hotel, travel nine kilometers south from Aire sur l'Adour on N134 in the direction of Pau and then continue on D260.

*DOMAINE DE BASSIBE*
*Hotelier: Jean Pierre Capelle*
*Segos, 32400 Riscle*
*Tel: 62.09.46.71 Telex: 531918*
*9 Rooms - Sgl from 495F Dbl to 835F*
*Open: mid-April to end November*
*Credit cards: AX, VS, DC*
*Restaurant, pool*
*Located 39 km N of Pau*
*Region: Basque*

This has proven to be a popular spot for our readers to stay in while exploring the Champagne district. The Bernard family who lovingly manage the Hotel du Cheval Blanc consider it principally a "restaurant with rooms". With fresh flowers, linen, china and silver dressing the tables, the restaurant is very attractive. The menu features regional specialities and the wine list is impressive in its selection and presentation of French wines. On a warm day, one can enjoy a before- or after-dinner drink in a garden setting at tables in front of the restaurant. The bedrooms of the Cheval Blanc are actually located in a separate building across the road. The location proves to be an advantage, as one is removed from the late-night chatter of the restaurant guests. There are twenty-one rooms, only a few of which are original to the inn: the newer rooms are found in a modern, though very tasteful, extension - one hardly notices the transition from the old to the new wing. All the bedrooms are decorated with pretty print wallpapers, matching bedspreads and antique reproduction furniture. The nicest feature of the hotel is that the rooms are surrounded by an expanse of garden. Guests spend many a leisurely afternoon lounging in the grounds or playing tennis on the hotel's clay court. The Cheval Blanc is not a luxurious hotel, but is comfortable, the restaurant has an excellent reputation and the setting is rural and tranquil.

*HOTEL DU CHEVAL BLANC*
*Hotelier: Robert Bernard*
*51400 Sept Saulx*
*Tel: 26.03.90.27 Telex: 830885*
*21 Rooms - Sgl from 288F Dbl to 486F*
*Closed: mid-January to mid-February*
*Credit cards: All major*
*Restaurant, park, tennis*
*Located 20 km SE of Reims*
*Region: Champagne*

If business or pleasure brings you to Nantes, stay in this converted thirteenth-century abbey on the town's outskirts.   L'Abbaye de Villeneuve might also serve as a good point to bridge the distance between a tour of Brittany and the Loire Valley. A tree-lined drive leads up to L'Abbaye de Villeneuve, a grand, two-story dwelling set a good distance from the main road.   High ceilings and handsome furnishings impose a formal air and fit the mood of this stately home.   Two intimate dining rooms offer guests a lovely atmosphere in which to dine. Service is very professional, befitting the elegant table settings and grand cuisine.   A massive stone stairway winds up to the abbey's eighteen bedrooms: these accommodations are luxuriously furnished, with vast windows offering views of the grounds.   Each room is equipped with direct dial phone, television and lovely, modern bathrooms. Although the grounds are lacking in color, there is a small circular wading pool on the back lawn.   Directions: travel southeast out of Nantes, towards Autoroute A801, and then take D178 to Route de Sables d'Olonne.

*L'ABBAYE DE VILLENEUVE*
*Hotelier: Philippe Savry*
*Manager: Lois Sevellec*
*Route de Sables d'Olonne*
*44840 Les Sorinieres*
*Tel: 40.04.40.25 Telex: 710451*
*  Fax: 40.31.28.45*
*18 Rooms - Dbl from 470F to 1100F*
*Open: All year*
*Credit cards: VS, AX, DC*
*Restaurant, wading pool*
*Located 10 km S of Nantes*
*Region: Loire Valley*

On a recent trip to France I discovered the Hotel des Rohan just around the corner from Strasbourg's stunning cathedral. On a pedestrian street, this charming hotel has a lovely foyer and a salon where breakfast is served. The thirty-six beautiful rooms have either private bath or shower, direct-dial phone, radio, television and mini-bar. The hotel is decorated in seventeenth- and eighteenth-century style. Tapestries adorn the walls, and in the bedrooms the style is either Louis XV or rustic. The location is quiet, ideal for exploring Strasbourg on foot. The narrow streets are a maze that winds in the shadow of leaning, timbered buildings and in the shade of the lacy trees that grow beside the river. The shops are delightful with their beautiful displays of Alsatian specialties such as wines, foie-gras, sausages and costumes. The Hotel des Rohan is without a restaurant and so one is free to investigate the numerous sidewalk cafes and cozy restaurants that Strasbourg is famous for. Being at the heart of the city's old quarter is also the hotel's one drawback - one must park elsewhere. Nearby parking areas convenient to the hotel are at the Place du Chateau, the Place Gutenberg (underground) and the Rue du Viel Hopital (except on Wednesdays and Saturdays when there is a flea market).

*HOTEL DES ROHAN*
*17-19, Rue du Morquin*
*67000 Strasbourg*
*Tel: 88.32.85.11 Telex: 870047*
*36 Rooms - Sgl from 265F Dbl to 540F*
*Open: All year*
*Credit cards: VS*
*No restaurant*
*Located at the center of town*
*Region: Alsace*

L'Auberge du Pere Bise combines a traditional welcome, exquisite cuisine (some of the best in the region) and a beautiful location to ensure an enjoyable holiday. This shingled, three-story, ivy-covered inn is charming through and through and has offered first class accommodation and service since 1901.   At the Auberge du Pere Bise, angled on a small peninsula with terraces and gardens that extend to the water's edge, one can enjoy an idyllic setting of lake, mountains and a large, wooded park.   Most of the rooms overlook the lake and many enjoy a private balcony. Accommodations are charming and at the same time luxurious in their comfort. This lovely auberge is not a discovery but rather long praised and recognized by many to be one of the finest inns in France.   Sadly, Francois Bise passed away in 1984, but his widow and daughter carry on the tradition of excellence that he established and has long been associated with this lakeside inn.   Even if the setting didn't warrant a visit, Michelin's three toque rating for the restaurant indicates that it alone is worth a dining detour.

*L'AUBERGE DU PERE BISE*
*Hotelier: Charlyne Bise*
*Route de Port, Talloires*
*74290 Veyrier du Lac*
*Tel: 50.60.72.01 Telex: 385812*
*34 Rooms - Sgl from 560F Dbl to 900F*
*    Apt to 2800F*
*Closed: 20 April to 7 May and*
*        15 December to 14 February*
*   Restaurant closed Tuesdays*
*Credit cards: AX, VS, DC*
*Restaurant, faces lake, park*
*Located 56 km S of Geneva*
*Region: Alps (listed on map under Rhone Valley)*

La Tonnellerie, renovated from a wine-merchant's house, is situated on a small road near the church in the country village of Tavers. Just three kilometers away from the medieval city of Beaugency and only an hour and a half's drive from Paris by the autoroute, the Hostellerie de la Tonnellerie proves to be an ideal starting point for visiting the chateaux of the Loire Valley. Although the inn is located on a village street, there is very little traffic through Tavers and most of the bedrooms overlook an oasis of garden. Two wings of the building extend back and border a central courtyard ablaze with flowers and a lovely, refreshing pool. On the first floor of one wing is La Tonnellerie's restaurant which features regional specialties as well as "nouvelle cuisine" and this is where, a century ago, coopers made barrels for the wine merchants. The atmosphere of this lovely restored home is enhanced by antiques, arrangements of flowers, lovely watercolors and decorative wallpapers. The decor is warm and inviting and the welcome extended by the Aulagnon family is very gracious. The hotel is situated three kilometers to the southwest of Beaugency on N152.

*HOSTELLERIE DE LA TONNELLERIE*
*Hotelier: M & Mme Aulagnon*
*12, Rue des Eaux-Bleues*
*Tavers*
*45190 Beaugency*
*Tel: 38.44.68.15*
*27 Rooms - Sgl from 370F Dbl to 530F*
*Open: May to October*
*Credit cards: DC, VS, MC*
*Restaurant, pool, garden*
*Located 28 km SW of Orleans*
*Region: Loire Valley*

The Bastide de Tourtour is situated on the outskirts of Tourtour, "le village dans le ciel", and actually guards a position even higher than the "village in the heavens". From its vantage point one can enjoy unobstructed vistas of the surrounding countryside of Haute Provence.   The region is lovely and the village with its cobbled streets, galleries, tempting shops, cozy restaurants and inviting cafes a delight to explore.   The location of the Bastide de Tourtour is ideal, and so I was therefore extremely disappointed to find it in need of refurbishing and the welcome somewhat stiff on a recent visit.   However, I was unable to find a better substitute, and so continue to include it in the book with the hopes that conditions will improve in the near future.   A grand circular staircase, with old implements for weaving, spinning, etc. - "brocante", adorning each floor's landing, winds up to the hotel's accommodations.   All of the Bastide's bedrooms have private terraces and profit from the hotel's greatest offering - its panoramic views: the scope and direction of the view is a direct factor in determining rates.   The decor as well as the view varies from room to room.   The restaurant is attractive, with tables set under arches and beamed ceilings and, when weather permits, tables are set on its terrace.

*BASTIDE DE TOURTOUR*
*Hotelier: M & Mme Laurent*
*Route Draguignan, Tourtour, 83690 Salernes*
*Tel: 94.70.57.30 Telex: 970827*
*26 Rooms - Sgl from 470F Dbl to 1090F*
*Open: 15 February to 10 November,*
  *Restaurant closed Mondays low season*
*Credit cards: AX, VS, DC*
*Restaurant, pool, tennis, jacuzzi, weight room*
*Located 20 km NW of Draguignan*
*Region: Haute Provence*

Secluded in the residential hills of Trebeurden, the Manoir de Lan Kerrellec is a very elegant and refined hotel.   It is a handsome stone manor with white shuttered windows and a grey slate roof - architecturally very typical of the region.   The Manoir de Lan Kerrellec was once the private home of Monsieur Daube's, the present owner's, grandparents.   During the war it opened up to guests as a "salon de the", but has expanded and perfected its services as a hotel over the past few decades.   The circular dining room is truly spectacular, with a high vaulted wooden ceiling and unobstructed views out to a secluded section of the coast.   Reminiscent of an English manor house, a salon-bar off the restaurant offers an ideal retreat. The hotel has ten bedrooms, seven on the ground floor, four on the top floor, all with marvellous views out to the open sea.   If you are travelling with children, it is also interesting to note that two additional bedrooms are available to rent, equipped only with a washbasin, located across from the larger rooms and overlooking the garden.   The ten principal bedrooms of the hotel are very comfortably appointed and lovely in their furnishings.   The Manoir de Lan Kerrellec offers a quiet and picturesque setting for a Breton holiday.

*MANOIR DE LAN KERRELLEC*
*Hotelier: M Daube*
*22560 Trebeurden*
*Tel: 96.23.50.09*
*10 Rooms - Sgl from 440F Dbl to 690F*
*Open: mid-March to 29 October*
  *Restaurant closed Mondays low season*
*Credit cards: AX, VS*
*Restaurant, coastal views*
*Located 9 km NW of Lannion*
*Region: Brittany*

On a hilltop overlooking neighboring islands is a charming hotel managed and run by a delightful couple.   In 1977 Gerard and Danielle Jouanny purchased a home, then put their energy and creative effort into renovating and opening it as a hotel in 1978.   The Ti Al-Lannec still feels like a home away from home, from the smell of croissants baking to the personal touches in the decor.   The restaurant is lovely and opens onto glorious views of the coast.   The public rooms have been thoughtfully equipped to accommodate the hobbies of the guests and the unpredictable moods of the weather.   There are jigsaw puzzles, books and games, in addition to a swing on the lawn and a large outdoor chess set.   From the back lawn there is a path that descends to the beach.   Children are obviously welcome. The hotel was full when I visited, but as I viewed a number of occupied rooms, there were few that did not have a cherished stuffed animal warming the pillow.   Most of the rooms look out to the sea and the Jouannys have recently completed the addition of balconies and terraces to almost all of them.   I saw an especially lovely corner room, eleven, with spacious twin beds and fantastic views.   I was very impressed by the Ti Al-Lannec but I am not at all certain the Jouannys' warm welcome didn't touch me even more.

*TI AL-LANNEC*
*Hotelier: Gerard & Danielle Jouanny*
*22560 Trebeurden*
*Tel: 96.23.57.26, Telex: 740656*
*23 Rooms - Sgl from 310F Dbl to 550F*
*Open: 21 March to 12 November*
*Credit cards: AX, VS*
*Restaurant*
*Lovely views of the sea*
*Located 9 km NW of Lannion*
*Region: Brittany*

A picturesque farm converted to hotel and restaurant, La Verte Campagne can offer you a delicious meal in a room with a cozy fireplace and comfortable accommodation. The dining room is intimate and charming. Under heavy beams, worn copper and decorative plates adorn the exposed stone walls of this eighteenth-century Normandy farmhouse. Tables huddle around the warmth of the room's large open fire. In centuries past the fireplace served as the stove and it was here that large kettles of food were cooked. La Verte Campagne has only eight bedrooms, most of them quite small, but then so is the price. Room seven with twin beds and bath, and six with a double bed and bath, are the largest bedrooms. Room one, on the other end of the scale, is the smallest; tiny in fact. It has a delicate pink print wallpaper and just enough room to sleep. Room three, one of the medium-sized rooms, is the one I liked most. It has one bed and is decorated with bright red and white checks. The hotel is a bit difficult to find, which is also the nature of its charm: travel southeast of Trelly, one and a half kilometers on D539.

*LA VERTE CAMPAGNE*
*Hotelier: Mme Meredith*
*Hameau Chevalier*
*Trelly, 50660 Quettreville*
*Tel: 33.47.65.33*
*8 Rooms - Sgl from 150F Dbl to 300F*
*Closed: 10 January to end February*
  *Restaurant closed Sunday Dinner -*
  *in low season*
*Credit cards: AX, VS*
*Charming restaurant, small farmhouse*
*Located 12 km S of Coutances*
*Region: Normandy*

Nestled on a picturesque bend of the Dordogne, referred to as the "Cingle de Tremolat", is the sleepy, tobacco-growing village of Tremolat. Tucked off a quiet street that leads into the center is Le Vieux Logis et Ses Logis des Champs. Opening up on one side to farmland, this charming hotel has a pretty back garden with a small stream. The Giraudel-Destord family has lived in this ancient, ivy-covered farm complex for four hundred years. The current Mme Giraudel-Destord opened the family home to guests thirty-five years ago; her charm dominates the atmosphere and she still arranges flower bouquets for the breakfast trays each morning. Her son Bernard continues her fine traditions. The bedrooms have recently been redecorated and are located in various buildings about the property. Each room has an individual theme for its decor and everything matches, down to the smallest detail. A favorite is decorated in large red and white checks: the duvets, the pillows, the curtains, the canopy on the four-poster bed. The restaurant is in the barn and the tables are cleverly positioned within each of the stalls.

*LE VIEUX LOGIS ET SES LOGIS DES CHAMPS*
*Hotelier: Bernard Giraudel-Destord*
*24510 Tremolat*
*Tel: 53.22.80.06 Telex: 541025*
*23 Rooms - Sgl from 649F Dbl to 815F*
*Open: All year*
*Credit cards: All major*
*Restaurant*
*Located 54 km S of Perigueux*
*Region: Dordogne*

In the middle of a beautiful valley, with mountains towering as much as five thousand feet on either side, the medieval town of Trigance clings to a rocky spur. The Chateau de la Trigance is found within the walls and ruins of the ancient castle that crowns the village. The restorations and extent of the work involved to prepare this eleventh-century fortress as a hotel are fully appreciated after seeing the before and after photographs. Additions are still being made and completion of an extra two rooms will be finished soon. At present there are eight rooms which are tucked behind thick stone walls of the ancient fortress. The accommodation is definitely not luxurious, often a bit dark and austere with beds tucked right up against the ancient stone walls, but the setting and atmosphere is unique with an authentic medieval flavor. The restaurant is renowned for its fine cuisine. Monsieur and Madame Thomas are in charge of the hotel in its magnificent setting under the warm blue skies of Haute Provence. The location is convenient for touring the spectacular Gorges du Verdon: pack a picnic and spend a day driving the canyon at leisure. Roads travel either side of the Gorges du Verdon. Views plunge down to narrow stretches where the river forges a path and to calmer, wider sections where the Verdon pauses to create glistening, dark, blue-green pools. A spectacular journey.

*CHATEAU DE LA TRIGANCE*
*Hotelier: M & Mme Jean Claude Thomas*
*Trigance, 83840 Comps sur Artuby*
*Tel: 94.76.91.18*
*8 Rooms - Sgl from 315F Dbl to 630F*
*Open: 21 March to 11 November*
*Credit cards: All major*
*Restaurant, enclosed in medieval walls*
*Located 41 km N of Draguignan*
*Region: Haute Provence*

On the northeastern boundaries of the Loire Valley and its numerous, more famous castles, the Chateau de Valencay is an impressive and less frequented chateau. Built on the vast terraces that dominate the Nahon Valley, this majestic Renaissance chateau is impressive, with a large central pavilion flanked by four imposing round dome towers. The expanse of grounds hosts a zoological garden. The Hotel d'Espagne is located adjacent to the gates that open up to the Chateau de Valencay. In Napoleon's time this marvellous villa was once the hideaway of the exiled Spanish princes. Isolated and enchanting with its vine-covered walls, cobbled courtyard, covered terrace bordered by beautiful flowers, gardens and elegant rooms, it is still possible to make it your own secret hideaway. Since 1875, the gracious Fourre family have been welcoming guests into their home and serving them royally. The bedrooms are attractive and comfortable, decorated with lovely prints and matching fabrics. Although individual in size and decor, the rooms are all equipped with private bathrooms and located in wings of the hotel that border a peaceful inner courtyard. The Hotel d'Espagne is highly regarded and praised for its cuisine and the dining room is romantic in its decor and atmosphere.

*HOTEL D'ESPAGNE*
*Hotelier: Fourre family*
*9, Rue Chateau*
*36600 Valencay*
*Tel: 54.00.00.02 Telex: 751675*
*17 Rooms - Sgl from 350F Dbl to 600F*
*Open: mid-March to mid-November*
*Credit cards: All major*
*Restaurant, inner courtyard*
*Located 55 km S of Blois*
*Region: Loire Valley*

*Hotel Descriptions*

In a region famous for its food, Restaurant Pic stands out for its excellent cuisine. This is in the true sense a "restaurant with rooms" as the hotel portion consists of two bedrooms and two apartments - all provided simply for the convenience and comfort of those fortunate guests who reserved early and who have come to sample the culinary delights of the restaurant. Father and son, Jacques and Alain, are masters in the kitchen, a reputation that is acclaimed the world over. Madame Pic is ever present to offer a welcoming smile and ensure that guests are content while her husband and son are busy creating in the kitchen. For such a renowned restaurant, the ambiance is surprizingly not stuffy or overly formal, but congenial - a direct reflection of and compliment to the Pic family. The Hotel-Restaurant Pic does not offer accommodation on a demi-pension basis, but does have three good value menus or one can always order a la carte. In summer meals are served in the shady garden. To reach the hotel take the Valence-Sud exit off the autoroute in the direction of "Centre Ville" and continue on to the Avenue Victor Hugo where you find Hotel-Restaurant Pic.

*HOTEL-RESTAURANT PIC*
*Hotelier: M Jacques Pic*
*285, Avenue Victor Hugo*
*26000 Valence*
*Tel: 75.44.15.32*
*4 Rooms - Sgl from 400F Dbl to 850F*
*Closed: August & 10 days in February*
  *Restaurant closed Wednesdays and Sunday nights*
*Credit cards: AX, DC, VS*
*Famous restaurant*
*Located 99 km S of Lyon*
*Region: Rhone Valley*

A beautiful drive winds up to this magnificent, grey-turreted chateau - the first impression is captivating.   The Chateau de Castel Novel offers superlative service and accommodation and, to top it off, the cuisine is superb.   This is the country of such delicacies as "foie gras", truffles, veal and a delightful variety of mushrooms. Jean Pierre Faucher, who served his chef's apprenticeship in the region and at some of France's finest restaurants, offers you a wonderful menu.   The bedrooms are cozy and beautifully maintained.   They are few in number, and I found as they were shown to me that each one became my "favorite" in the order visited.   They are all marvellous, but different.   One is impressive if you like to sleep in a turret; another has a pair of magnificent, spiraling wooden four-poster beds; and yet another has twin beds, two balconies and a lovely view.   The Parveaux family have added ten garret rooms in an annex called La Metarie du Chateau.   These rooms are less luxurious in furnishings but are offered at a reduced rate.   Built in the fourteenth and fifteenth centuries, the Chateau de Castel Novel is set in a garden of fifteen acres with a swimming pool, tennis courts and a practice area of three holes for golfers.   The hotel is professionally and graciously managed by Albert Parveaux and his charming wife, Christine.   Directions: travel ten kilometers to the northwest from Brive la Gaillarde on D901 and D152.

*CHATEAU DE CASTEL NOVEL*
*Hotelier: M Albert Parveaux*
*Varetz, 19240 Allassac*
*Tel: 55.85.00.01 Telex: 590065*
*38 Rooms - Sgl from 335F Dbl to 935F*
*Open: 11 April to 20 October*
*Credit cards: AX, VS, DC*
*Restaurant, pool, tennis*
*Located 10 km NW of Brive*
*Region: Dordogne*

*Hotel Descriptions*

Vence is a quaint little town of narrow streets, intriguing passageways and tempting craft and specialty shops.   Located in the hills above the resort towns of the Riviera, Vence enjoys a quieter setting and medieval ambiance.   It is a perfect base from which to explore neighboring hilltop villages such as the fortified St Paul de Vence and its Maeght Foundation, the perfume center of Grasse, and the charming Biot which has recently earned a reputation for fine glassware.   Look for the largest tree in Vence and there you will find L'Auberge des Seigneurs.   This is a delightful inn, located on a quiet side street at the center of Vence.   The inn is charming in its decor and country ambiance: heavy old beams are exposed in the ceilings and walls are whitewashed.   Copper plates, pans and bedwarmers adorn the walls, while provincial prints cover the tables and lovely antique pieces are used handsomely.   Wooden doors, rich in their patina, a large stone fireplace and striking flower arrangements complete a scene in the restaurant and salon that is intimate and cozy.   Up a creaking stairway are ten delightful, small rooms. Inexpensive in price, the bedrooms are a true bargain - comfortable and simply decorated with pretty country prints.

*L'AUBERGE DES SEIGNEURS ET DU LION D'OR*
*Hotelier: M Rodi*
*Place Frene*
*06140 Vence*
*Tel: 93.58.04.24*
*10 Rooms - Sgl from 220F Dbl to 274F*
*Closed: mid-October to end November*
*   Restaurant closed Tuesdays*
*Restaurant*
*Located 22 km NW of Nice*
*Region: Riviera*

Looking up from the town of Vence you can see the Chateau St Martin sitting on the hillside a few kilometers away. (From Vence, travel to the north, two and a half kilometers on D2, the Route Coursegoules.) The Chateau St Martin stands behind the historical ruins of an old drawbridge, tower and wall, giving the hotel a feeling of the past, while a beautifully located swimming pool and tennis courts provide the pleasures of the present. The castle ruins hint at a past which stretches back to Roman times. The present castle was built in 1936 to combine the maximum in comfort with the refinement and beauty of residences of old. The accommodation is so luxurious and spacious the rooms are appropriately referred to as suites. If you prefer solitude, there are also small Provencal country houses on the estate. A well-known cook is in charge of this most famous kitchen. All products from the estate are at his disposal: fresh eggs, fruit and vegetables picked daily and oil from one thousand-year-old olive trees. Sample his splendors at tables set on a wide, outdoor terrace and enjoy a one hundred-kilometers vista down to the Cote d'Azur. Although indoors, an elegant restaurant looks out through floor to ceiling windows and enjoys the same breathtaking panorama. The Chateau St Martin is for those seeking sheer luxury and the finest of service.

*CHATEAU ST MARTIN*
*Hotelier: Mlle Brunet*
*Route Coursegoules, 06140 Vence*
*Tel: 93.58.02.02 Telex: 470282*
*25 Rooms - Sgl from 1587F Dbl to 2195F*
*Open: March to 20 November*
*  Restaurant closed Wednesdays, low season*
*Credit cards: All major*
*Restaurant, pool, tennis, park*
*Located 22 km NW of Nice*
*Region: Riviera*

The Dordogne, a favorite region of France, has an abundance of small country inns. It is difficult to isolate a favorite hotel as each has an individual style, charm and appeal. Since each deserves special attention, the only "sensible" solution is to make repeated visits to the Dordogne in the hopes of savoring them all. As a result I have one more "gem" - the Manoir de Rochecourbe. It is with special pleasure that I include and recommend it, as the wife of the owner, Madame Roger, is also the sister of Madame Bonnet of the delightful Hotel Bonnet in Beynac. The Manoir de Rochecourbe, a dainty chateau with its one single turret, belonged to Madame Roger's grandmother and most of the furnishings are original or from Monsieur Roger's family. Surrounded by its own lacy garden, it seems appropriate that each of the seven rooms is named after a flower. Climb the turret to your chamber. Only the smallest room does not have an en-suite bathroom. Although the hotel does not have a restaurant, simple meals are sometimes prepared by request and served in the small, intimate dining room. This is indeed a lovely hotel and the welcome is delightfully consistent and characteristic of this gracious family.

*MANOIR DE ROCHECOURBE*
*Hotelier: M & Mme Roger*
*Vezac, 24220 St Cyprien*
*Tel: 53.29.50.79*
*7 Rooms - Sgl from 265F Dbl to 434F*
*Open: 18 April to 1 November*
*Credit cards: VS*
*No restaurant*
*Located 64 km SE of Perigueux*
*Region: Dordogne*

Considered to be one of France's most picturesque villages, Vezelay is a "must" today just as it was in the Middle Ages when it was considered an important pilgrimage stop. Perched on the hillside overlooking the romantic valley of the Cousin, Vezelay is a wonderful place to spend the afternoon, enjoy a countryside picnic, or, if afforded the luxury of time, to linger and spend the evening. A popular choice for a hotel is the Poste et Lion d'Or, a hillside inn that sits just outside the village gates and walls. Poste et Lion d'Or is believed to have existed as a post house in the Middle Ages, accommodating those who awaited the opening of the village drawbridge. Throughout the hotel there are remembrances from times more recent than the days of knights in armor. The bedrooms in the main building are lovely and decorated with handsome antiques. The furniture has been collected piece by piece since the current owner's grandmother purchased the inn almost sixty years ago. An ivy-clad annex is surrounded by a sprawling English garden. Here the rooms are quiet but the decor is modern. Like the hotel, the restaurant has an intriguing blend of old and modern decor. The Danguy family are on the premises to welcome you and expertly manage this comfortable hillside inn.

*HOTEL POSTE ET LION D'OR*
*Hotelier: Danguy family*
*Place du Champ de Foire*
*89450 Vezelay*
*Tel: 86.33.21.23 Telex: 800949*
*45 Rooms - Sgl from 232F Dbl to 564F*
*Open: 18 April to 3 November*
*Credit cards: AX, VS*
*Restaurant*
*Located 15 km W of Avallon*
*Region: Burgundy*

It is fitting that the engaging hilltown of Vezelay with its acclaimed Romanesque basilica should also offer the Residence Hotel le Pontot.  This is an unusual hotel, perhaps best summed up in the words of our host, Christian Abadie, "All is very simple here, nothing but the best!"  And when I commented that the residence was "like a museum" he immediately countered, "No, it *is* a museum!".  We learned that Monsieur Abadie does not exaggerate as we toured this medieval townhouse, a registered historical landmark whose oldest part dates from the eleventh century. The entry salon is Louis XVI and displays a parquet floor patterned after Versailles, surrounded by walls of wooden relief depicting the four seasons, love, the sciences and the arts, but their beauty is eclipsed by the salon's "piece de resistance" - its Baccarat crystal chandelier.  Upstairs, the bedrooms which date from the sixteenth century are all decorated with antique pieces, impeccable style and the finest linens.  A comfortable lounge is found in a part of the home that bridges the street below.  Breakfast is a rare treat, served on cobalt blue Limoges china encrusted with gold, flanked by silver pitchers and flatware.  On a summer morning, breakfast is served outdoors in the flower-filled garden.  The Residence Hotel le Pontot is for those seeking a truly unique lodging experience and who appreciate the fine taste and museum quality pieces exhibited.

*RESIDENCE HOTEL LE PONTOT*
*Hotelier: Christian Abadie*
*Place de la Marie, 89450 Vezelay*
*Tel: 86.33.24.40*
*8 Rooms - Sgl from 550F, Dbl to 900F*
*Open: 9 April to 15 November*
*Credit cards: AX, MC, VS*
*No restaurant, boutique*
*Located 15 km W of Avallon*
*Region: Burgundy*

I was pleased to discover that the potential of this little inn has been realized under the direction of Monsieur Garnier.   In the sixteenth century the walls of L'Atelier sheltered fabric workshops.   The front room has been converted into a lovely sitting room with a tapestry chairs set on an Oriental rug before a large fireplace. A central stairway that led to the individual workshops in what was once an outdoor courtyard - exterior balconies remain as evidence on each of the floors - now climbs to the hotel's nineteen bedrooms.   No two rooms are alike, but each is with private bath, charming and very reasonably priced.   Old wooden ceiling beams have been re-exposed, walls are papered or freshly painted to contrast with supporting timbers, antiques contribute handsomely to the furnishings and a few rooms have a fireplace.   One room is unique in that its top floor location and skylight window affords a view out over rooftops, across the river to the City of the Popes in Avignon.   Sheltered in back is a delightful, quiet courtyard where one can enjoy a breakfast of croissants and "cafe au lait" and also two additional rooms of the hotel, each with a private terrace.   If you have an afternoon at leisure, climb the old, exterior stone stairway off the courtyard to a peaceful terrace that overlooks the walls of the fort and village rooftops - a perfect spot to hide away with a book.

*L'ATELIER*
*Hotelier: M Garnier*
*5, Rue de la Foire*
*30400 Villeneuve les Avignon*
*Tel: 90.25.01.84*
*19 Rooms - Sgl from 228F Dbl to 340F*
*Closed: January*
*Credit cards: All major*
*No restaurant*
*Located 3 km N of Avignon*
*Region: Provence*

Le Prieure, constructed in 1322 on the orders of Cardinal Armand de Via, was purchased in 1943 by Roger Mille who transformed it into a small inviting hotel. At the heart of the lovely medieval village of Villeneuve les Avignon, Le Prieure is charming. Ivy clings to its warm stone exterior, green shutters dress its windows and sun-baked tiles adorn its roof. The hotel has expanded and changed over the years. The chapel was completely remodelled, creating five pretty twin rooms with bathrooms and two lovely suites. The dining room was enlarged by moving the fireplace and adding large picture windows. Most recently, in 1987, the Milles renovated the last five "old" bathrooms in the original wing of the inn. Always with pride and a concern for the comforts of their guests, the Milles conduct everything with refinement and taste. Throughout Le Prieure beautiful antiques add charm and beauty to the ambiance and setting. When blessed with the balmy weather of Provence, dine on the terrace surrounded by foliage and soft lighting in the subtle elegance of a summer night. Marie-France and Jacques are present to welcome you and assist with selections from the wine list and menu. They are good hosts and their presence lends a personal and special touch to the very competent and professional service.

*LE PRIEURE*
*Hotelier: M Jacques Mille*
*7, Place de Chapitre*
*30400 Villeneuve les Avignon*
*Tel: 90.25.18.20 Telex: 431042*
*36 Rooms - Sgl from 450F Dbl to 950F, Apt 1600F*
*Open: 11 March to 9 November*
*Credit cards: All major*
*Restaurant, pool, tennis, park*
*Located 3 km N of Avignon*
*Region: Provence*

Deep in the Burgundy countryside, the elegant and highly comfortable Hotel-Restaurant Georges Blanc offers gastronomical delights amidst luxurious surroundings. For three generations the Blanc family have been well known restauranteurs and innkeepers, a tradition now continued by the family's youngest son, Georges, a world-renowned chef. Sample his culinary skills in one of the two pretty riverside dining rooms, while seated in rosy-hued tapestry chairs at tables set elegantly with fine china, silver and glassware. Polished antique sideboards and chests display stunning flower arrangements and a beautiful tapestry covers the wall next to an expanse of windows. The extensive wine cellar is impressively displayed through its glass walls. Our welcome to the Georges Blanc was very professional and accommodating. Flowerboxes spilling over with geraniums line the walkway to the back wing of the hotel where a good part of the rooms are located alongside the peaceful river. All of the fresh, clean bedrooms have private bath or shower and are tastefully furnished with antique reproductions and fine fabrics. The very large and luxurious suite with two floors and two smaller apartments are good options for those seeking more spacious accommodations as the standard rooms can be small. An inviting swimming pool, tennis court and even a helicopter landing pad are also found behind the hotel.

*HOTEL-RESTAURANT GEORGES BLANC*
*Hotelier: Georges Blanc*
*01540 Vonnas*
*Tel: 74.50.00.10 Telex: 380 776*
*30 Rooms - Dbl from 500F, Suite to 1900F*
*Open: 12 February to 2 January*
*Credit cards: AX, VS, DC*
*Superb restaurant, pool, tennis*
*Located 19 km SE of Macon*
*Region: Rhone Valley*

# Inn Discoveries from Our Readers

Many hotel recommendations have been sent to us by you, our readers. Some we have included in this edition, others we have not yet had the opportunity to see. We have a rule never to include any hotel, no matter how perfect it sounds, until we have made a personal inspection. This seems a waste of some excellent "tips", so, to solve this dilemma, we are adding to each of our guides a new section of hotels you have seen and loved and have shared with us, but which we have not yet inspected. Thank you for your contributions. Please keep them coming.

## AIGUES MORTES        HOSTELLERIE DES REMPARTS   Provence

Hostellerie des Remparts, Hotelier: Chantal & Peer Kansten, 6, Place des Armes, 30220 Aigues Mortes, Tel: 66.51.82.77, Dbl from 300F to 450F

"South of Provence is a region known as the Camargue, a land of gypsies, marshlands and white horses. Aigues Mortes is a medieval village and the Hostellerie des Remparts is found within its protective walls. The Hostellerie des Remparts is located in an eighteenth-century house, the former garrison of a famous knight. Although not luxurious, the hotel has nineteen comfortable rooms and I am certain we enjoyed one of the choicest - a spacious corner room with handsome furnishings and large floor-to-ceiling windows. The restaurant was attractive but the food mediocre. However, there are lots of sidewalk cafes and restaurants tucked along the village's medieval, narrow streets. Aigues Mortes is perhaps the most interesting destination of the Camargue and the Hostellerie des Remparts seemed to offer the most comfortable lodging." *Recommendation - Anonymous, New York*

**ARLES**     **LA FENIERE**                Provence

La Feniere, (7.5 km east of Arles on N453), 13200 Arles, Tel: 90.98.47.44, Telex: 441237, Dbl from 275F to 550F

La Feniere is recommended as a reasonably priced hotel - "a charmer, located in the middle of a wheat field. The people were absolutely hometown friendly, and the restaurant served provincial food such as delicious beef stew. We had travelled along the coast to St Raphael and then inland in considerable heat. La Feniere was like an oasis. I loved staying outside the busy, tourist city of Arles." *Recommended by Sherrill Root, California*

**AZAY LE RIDEAU**    **HOTEL DU GRAND MONARQUE**    Loire Valley

Hotel du Grand Monarque, Hotelier: Jacquet family, 37190 Azay le Rideau, Tel: 47.45.40.08, Sgl from 150F Dbl to 400F

"Azay is our favorite chateau and the Hotel du Grand Monarque is happily located at the town's center. We enjoyed our stay here largely because of the congenial atmosphere and the mood set by the owners. Three generations of the Jacquet family have proudly managed the inn and offer a mosaic of simply decorated but pretty rooms and a delightful restaurant. We won't return to the Loire without visiting the Chateau d'Azay le Rideau and when we do we will gladly settle once more at the Hotel du Grand Monarque." Editor's note: I stayed here more than a decade ago, before ever travelling to France on a research trip. Mrs. Peters' description recalls my own memories of a lovely inn and I will be eager to revisit and consider the Hotel du Grand Monarque for a future edition. *Recommended by Jane Peters, Connecticut*

**BARBIZON**  **HOSTELLERIE DE LA CLE D'OR**  Ile de Paris

Hostellerie de la Cle d'Or, Hotelier: J. Karampournis, 73, Grande Rue, 77630 Barbizon, Tel: (1) 60.66.40.96, Dbl from 300F to 500F

"We stopped in Barbizon to stretch our legs after a long flight from New York. We enjoyed the quiet of this peaceful village and were pleased to discover the charming Hostellerie de la Cle d'Or. We decided to lunch at the inn and each course was delicious and so delightfully French. Our meal began with pate and ended with an assortment of cheeses accompanied by crusty French bread. Rain threatened on the day of our visit but tables were optimistically set in a peaceful inner courtyard - perhaps next time. We snuck a peek at a number of the bedrooms found in a wing at the back of the inn. The rooms looked comfortable and when we inquired as to their price found them to be quite reasonable." *Recommendation - Anonymous, New York*

**BEAUMONT**  **MANOIR DE MONTOUR**  Loire Valley

Manoir de Montour, Hotelier: Mme Krebs, Beaumont en Veron, 37420 Avoine, Tel: 47.58.43.76, Dbl from 180F per day, Apt to 1400F per week

Staying at the Manoir de Montour is truly experiencing a French home. This is Madame Krebs' home and she rents out just two rooms in her lovely stone manor and has two individual buildings that will each comfortably accommodate up to four persons. The manor comes highly recommended by another hotelier, Francois de Valbray. He describes it as very bohemian in decor, comfortable and cozy, and explains that Madame Krebs extends a warm and genuine welcome. He warns that the manor is difficult to find as it is located on the outskirts of the village and advises that one ask directions upon arrival in town and avoid a frustrating search. *Recommended by Francois de Valbray, Champigne*

*Inn Discoveries from Our Readers*

## DISSAY SOUS COURCILLON  CHATEAU DE COURCILLON Loire Valley

Le Chateau de Courcillon, Hotelier: Mme Claire Jacquard,
72500 Dissay sous Courcillon, Tel: 43.44.10.00, Rates: Unknown

"We highly recommend that you visit this delightful chateau and experience first
hand the beautiful and peaceful setting of this building that dates back to the fifth
and sixth centuries.  Having widely travelled in Europe, we were astonished to
discover, by pure chance, this completely unpublicized restaurant and hotel, which
has been, to our great interest, frequented by royalty from overseas on recent visits
to Le Mans.  It has operated as a hotel for some time, but in January 1987 the
original "Guards' Room" was operated as an exclusive restaurant offering a choice
for the discerning connoisseur or the budget conscious tourist.  To complement
the exquisite local fare two set menus are on offer, together with a la carte.  The
proprietress, Madame Claire Jacquard, extends a most warm and sincere welcome
to all her guests." *Recommended by Philip & Melanie Seymour-Smith, England*

## PARIS       HOTEL LE SAINTE BEUVE       Sixth Arrondissement

Hotel le Sainte Beuve, 9, Rue Sainte Beuve, 75006 Paris, Tel: (1) 45.48.20.07,
Sgl from 600F Dbl to 1000F

This intimate hotel comes highly recommended.  It is located on the left bank on a
small street tucked between the Boulevard Raspail and the Rue Notre Dame des
Champs.  The Hotel le Sainte Beuve has only twenty-three rooms which are
described as deluxe and luxuriously furnished with antiques.  Although the hotel
does not have a restaurant it does have a lovely cocktail lounge and salon where a
log fire creates an inviting ambiance.  Service is stressed as attentive, helpful and
personal. *Recommended by Mr & Mrs Stahl, California*

## ST SYMPHORIEN    CHATEAU D'ESCLIMONT    Ile de Paris

Chateau d'Esclimont, 28700 St Symphorien, Tel: 37.31.15.15, Telex: 780560, Sgl from 600F Dbl to 1300F, Apt to 2100F

A number of readers have written in to recommend and highly praise the Chateau d'Esclimont. Located sixty kilometers to the southwest of Paris, this lovely and elegant chateau is described as striking in appearance and setting. With a slate grey roof capped by turrets, the Chateau d'Esclimont is bounded by a moat and surrounded by one hundred and fifty acres of private parkland. Everything about the chateau sounds grand - the luxurious accommodation, the first class regally furnished restaurant and the refined service. So close to Paris, this is targeted as a "must" for our next research trip.

## TOURTOUR    AUBERGE ST PIERRE    Haute Provence

Auberge St Pierre, Hotelier: Mme Marcellin, (3 km E of town on D51) 83690 Tourtour, Tel: 94.70.57.17, Sgl from 280F Dbl to 350F

"A dream spot in a beautiful bucolic setting with deer, sheep and cows - all on the farm. The Auberge St Pierre has tennis courts, a pool and a sauna and there are numerous hiking trails. The restaurant prides itself on using the farm's own excellent fresh produce. A charming French family own and operate the auberge. Found the rates to be quite reasonable." Editor's note: Tourtour is a lovely, enchanting hilltop village referred to as "le village dans le ciel". Recommended in the book is the Bastide de Tourtour which we found to be a bit run-down on our last visit and so would greatly appreciate further comments on this inn. *Recommended by Mrs. E.B. Tray, New York*

La Source Bleue, Touzac, 46700 Puy l'Eveque, Tel: 65.36.52.01,
Sgl from 200F Dbl to 350F

"We have just returned from a trip through the Lot and Dordogne Valleys. One of
our stops was at an inn which we thought one of the loveliest we have ever
encountered. The enclosed brochure cannot begin to do justice to this charming
mill. The grounds bordering on the Lot are very beautiful - the accommodations
in the mill and the dining room are delightful - the management and service
gracious and friendly. We hope you will be able to visit the mill and include it in a
future edition." *Recommendation - Anonymous, New York*

# Hotels with U.S. Representatives

## B & D DE VOGÜÉ TOURS

P.O. Box 1998, Visalia, California 93279
Tel: 800 727-4748 / 209 733-7119, Fax: 209 733-4094

| TOWN | HOTEL | MAP | PAGE(S) |
|------|-------|-----|---------|
| BEAUMONT | CHATEAU DE DANZAY | I | 167 |
| BEAUMONT | MANOIR DE MONTOUR | n/a | 317 |
| BOURGUEIL | CHATEAU DES REAUX | I | 179 |
| CHAMPIGNE | LES BRIOTTIERES | I | 193 |
| COLY | MANOIR D'HAUTEGENTE | IV | 206 |
| LA JAILLE-YVON | CHATEAU DU PLESSIS | I | 232 |
| PLEUGUENEUC | CHATEAU MOTTE BEAUMANOIR | I | 31 266 |

## BEST WESTERN

P.O. Box 10203, Phoenix, Arizona 85064
Tel: 800 528-1234, Telex: 165743

| TOWN | HOTEL | MAP | PAGE(S) |
|------|-------|-----|---------|
| CORDES | HOTEL DU GRAND ECUYER | IV | 74 209 |
| PARIS (8th) | HOTEL LIDO | II | 135 |

## DAVID MITCHELL

200 Madison Avenue, New York, New York 10016
Tel: 212 696-1323, Telex: 422123, Fax: 212 213-2297

| TOWN | HOTEL | MAP | PAGE(S) |
|------|-------|-----|---------|
| ARLES | HOTEL JULES CESAR | III | 152 |
| AUDRIEU | CHATEAU D'AUDRIEU | I | 154 |
| BAIX | CARDINALE & RESIDENCE | III | 160 |

## DAVID MITCHELL (continued)

| TOWN | HOTEL | MAP | PAGE(S) | |
|------|-------|-----|---------|---|
| BARBIZON | *HOSTELLERIE DU BAS-BREAU* | II | | 161 |
| LES BAUX DE PROVENCE | *LA CABRO D'OR* | III | | 163 |
| LES BAUX DE PROVENCE | *L'OUSTAU BAUMANIERE* | III | 85 | 164 |
| LES BEZARDS | *L'AUBERGE LES TEMPLIERS* | II | | 173 |
| BRANTOME | *HOST. MOULIN DE L'ABBAYE* | IV | | 181 |
| CABRERETS | *LA PESCALERIE* | IV | 63 | 183 |
| CAGNES SUR MER | *LE CAGNARD* | III | | 184 |
| CARCASSONNE | *DOMAINE D'AURIAC* | IV | | 186 |
| CASTILLON DU GARD | *LE VIEUX CASTILLON* | III | 86 | 188 |
| CHAMPILLON BELLEVUE | *ROYAL CHAMPAGNE* | II | | 194 |
| CHATEAU ARNOUX | *LA BONNE ETAPE* | III | | 195 |
| CHENEHUTTE LES TUFFEAUX | *LE PRIEURE* | I | 43 | 199 |
| COLROY LA ROCHE | *HOST. LA CHENEAUDIERE* | II | | 205 |
| EZE VILLAGE | *CHATEAU DE LA CHEVRE D'OR* | III | 102 | 215 |
| FERE EN TARDENOIS | *HOSTELLERIE DU CHATEAU* | II | 107 | 217 |
| FONTVIEILLE | *LA REGALIDO* | III | | 219 |
| GRAMAT | *CHATEAU DE ROUMEGOUSE* | IV | 56 | 225 |
| HENNEBONT | *CHATEAU DE LOCGUENOLE* | I | | 226 |
| HONFLEUR | *LA FERME ST SIMEON* | I | 20 | 229 |
| IGE | *CHATEAU D'IGE* | III | | 230 |
| LAC DE BRINDOS | *CHATEAU DE BRINDOS* | IV | | 237 |
| LUYNES | *DOMAINE DE BEAUVOIS* | I | 42 | 241 |
| MARCAY | *CHATEAU DE MARCAY* | I | | 244 |
| MERCUES | *CHATEAU DE MERCUES* | IV | 61 | 247 |
| MONTBAZON | *CHATEAU D'ARTIGNY* | I | | 253 |
| NIEUIL | *CHATEAU DE NIEUIL* | IV | | 261 |
| ONZAIN | *DOM. DES HAUTS DE LOIRE* | I | | 263 |
| ROUFFACH | *CHATEAU D'ISENBOURG* | II | 119 | 272 |
| ST MARTIN DU FAULT | *LA CHAPELLE ST MARTIN* | IV | | 281 |

*Hotels with U.S. Representatives*

# DAVID MITCHELL (continued)

| TOWN | HOTEL | MAP | | PAGE(S) |
|------|-------|-----|---|---------|
| ST PERE SOUS VEZELAY | L'ESPERANCE | II | 108 | 285 |
| SALON DE PROVENCE | ABBAYE DE STE CROIX | III | | 289 |
| SEGOS | DOMAINE DE BASSIBE | IV | | 291 |
| TALLOIRES | L'AUBERGE DU PERE BISE | III | | 295 |
| TOURTOUR | BASTIDE DE TOURTOUR | III | 90 | 297 |
| TREBEURDEN | MANOIR DE LAN KERELLEC | I | | 298 |
| TREMOLAT | LE VIEUX LOGIS | IV | 53 | 301 |
| TRIGANCE | CHATEAU DE LA TRIGANCE | III | 90 | 302 |
| VALENCAY | HOTEL D'ESPAGNE | I | | 303 |
| VALENCE | HOTEL-RESTAURANT PIC | III | | 304 |
| VARETZ | CHATEAU DE CASTEL NOVEL | IV | 57 | 305 |
| VENCE | CHATEAU ST MARTIN | III | | 307 |
| VILLENEUVE LES AVIGNON | LE PRIEURE | III | 84 | 312 |
| VONNAS | HOTEL REST. GEORGES BLANC | III | | 313 |

# JACQUES DE LARSAY

622 Broadway, New York, New York 10012
Tel: 212 477-1600 / 800 366-1510, Fax: 212 995-0286

| TOWN | HOTEL | MAP | | PAGE(S) |
|------|-------|-----|---|---------|
| AMBOISE | CHATEAU DE PRAY | I | | 149 |
| AVALLON | LE MOULIN DES RUATS | II | | 156 |
| AVIGNON | HOTEL D'EUROPE | III | | 158 |
| LES BAUX DE PROVENCE | L'AUB. DE LA BENVENGUDO | III | | 162 |
| BEAULIEU SUR MER | HOTEL LA RESERVE | III | 100 | 166 |
| BEAUMONT | CHATEAU DE DANZAY | I | | 167 |
| BEAUNE | HOTEL LE CEP | II | 112 | 169 |
| BEAUNE | HOTEL DE LA POSTE | II | | 170 |
| CARCASSONNE | HOTEL DE LA CITE | IV | | 187 |
| CHAGNY | HOTEL LAMELOISE | II | 113 | 190 |

*Hotels with U.S. Representatives*

## JACQUES DE LARSAY (continued)

| TOWN | HOTEL | MAP | PAGE(S) |
|------|-------|-----|---------|
| CHAUMONT SUR LOIRE | HOSTELLERIE DU CHATEAU | I | 198 |
| CHENONCEAUX | HOTEL DU BON LABOUREUR | I | 47 200 |
| EZE VILLAGE | CHATEAU EZA | IV | 216 |
| LA MALENE | CHATEAU DE LA CAZE | III | 71 242 |
| MERCUES | CHATEAU DE MERCUES | IV | 61 247 |
| MONT ST MICHEL | HOTEL MERE POULARD | I | 25 29 257 |
| MOUGINS | LE MOULIN DE MOUGINS | III | 98 260 |
| PARIS (16th) | HOTEL ALEXANDER | II | 137 |
| PARIS (5th) | HOTEL COLBERT | II | 128 |
| PARIS (1st) | HOTEL MAYFAIR | II | 123 |
| PARIS (4th) | PAVILLON DE LA REINE | II | 123 |
| PARIS (6th) | RELAIS CHRISTINE | II | 131 |
| PARIS (4th) | HOTEL ST LOUIS | II | 127 |
| PARIS (6th) | HOTEL DES SAINTS PERES | II | 132 |
| PARIS (7th) | HOTEL ST SIMON | II | 133 |
| PARIS (8th) | HOTEL SAN REGIS | II | 136 |
| PARIS (1st) | HOTEL VENDOME | II | 124 |
| PEROUGES | OST. DU VIEUX PEROUGES | III | 114 264 |
| ST PAUL DE VENCE | HOTEL LA COLOMBE D'OR | III | 95 282 |
| TALLOIRES | L'AUBERGE DU PERE BISE | III | 295 |

## ROMANTIK HOTELS RESERVATIONS

14178 Woodinville-Duvall Road, P.O. Box 1278, Woodinville, Washington 98072
Tel: 206 486-9394 / 800 826-0015, Fax: 206 481-4079

| TOWN | HOTEL | MAP | PAGE(S) |
|------|-------|-----|---------|
| PARIS (5th) | HOTEL COLBERT | II | 128 |
| TAVERS | HOST. DE LA TONNELLERIE | I | 296 |
| TREBEURDEN | TI AL-LANNEC | I | 33 299 |

*Hotels with U.S. Representatives*

| HOTEL | TOWN | MAP# | page(s) |
|-------|------|------|---------|
| | Bagnoles de l'Orne | I | 159 |
| BOIS JOLI, Hotel | Chenonceaux | I | 47 200 |
| BON LABOUREUR | Chateau Arnoux | III | 195 |
| BONNE ETAPE, La | Beynac et Cazenac | IV | 55 172 |
| BONNET, Hotel | Gordes | III | 222 |
| BORIES, Les | Champigne | I | 193 |
| BRIOTTIERES, Les | Lac de Brindos | IV | 237 |
| BRINDOS, Chateau de | Les Baux de Provence | III | 163 |
| CABRO D'OR, La | Cagnes sur Mer | III | 184 |
| CAGNARD, Le | Moissac Bellevue | III | 252 |
| CALALOU, Hotel le | Cany Barville | I | 185 |
| CANIEL, Manoir de | Baix | III | 160 |
| CARDINAL & RESIDENCE | Varetz | IV | 57 305 |
| CASTEL NOVEL, Chateau de | Livarot | I | 240 |
| CAUDEMONNE, Le Manoir de | La Malene (La Caze) | III | 71 242 |
| CAZE, Chateau de la | Beaune | II | 112 169 |
| CEP, Hotel le | Marlenheim | II | 245 |
| CERF, Hostellerie du | Les Andelys | I | 150 |
| CHAINE D'OR, Hotel la | St Jean de Luz | IV | 279 |
| CHANTACO, Hotel de | St Martin du Fault | IV | 281 |
| CHAPELLE ST MARTIN, La | Chaumont sur Loire | I | 198 |
| CHATEAU, Hostellerie du | Fere en Tardenois | II | 107 217 |
| CHATEAU, Hostellerie du | Brantome | IV | 180 |
| CHATENET, Le | Chaumontel | II | 197 |
| CHAUMONTEL, Chateau de | Colroy la Roche | II | 205 |
| CHENEAUDIERE, Host. La | Sept Saulx | II | 292 |
| CHEVAL BLANC, Hotel du | Blere | I | 176 |
| CHEVAL BLANC, Le | Eze Village | III | 102 215 |
| CHEVRE D'OR, Chateau de la | Riec sur Belon | I | 35 270 |
| CHEZ MELANIE | Chissay | I | 203 |
| CHISSAY, Chateau de | Carcassonne | IV | 187 |
| CITE, Hotel de la | | | |

| HOTEL | TOWN | MAP# | | page(s) |
|---|---|---|---|---|
| HAUTERIVE, Moulin d' | St Gervais en Valliere | II | | 278 |
| HAUTS DE LOIRE, Dom. des | Onzain | I | | 263 |
| HOTEL, L' | Paris (6th) | II | | 131 |
| IGE, Chateau d' | Ige | III | | 230 |
| ISENBOURG, Chateau d' | Rouffach | II | 119 | 272 |
| JEANNE D'ARC, Grand Hotel | Paris (4th) | II | | 126 |
| JULES CESAR, Hotel | Arles | III | | 152 |
| LAMELOISE, Hotel | Chagny | II | 113 | 190 |
| LANCASTER, Hotel | Paris (8th) | II | | 135 |
| LAN KERRELLEC, Man. de | Trebeurden | I | | 298 |
| LEVEZOU, Hostellerie du | Salles Curan | IV | | 288 |
| LIDO, Hotel | Paris (8th) | II | | 135 |
| LIEVRE AMOUREUX, Le | St Lattier | III | | 280 |
| LOCGUENOLE, Chateau de | Hennebont | I | | 226 |
| LUTECE, Hotel de | Paris (4th) | II | | 127 |
| MANOIR, Hotel du | Chenonceaux | I | | 201 |
| MARCAY, Chateau de | Marcay | I | | 244 |
| MAYANELLE, La | Gordes | III | | 224 |
| MAYFAIR, Hotel | Paris (1st) | II | | 123 |
| MERCUES, Chateau de | Mercues | IV | 61 | 247 |
| MERE POULARD, Hotel | Mont St Michel | I | 25 29 | 257 |
| METAIRIE, Relais la | Millac | IV | | 250 |
| MEYRARGUES, Chateau de | Meyrargues | III | 92 | 248 |
| MONTESQUIOU, Manoir de | La Malene | III | | 243 |
| MONTLEDIER, Chateau de | Pont de Larn | IV | 74 | 268 |
| MONVIEL, Chateau de | Monviel | IV | | 258 |
| MORPHEE, Le | Gace | I | | 221 |
| MOTTE BEAUMANOIR, Chateau | Pleugueneuc | I | 31 | 266 |
| MOUGINS, Le Moulin de | Mougins | III | 98 | 260 |
| NIEUIL, Chateau de | Nieuil | IV | | 261 |
| NOYER, Auberge du | Le Bugue | IV | | 182 |

*Index Alphabetically by Hotel*

| HOTEL | TOWN | MAP# | page(s) |
|---|---|---|---|
| ROCHE TORIN, Manoir de la | Courtils | I | 210 |
| ROCHEVILAINE, Domaine de | Billiers | I | 38 174 |
| ROHAN, Hotel des | Strasbourg | II | 294 |
| ROUMEGOUSE, Chateau de | Gramat | IV | 56 225 |
| ROYAL CHAMPAGNE | Champillon Bellevue | II | 194 |
| RUATS, Le Moulin des | Avallon | II | 156 |
| ST JAMES CLUB, The | Paris (16th) | II | 137 |
| ST LOUIS, Hotel | Paris (4th) | II | 127 |
| ST MARTIN, Chateau | Vence | III | 307 |
| ST MICHEL, Hostellerie | Chambord | I | 191 |
| ST SIMON, Hotel | Paris (7th) | II | 133 |
| STE FOY, Hotel | Conques | IV | 66 208 |
| SAINTS PERES, Hotel des | Paris (6th) | II | 132 |
| SALLE, Chateau de la | Montpinchon | I | 24 256 |
| SAN REGIS, Hotel | Paris (8th) | II | 136 |
| SEIGNEURS & LION D'OR | Vence | III | 306 |
| SOMBRAL, Auberge du | St Cirq Lapopie | IV | 276 |
| STANG, Manoir du | La Foret Fouesnant | I | 35 220 |
| TEMPLIERS, L'Auberge les | Les Bezards | II | 173 |
| TEMPLIERS, Le Moulin des | Avallon | II | 157 |
| TI AL-LANNEC | Trebeurden | I | 33 299 |
| TONNELLERIE, Host. de la | Tavers | I | 296 |
| TORTINIERE, Dom. de la | Montbazon | I | 45 254 |
| TRES-GIRARD, Castel de | Morey St Denis | II | 259 |
| TREYNE, Chateau de la | Lacave | IV | 236 |
| TRIGANCE, Chateau de la | Trigance | III | 90 302 |
| URBILHAC, Chateau d' | Lamastre | III | 238 |
| VARENNE, Hotel de | Paris (7th) | II | 134 |
| VENDOME, Hotel | Paris (1st) | II | 124 |
| VERTE CAMPAGNE, La | Trelly | I | 300 |
| VEY, Le Moulin du | Clecy le Vey | I | 204 |

| HOTEL | TOWN | MAP# | | page(s) |
|---|---|---|---|---|
| VIEUX CASTILLON, Le | Castillon du Gard | III | 86 | 188 |
| VIEUX LOGIS, Le | Tremolat | IV | 53 | 301 |
| VIEUX PEROUGES, Ost. du | Perouges | III | 114 | 264 |
| VIEUX PUITS, Auberge du | Pont Audemer | I | | 267 |
| VIOLET, Chateau de | Peyriac Minervois | IV | | 265 |

# SAMPLE RESERVATION REQUEST LETTER

Hotel Name & Address

Messieurs, Mesdames:

Nous voudrions réserver pour _____ nuit(s),
*We would like to reserve for* *(number of)* *nights,*

    du _____ au _____,
    *from* *(date of arrival)* *to (date of departure),*

\_\_\_\_\_ une chambre à deux lits,
    *a room(s) with twin beds*

\_\_\_\_\_ une chambre au grand lit
    *room(s) with double bed*

\_\_\_\_\_ une chambre avec un lit supplémentaire,
    *room(s) with an extra bed*

\_\_\_\_\_ avec salle de bains et toilette privée,
    *with a bathroom and private toilet*

Nous sommes_____ personnes.
*We have* *(number)* *of persons in our party.*

Veuilliez confirmer la réservation en nous communicant le prix de la chambre, et le dépôt forfaitaire que vous exigez. Dans l'attente de vos nouvelles, nous vous prions d'agreer, Messieurs, Mesdames, l'expression de nos sentiments distingués.

*Please advise availability, rate of room and deposit needed. We will be waiting for you confirmation and send our kindest regards.*

Your Name & Address

# INN DISCOVERIES FROM OUR READERS

Future editions of *KAREN BROWN'S COUNTRY INN GUIDES* are going to include a new feature - a list of hotels recommended by our readers. We have received many letters describing wonderful inns you have discovered; however, we have never included them until we had the opportunity to make a personal inspection. This seemed a waste of some marvelous "tips". Therefore, in order to feature them we have decided to add a new section called "Inn Discoveries from Our Readers".

If you have a favorite discovery you would be willing to share with other travellers who love to travel the "inn way", please let us hear from you and include the following information:

1. *Your name, address and telephone number.*

2. *Name, address and telephone number of "your inn".*

3. *Brochure or picture of inn (we cannot return material).*

4. *Written permission to use an edited version of your description.*

5. *Would you want your name, city and state included in the book?*

We are constantly updating and revising all of our guide books. We would appreciate comments on any of your favorites. The types of inns we would love to hear about are those with special old-world ambiance, charm and atmosphere. We need a brochure or picture so that we can select those which most closely follow the mood of our guides. We look forward to hearing from you. Thank you.

# Karen Brown's Country Inn Guides

## The Most Reliable & Informative Series on Country Inns

Detailed itineraries guide you through the countryside and suggest a cozy inn for each night's stay. In the hotel section, every listing has been inspected and chosen for its romantic ambiance. Charming accommodations reflect every price range, from budget hideaways to deluxe palaces.

# *Order Form*

## KAREN BROWN'S COUNTRY INN GUIDES

Please ask in your local bookstore for **KAREN BROWN'S COUNTRY INN** guides. If the books you want are unavailable, you may order directly from the publisher.

*AUSTRIAN COUNTRY INNS & CASTLES $12.95*
*CALIFORNIA COUNTRY INNS & ITINERARIES $12.95*
*ENGLISH, WELSH & SCOTTISH COUNTRY INNS $12.95*
*EUROPEAN COUNTRY CUISINE - ROMANTIC INNS & RECIPES $10.95*
*EUROPEAN COUNTRY INNS - BEST ON A BUDGET $14.95*
*FRENCH COUNTRY BED & BREAKFASTS $12.95*
*FRENCH COUNTRY INNS & CHATEAUX $12.95*
*GERMAN COUNTRY INNS & CASTLES $12.95*
*IRISH COUNTRY INNS $12.95*
*ITALIAN COUNTRY INNS & VILLAS $12.95*
*PORTUGUESE COUNTRY INNS & POUSADAS $12.95*
*SCANDINAVIAN COUNTRY INNS & MANORS $12.95*
*SPANISH COUNTRY INNS & PARADORS $12.95*
*SWISS COUNTRY INNS & CHALETS $12.95*

*Name* _____  *Street* _____

*City* _____  *State* _____  *Zip* _____

*Add $2.00 for the first book and .50 for each additional book for postage & packing.*
*California residents add 6 1/2% sales tax.*
*Indicate the number of copies of each title.  Send in form with your check to:*

KAREN BROWN'S COUNTRY INN GUIDES
P.O Box 70
San Mateo, CA 94401
(415) 342-9117

# Bed & Breakfast Travel in France

### The Latest & Delightfully Inexpensive Way
### To Experience the French Countryside

**French Country Bed & Breakfasts** was written as a companion guide to Karen's first book, *French Country Inns & Chateaux*. Bed & Breakfast accommodation is a relatively new trend in France, gaining popularity in the last five to ten years and affords travellers a marvelous way to experience France. *French Country Bed & Breakfasts* is the only guide with a selective list to some of the country's most charming and welcoming homes. Featured are over 160 places to stay with illustrations and descriptions that include important information as to the level of English spoken, facilities, driving directions, rates and whether evening meals are offered.

The Bed & Breakfast formula is for the traveller who wants to experience the "real" France, its people and culture. Couples will love the sense of discovery of some truly enchanting hideaways. Single travellers will relish the social aspect of bed & breakfast stays: there are ample opportunities to meet other travellers, usually Europeans, as well as the hosts and their families. Families with children will enjoy the informality, convenience and reasonable rates. Spend a night in a chateau dating from the Middle Ages whose stone walls ooze with history, dine on family china and silver passed down through the generations, and the next night experience the sights and sounds of a simple farm in a bucolic setting and savor a hearty repast served "en famille". Your hosts cover the entire spectrum of French society, from titled counts and countesses to gentlemen farmers. Each home is unique, offering its own special charm and a warm and genuine welcome.

Karen Brown (Herbert) was born in Denver, but has spent most of her life in the San Francisco Bay area where she now lives with her husband, Rick, their little girl, Alexandra, and baby son, Richard. Taking a year off from college, Karen travelled to Europe and wrote *French Country Inns & Chateaux*, the first in what has grown to be an extremely successful series of 14 guide books on charming places to stay. For many years Karen has been planning to open her own country inn. Her dream will soon come to reality - Karen and her husband, Rick, have bought a beautiful piece of property on the coast south of San Francisco and are working with an architect to design the "perfect" little inn which will be furnished with the antiques she has been collecting for many years and will incorporate her wealth of information on just what makes an inn very special. Karen and Rick are looking forward to welcoming guests and friends to their inn.